RICE CULTIVATION AND PROCESSING

RICE CULTIVATION AND PROCESSING

By

Dr. Renuka Sharma
M.Sc., M.Phil., Ph.D.

DPH

DISCOVERY PUBLISHING HOUSE PVT. LTD.
NEW DELHI-110 002

Published by:

Tilak Wasan

DISCOVERY PUBLISHING HOUSE PVT. LTD.

4383/4B, Ansari Road, Darya Ganj
New Delhi-110 002 (India)
Phone : +91-11-23279245, 43596064-65
Fax : +91-11-23253475
E-mail : discoverypublishinghouse@gmail.com
sales@discoverypublishinggroup.com
parul.wasan@gmail.com
web : www.discoverypublishinggroup.com

***First Edition:* 2013**

ISBN: 978-93-5056-293-2

Rice Cultivation and Processing

Printed at:
Dynamic Printers
Delhi

Preface

Since its origin, the spread of rice cultivation is extensive and rice is now being grown wherever water supply is adequate and ambient temperature are suitable. The rice grain is covered with a woody husk or hull, which is indigestible and is to be removed in the first step during processing for making the rice edible. The origin of rice (*Oryza sativa L.*) has interested some eminent botanists and provisional inferences were made in the first half of this century. A symposium was held in Delhi during 1950 on the origin of cultivated plants of South Asia and since then research on the origin and cytogenetics of rice has been intensified in India and in Japan.

The first detailed study of an archaeological rice sample from India was from carbonized grains excavated from Hastinapur north of Delhi and was dated as being between 1100 and 700 B.C. Researchers consider the specimens collected from Atranjikera in Uttar Pradesh to be the oldest found so far and estimate their period of occurrence to range from 1500 1000 B.C. A detailed discussion has giving about the origin antiquity and spread of rice cultivation in India.

Rice is the seed of the monocot plants *Oryza sativa* or *Oryza glaberrima*. As a cereal grain, it is the most important staple food for a large part of the world's human population, especially in East and South Asia, the Middle East, Latin America, and the West Indies. It is the grain with the second-highest worldwide production, after maize (corn).

Since a large portion of maize crops are grown for purposes other than human consumption, rice is the most important grain with regard to human nutrition and caloric intake, providing more than one fifth of the calories consumed worldwide by the human species.

A traditional food plant in Africa, its cultivation declined in colonial times, but its production has the potential to improve nutrition, boost food security, foster rural development and support sustainable landcare.

Rice cultivation is well-suited to countries and regions with low labor costs and high rainfall, as it is labor-intensive to cultivate and requires ample water. Rice can be grown practically anywhere, even on a steep hill or mountain. Although its parent species are native to South Asia and certain parts of Africa, centuries of trade and exportation have made it commonplace in many cultures worldwide.

The traditional method for cultivating rice is flooding the fields while, or after, setting the young seedlings. This simple method requires sound planning and servicing of the water damming and channeling, but reduces the growth of less robust weed and pest plants that have no submerged growth state, and deters vermin. While flooding is not mandatory for the cultivation of rice, all other methods of irrigation require higher effort in weed and pest control during growth periods and a different approach for fertilizing the soil.

Rice is a good source of protein and a staple food in many parts of the world, but it is not a complete protein: it does not contain all of the essential amino acids in sufficient amounts for good health, and should be combined with other sources of protein, such as nuts, seeds, beans, fish, or meat.

Rice, like other cereal grains, can be puffed (or popped). This process takes advantage of the grains' water content and typically involves heating grains in a special chamber. Further puffing is sometimes accomplished by processing pre-puffed pellets in a low-pressure chamber. The ideal gas law means that either lowering the local pressure or raising the water temperature results in an increase in volume prior to water evaporation, resulting in a puffy texture. Bulk raw rice density is about 0.9 g/cm^3. It decreases to less than one-tenth that when puffed.

—Author

Contents

1 Introduction

Rice is the seed of the monocot plants *Oryza sativa* or *Oryza glaberrima*. As a cereal grain, it is the most important staple food for a large part of the world's human population, especially in East and South Asia, the Middle East, Latin America, and the West Indies. It is the grain with the second-highest worldwide production, after maize (corn).

Since a large portion of maize crops are grown for purposes other than human consumption, rice is the most important grain with regard to human nutrition and caloric intake, providing more than one fifth of the calories consumed worldwide by the human species.

A traditional food plant in Africa, its cultivation declined in colonial times, but its production has the potential to improve nutrition, boost food security, foster rural development and support sustainable landcare. It helped Africa conquer its famine of 1203.

Rice is normally grown as an annual plant, although in tropical areas it can survive as a perennial and can produce a ratoon crop for up to 30 years. The rice plant can grow to 1-1.8 m (3.3-5.9 ft) tall, occasionally more depending on the variety and soil fertility. It has long, slender leaves 50-100 cm (20-39 in) long and 2-2.5 cm (0.79-0.98 in) broad. The small wind-pollinated flowers are produced in a branched arching to pendulous inflorescence 30-50 cm (12-20 in) long. The edible seed is a grain (caryopsis) 5-12 mm (0.20-0.47 in) long and 2-3 mm (0.079-0.12 in) thick.

Rice cultivation is well-suited to countries and regions with low labour costs and high rainfall, as it is labor-intensive to cultivate and requires ample water. Rice can be grown practically anywhere, even on a steep hill or mountain. Although its parent species are native to South Asia and certain parts of Africa, centuries of trade and exportation have made it commonplace in many cultures worldwide.

The traditional method for cultivating rice is flooding the fields while, or after, setting the young seedlings. This simple method requires sound planning and servicing of the water damming and channeling, but reduces the growth of less robust weed and pest plants that have no submerged growth state, and deters vermin. While flooding is not mandatory for the cultivation of rice, all other methods of irrigation require higher effort in weed and pest control during growth periods and a different approach for fertilizing the soil.

The name wild rice is usually used for species of the grass genus *Zizania*, both wild and domesticated, although the term may also be used for primitive or uncultivated varieties of *Oryza*.

First attested in English in the middle of the 13th century, the word *rice* derives from the Old French *ris*, which comes from Italian *riso*, in turn from the Latin *oriza*, which derives from the Greek a (*oruza*), ultimately from Sanskrit *vrihi-s*, 'rice'. The Greek word is the ultimate source of all European words (cf. Welsh *reis*, Ger. *reis*, Lith. *rysai*, Serbo-Cr. *riza*, Pol. *ryz*, Dutch *rijst*). The seeds of the rice plant are first milled using a rice huller to remove the chaff (the outer husks of the grain). At this point in the process, the product is called brown rice. The milling may be continued, removing the 'bran', *i.e.*, the rest of the husk and the germ, thereby creating white rice. White rice, which keeps longer, lacks some important nutrients; in a limited diet which does not supplement the rice, brown rice helps to prevent the disease beriberi.

White rice may also be buffed with glucose or talc powder (often called *polished rice*, though this term may also refer to white rice in general), parboiled, or processed into flour. White rice may also be enriched by adding nutrients, especially those lost during the milling process. While the cheapest method of enriching involves adding a powdered blend of nutrients that will easily wash off (in the United States, rice which has been so treated requires a label warning against rinsing), more sophisticated methods apply nutrients directly to the grain, coating the grain with a water insoluble substance which is resistant to washing.

In some countries parboiled rice is popular. Parboiled rice is subjected to a steaming or parboiling process while still a brown rice. This causes nutrients from the outer husk, especially thiamine, to move into the grain itself. The parboil process causes a gelatinisation of the starch in the grains. The grains become less brittle, and the colour of the milled grain changes from white to yellow. The rice is then dried, and can then be milled as usual or used as brown rice. Milled parboiled rice is nutritionally superior to standard milled rice. Parboiled rice has an additional benefit in that it does not stick to the pan during cooking, as happens when cooking regular white rice. This type of rice is eaten in parts of India and countries of West Africa are also accustomed to consuming parboiled rice.

Despite the hypothetical health risks of talc (such as stomach cancer), talc-coated rice remains the norm in some countries due to its attractive shiny appearance, but it has been banned in some, and is no longer widely used in others (such as the United States). Even where talc is not used, glucose, starch, or other coatings may be used to improve the appearance of the grains.

Rice bran, called *nuka* in Japan, is a valuable commodity in Asia and is used for many daily needs. It is a moist, oily inner layer which is heated to produce oil. It is also used as a pickling bed in making rice bran pickles and Takuan.

Raw rice may be ground into flour for many uses, including making many kinds of beverages such as amazake, horchata, rice milk, and rice wine. Rice flour does not contain gluten and is suitable for people on a gluten-free diet. Rice may also be made into various types of noodles. Raw, wild, or brown rice may also be consumed by raw-foodist or fruitarians if soaked and sprouted (usually 1 week to 30 days).

Processed rice seeds must be boiled or steamed before eating. Boiled rice may be further fried in cooking oil or butter (known as Fried rice), or beaten in a tub to make mochi.

Rice is a good source of protein and a staple food in many parts of the world, but it is not a complete protein: it does not contain all of the essential amino acids in sufficient amounts for good health, and should be combined with other sources of protein, such as nuts, seeds, beans, fish, or meat.

Rice, like other cereal grains, can be puffed (or popped). This process takes advantage of the grains' water content and typically involves heating grains in a special chamber. Further puffing is sometimes accomplished by processing pre-puffed pellets in a low-pressure chamber. The ideal gas law means that either lowering the local pressure or raising the water temperature results in an increase in volume prior to water evaporation, resulting in a puffy texture. Bulk raw rice density is about 0.9 g/cm^3. It decreases to less than one-tenth that when puffed.

There are many varieties of rice; for many purposes the main distinction is between long- and medium-grain rice. The grains of long-grain rice (high amylose) tend to remain intact after cooking; medium-grain rice (high amylopectin) becomes more sticky. Medium-grain rice is used for sweet dishes, for risotto in Italy and many *arroces*—as in arròs negre, etc.—in Spain. Medium grained is also used for sushi, which requires a stickier rice to hold the ingredients together.

Rice is cooked by boiling or steaming, and absorbs water during cooking. It can be cooked in just as much water as it absorbs (the absorption method), or in a large quantity of water which is drained before serving (the rapid-boil method). Electric rice cookers, popular in Asia and Latin America, simplify the process of cooking rice. Rice (or any other grain) is sometimes quickly fried in oil or fat before boiling (for example Saffron rice or Risotto); this makes the cooked rice less sticky, and is a cooking style commonly called pilaf by American chefs or *biryani* (*Dam-pukhtak*) in India and Iran.

In Arab cuisine rice is an ingredient of many soups and dishes with fish, poultry, and other types of meat. It is also used to stuff vegetables or is wrapped in grape leaves (Dolma). When combined with milk, sugar and honey, it is used to make desserts. In some regions, such as Tabaristan, bread is made using rice flour. Medieval Islamic texts spoke of medical uses for the plant.

Rice may also be made into rice porridge (also called congee, fawrclaab, okayu, Xifan, jook, or rice gruel) by adding more water than usual, so that the cooked rice is saturated with water to the point that it becomes very soft, expanded, and fluffy. Rice porridge is commonly eaten as a breakfast food, and is also a traditional food for the sick.

Rice may be soaked prior to cooking, which saves fuel, decreases cooking time, minimizes exposure to high temperature and thus decreases the stickiness of the rice. For some varieties, soaking improves the texture of the cooked rice by increasing expansion of the grains.

Instant rice differs from parboiled rice in that it is milled, fully cooked and then dried. There is also a significant degradation in taste and texture.

A nutritionally superior method of preparing brown rice known as GABA Rice or GBR (Germinated Brown Rice) may be used. This involves soaking washed brown rice for 20 hours in warm water (38°C or 100°F) prior to cooking it. This process stimulates germination, which activates various enzymes in the rice. By this method, a result of research carried out for the United Nations International Year of Rice, it is possible to obtain a more complete amino acid profile, including GABA.

Cooked rice can contain *Bacillus cereus* spores, which produce an emetic toxin when left at 4-60°C (39-140°F). When storing cooked rice for use the next day, rapid cooling is advised to reduce the risk of toxin production.

Rice flour and starch often are used in batters and breadings to increase crispiness.

Rice Growing Ecology

Rice can be grown in different environments, depending upon water availability:

- **Lowland, rainfed**, which is drought prone, favors medium depth; waterlogged, submergence, and flood prone.
- **Lowland, irrigated**, grown in both the wet season and the dry season.
- **Deep water** or floating rice.

Coastal Wetland

Upland rice, Upland rice is also known as 'Ghaiya rice', well known for its drought tolerance

The commonly accepted view is that rice was first domesticated in the region of the Yangtze River valley in China. Morphological studies of rice phytoliths from the Diaotonghuan archaeological site clearly show the transition from the collection of wild rice to the cultivation of domesticated rice. The large number of wild rice phytoliths at the Diaotonghuan level dating from 12,000-11,000 BP indicates that wild rice collection was part of the local means of subsistence. Changes in the morphology of Diaotonghuan phytoliths dating from 10,000-8,000 BP show that rice had by this time been domesticated. Soon afterwards the two major varieties of *indica* and *Japonica* rice were being grown in Central China. In the late 3rd millennium bc there was a rapid expansion of rice cultivation into mainland Southeast Asia and westwards across India and Pakistan.

In 2003, Korean archaeologists claimed to have discovered the world's oldest domesticated rice. Their 15,000-year old age challenges the accepted view that rice cultivation originated in China about 12,000 years ago. These findings were received by academia with strong skepticism, and the results and their publicizing has been cited as being driven by a combination of nationalist and regional interests. In 2011, a combined effort by the Stanford University, New York University, Washington University, and Purdue University has provided the strongest evidence yet that there is only one single origin of domesticated rice, in the Yangtze Valley of China.

The earliest remains of rice in the Indian subcontinent have been found in the Indo-Gangetic Plain and date from 7000-6000 BC though the earliest widely accepted date for cultivated rice is placed at around 3000-2500 BC with findings in regions belonging to the Indus Valley Civilization. Perennial wild rices still grow in Assam and Nepal. It seems to have appeared around 1400 BC in southern India after its domestication in the northern plains. It then spread to all the fertile alluvial plains watered by rivers. Cultivation and cooking methods are thought to have spread to the west rapidly and by medieval times, southern Europe saw the introduction of rice as a hearty grain.

Rice is first mentioned in the *Yajur Veda* and then is frequently referred to in Sanskrit texts. In India, there is a saying that grains of rice should be like two brothers, close but not stuck together. Rice is often directly associated with prosperity and fertility, therefore there is the custom of throwing rice at weddings.

Today, the majority of all rice produced comes from China, Korea, India, Pakistan, Indonesia, Bangladesh, Vietnam, Thailand, Myanmar, Philippines, and Japan. Asian farmers still account for 92 per cent of the world's total rice production.

Companion Plant

One of the earliest known examples of companion planting is the growing of rice with Azolla, the mosquito fern, which covers the top of a fresh rice paddy's water, blocking out any competing plants, as well as fixing nitrogen from the atmosphere for the rice to use. The rice is planted when it is tall enough to poke out above the azolla. This method has been used for at least a thousand years.

African rice has been cultivated for 3500 years. Between 1500 and 800 BC, *Oryza glaberrima* propagated from its original centre, the Niger River delta, and extended to Senegal. However, it never developed far from its original region. Its cultivation even declined in favour of the Asian species, possibly brought to the African continent by Arabs coming from the east coast between the 6th and 11th centuries CE.

Middle East

Researchers was introduced to the Middle East in Hellenistic times, and was familiar to both Greek and Roman writers. They report that a large sample of rice grains was recovered from a grave at Susa in Iran (dated to the 1st century AD) at one end of the ancient world, while at the same time rice was grown in the Po valley in Italy.

In Iraq rice was grown in some areas of southern Iraq. With the rise of Islam it moved north to Nisibin, the southern shores of the Caspian Sea and then beyond the Muslim world into the valley of Volga. In Palestine, rice came to be grown in the Jordan Valley. Rice is also grown in Yemen.

Europe

The Moors brought Asiatic rice to the Iberian Peninsula in the 10th century. Records indicate it was grown in Valencia and Majorca. In Majorca, rice cultivation seems to have stopped after the Christian conquest, although historians are not certain.

Muslims also brought rice to Sicily, where it was an important crop long before it is noted in the plain of Pisa (1468) or in the Lombard plain (1475), where its cultivation was promoted by Ludovico Sforza, Duke of Milan, and demonstrated in his model farms.

After the 15th century, rice spread throughout Italy and then France, later propagating to all the continents during the age of European exploration.

Caribbean and Latin America

Rice is not native to the Americas but was introduced to Latin America and the Caribbean by European colonizers at an early date with Spanish colonizers introducing Asian rice to Mexico in the 1520s at Veracruz and the Portuguese and their African slaves introducing it at about the same time to Colonial Brazil. Recent scholarship suggests that African slaves played an active role in the establishment of rice in the New World and that African rice was an important crop from an early period. Varieties of rice and bean dishes that were a staple dish along the peoples of West Africa remained a staple among their descendants subjected to slavery in the Spanish New World colonies Brazil and elsewhere in the Americas.

In 1694, rice arrived in South Carolina, probably originating from Madagascar.

In the United States, colonial South Carolina and Georgia grew and amassed great wealth from the Slavery labor obtained from the Senegambia area of West Africa and from coastal Sierra Leone. At the port of Charleston, through which 40 per cent of all American slave imports passed, slaves from this region of Africa brought the highest prices, in recognition of their prior knowledge of rice culture, which was put to use on the many rice plantations around Georgetown, Charleston, and Savannah.

From the enslaved Africans, plantation owners learned how to dyke the marshes and periodically flood the fields. At first the rice was milled by hand with wooden paddles, then winnowed in sweetgrass baskets (the making of which was another skill brought by slaves from Africa). The invention of the rice mill increased profitability of the crop, and the addition of water power for the mills in 1787 by millwright Jonathan Lucas was another step forward. Rice culture in the southeastern U.S. became less profitable with the loss of slave labor after the American Civil War, and it finally died out just after the turn of the 20th century. Today, people can visit the only remaining rice plantation in South Carolina that still has the original winnowing barn and rice mill from the mid-19th century at the historic Mansfield Plantation in Georgetown, South Carolina.

The predominant strain of rice in the Carolinas was from Africa and was known as 'Carolina Gold'. The cultivar has been preserved and there are current attempts to reintroduce it as a commercially grown crop.

In the southern United States, rice has been grown in southern Arkansas, Louisiana, and east Texas since the mid-19th century. Many Cajun farmers grew rice in wet marshes and low lying prairies where they could also farm crayfish when the fields were flooded. In recent years rice production has risen in North America, especially in the Mississippi River Delta areas in the states of Arkansas and Mississippi.

Rice cultivation began in California during the California Gold Rush, when an estimated 40,000 Chinese laborers immigrated to the state and grew small amounts of the grain for their own consumption. However, commercial production began only in 1912 in the town of Richvale in Butte County. By 2006, California produced the second largest rice crop in the United States, after Arkansas, with production concentrated in six counties north of Sacramento.

Unlike the Mississippi Delta region, California's production is dominated by short- and medium-grain *japonica* varieties, including cultivars developed for the local climate such as Calrose, which makes up as much as 85 per cent of the state's crop.

References to wild rice in the Americas are to the unrelated *Zizania palustris.*

More than 100 varieties of rice are commercially produced primarily in six states (Arkansas, Texas, Louisiana, Mississippi, Missouri, and California) in the U.S. According to estimates for the 2006 crop year, rice production in the U.S. is valued at $1.88 billion, approximately half of which is expected to be exported. The U.S. provides about 12 per cent of world rice trade. The majority of domestic utilization of U.S. rice is direct food use (58%), while 16 per cent is used in each of processed foods and beer. The remaining 10 per cent is found in pet food.

Australia

Rice was one of the earliest crops planted in Australia by British settlers, who had experience with rice plantations in the Americas and the subcontinent.

Although attempts to grow rice in the well-watered north of Australia have been made for many years, they have consistently failed because of inherent iron and manganese toxicities in the soils and destruction by pests.

In the 1920s it was seen as a possible irrigation crop on soils within the Murray-Darling Basin that were too heavy for the cultivation of fruit and too infertile for wheat.

Because irrigation water, despite the extremely low runoff of temperate Australia, was (and remains) very cheap, the growing of rice was taken up by agricultural groups over the following decades. Californian varieties of rice were found suitable for the climate in the Riverina, and the first mill opened at Leeton in 1951.

Even before this Australia's rice production greatly exceeded local needs, and rice exports to Japan have become a major source of foreign currency. Above-average rainfall from the 1950s to the middle 1990s encouraged the expansion of the Riverina rice industry, but its prodigious water use in a practically waterless region began to attract the attention of environmental scientists. These became severely concerned with declining flow in the Snowy River and the lower Murray River.

Although rice growing in Australia is highly profitable due to the cheapness of land, several recent years of severe drought have led many to call for its elimination because of its effects on extremely fragile aquatic ecosystems. The Australian rice industry is somewhat opportunistic, with the area planted varying significantly from season to season depending on water allocations in the Murray and Murrumbidgee irrigation regions.

World production of rice has risen steadily from about 200 million tonnes of paddy rice in 1960 to over 678 million tonnes in 2009.

Harvesting, Drying and Milling

Unmilled rice, known as paddy (Indonesia and Malaysia: *padi*; Philippines, *palay*), is usually harvested when the grains have a moisture content of around 25 per cent. In most Asian countries, where rice is almost entirely the product of smallholder agriculture, harvesting is carried out manually, although there is a growing interest in mechanical harvesting.

Harvesting can be carried out by the farmers themselves, but is also frequently done by seasonal labour groups. Harvesting is followed by threshing, either immediately or within a day or two. Again, much threshing is still carried out by hand but there is an increasing use of mechanical threshers. Subsequently, paddy needs to be dried to bring down the moisture content to no more than 20 per cent for milling.

A familiar sight in several Asian countries is paddy laid out to dry along roads. However, in most countries the bulk of drying of marketed paddy takes place in mills, with village-level drying being used for paddy to be consumed by farm families. Mills either sun dry or use mechanical driers or both. Drying has to be carried out quickly to avoid the formation of moulds. Mills range from simple hullers, with a throughput of a couple of tons a day, that simply remove the outer husk, to enormous operations that can process 4,000 tons a day and produce highly polished rice.

A good mill can achieve a paddy-to-rice conversion rate of up to 72 per cent but smaller, inefficient mills often struggle to achieve 60 per cent. These smaller mills often do not buy paddy and sell rice but only service farmers who want to mill their paddy for their own consumption.

Distribution

Because of the importance of rice to human nutrition and food security in Asia, the domestic rice markets tend to be subject to considerable state involvement. While the private sector plays a leading role in most countries, agencies such as BULOG in Indonesia, the NFA in the Philippines, VINAFOOD in Vietnam and the Food Corporation of India are all heavily involved in purchasing of paddy from farmers or rice from mills and in distributing rice to poorer people. BULOG and NFA monopolise rice imports into their countries while VINAFOOD controls all exports from Vietnam.

Trade

World trade figures are very different to those for production, as only about 5-6 per cent of rice produced is traded internationally. The largest three exporting countries are Thailand, Vietnam, and the United States. Major importers usually include Bangladesh, the Philippines, Brazil and some African and Persian Gulf countries. Although China and India are the two largest producers of rice in the world, both countries consume the majority of the rice produced domestically, leaving little to be traded internationally.

Price

In late 2007 to May 2008, the price of grains rose greatly due to droughts in major producing countries (particularly Australia), increased use of grains for animal feed and US subsidies for bio-fuel production. Although there was no shortage of rice on world markets this general upward trend in grain prices led to panic buying by consumers, government rice export bans (in particular, by Vietnam and India) and inflated import orders by the Philippines marketing board, the National Food Authority. This caused significant rises in rice prices.

In late April 2008, prices hit 24 US cents a pound, twice the price of seven months earlier. On April 30, 2008, Thailand announced plans for the creation of the Organisation of Rice Exporting Countries (OREC) with the intention that this should develop into a price-fixing cartel for rice. However, little progress had been made by mid-2011 to achieve this.

Between 1961 and 2002, per capita consumption of rice increased by 40 per cent.

Rice is the most important crop in Asia. In Cambodia, for example, 90 per cent of the total agricultural area is used for rice production.

U.S. rice consumption has risen sharply over the past 25 years, fueled in part by commercial applications such as beer production. Almost one in five adult Americans now report eating at least half a serving of white or brown rice per day.

Environmental Impacts

In many countries where rice is the main cereal crop, rice cultivation is responsible for most of the methane emissions. Rice requires slightly more water to produce than other grains.

As sea levels rise, rice will become more inclined to remain flooded for longer periods of time. The longer it stays in water, it cuts the soil off from atmospheric oxygen and causes fermentation of organic matter in the soil. During the wet season, rice cannot hold the carbon in anaerobic conditions.

The microbes in the soil convert the carbon into methane which is then released through the respiration of the rice plant or through diffusion of water. Current contributions of methane from agriculture is ~15 per cent of anthropogenic greenhouse gases, as estimated by the IPCC. A further rise in sea level of 10-85 centimeters would then stimulate the release of more methane into the air by rice plants. Methane is twenty times more potent a greenhouse gas than carbon dioxide.

A 2010 study found that, as a result of rising temperatures and decreasing solar radiation during the later years of the 20th century, the rice yield growth rate has decreased in many parts of Asia, compared to what would have been observed had the temperature and solar radiation trends not occurred. The yield growth rate had fallen 10-20 per cent at some locations. The study was based on records from 227 farms in Thailand, Vietnam, India, China, Bangladesh and Pakistan. The mechanism of this falling yield was not clear but might involve increased respiration during warm nights, so expending energy without being able to photosynthesise.

Rice pests are any organisms or microbes with the potential to reduce the yield or value of the rice crop (or of rice seeds). Rice pests include weeds, pathogens, insects, rodents, and birds. A variety of factors can contribute to pest outbreaks, including the overuse of pesticides and high rates of nitrogen fertilizer application. Weather conditions also contribute to pest outbreaks. For example, rice gall midge and army worm outbreaks tend to follow periods of high rainfall early in the wet season, while thrips outbreaks are associated with drought.

Crop protection scientists are trying to develop rice pest management techniques which are sustainable. In other words, to manage crop pests in such a manner that future crop production is not threatened.

At present, rice pest management includes cultural techniques, pest-resistant rice varieties, and pesticides (which include insecticide). Increasingly, there is evidence that farmers' pesticide applications are often unnecessary, and even facilitate pest outbreaks. By reducing the populations of natural enemies of rice pests, misuse of insecticides can actually lead to pest outbreaks.

Botanicals, so-called 'natural pesticides', are used by some farmers in an attempt to control rice pests. Botanicals include extracts of leaves, or a mulch of the leaves themselves. Some upland rice farmers in Cambodia spread chopped leaves of the bitter bush (*Chromolaena odorata*) over the surface of fields after planting. This practice probably helps the soil retain moisture and thereby facilitates seed germination. Farmers also claim the leaves are a natural fertilizer and helps suppress weed and insect infestations.

Among rice cultivars there are differences in the responses to, and recovery from, pest damage. Therefore, particular cultivars are recommended for areas prone to certain pest problems. The genetically based ability of a rice variety to withstand pest attacks is called resistance.

Three main types of plant resistance to pests are recognized as nonpreference, antibiosis, and tolerance. Nonpreference (or antixenosis) describes host plants which insects prefer to avoid; antibiosis is where insect survival is reduced after the ingestion of host tissue; and tolerance is the capacity of a plant to produce high yield or retain high quality despite insect infestation. Over time, the use of pest resistant rice varieties selects for pests that are able to overcome these mechanisms of resistance.

When a rice variety is no longer able to resist pest infestations, resistance is said to have broken down. Rice varieties that can be widely grown for many years in the presence of pests, and retain their ability to withstand the pests are said to have durable resistance. Mutants of popular rice varieties are regularly screened by plant breeders to discover new sources of durable resistance.

Major rice pests include the brown planthopper, the rice gall midge, the rice bug, the rice leafroller, rice weevils, stemborer, panicle rice mite, rats, and the weed *Echinochloa crusgali*.

Major rice diseases include Rice ragged stunt, Sheath Blight and tungro. Rice blast, caused by the fungus *Magnaporthe grisea*, is the most significant disease affecting rice cultivation. There is also an ascomycete fungus, *Cochliobolus miyabeanus*, that causes brown spot disease in rice.

Parasitic Weeds

Rice is parasitized by the weed eudicot *Striga hermonthica*. This parasitic weed is a devastating pest on the crop.

While most rice is bred for crop quality and productivity, there are varieties selected for characteristics such as texture, smell, and firmness. Cultivars exist that are adapted to deep flooding, and these are generally called 'floating rice'.

There are four major categories of rice worldwide:

1. *Indica*,
2. *Japonica*,
3. *Aromatic*; and
4. *Glutinous*.

The different varieties of rice are not considered interchangeable, either in food preparation or agriculture, so as a result, each major variety is a completely separate market from other varieties. It is common for one variety of rice to rise in price while another one drops in price.

The largest collection of rice cultivars is at the International Rice Research Institute in the Philippines, with over 100,000 rice accessions held in the International Rice Genebank. Rice cultivars are often classified by their grain shapes and texture. For example, Thai Jasmine rice is long-grain and relatively less sticky, as long-grain rice contains less amylopectin than short-grain cultivars. Chinese restaurants often serve long-grain as plain unseasoned steamed rice though short-grain rice is common as well. Japanese mochi rice and Chinese sticky rice are short-grain. Chinese people use sticky rice which is properly known as 'glutinous rice' (note: glutinous refer to the glue-like characteristic of rice; does not refer to 'gluten') to make zongzi. The Japanese table rice is a sticky, short-grain rice. Japanese sake rice is another kind as well.

Indian rice cultivars include long-grained and aromatic Basmati (grown in the North), long and medium-grained Patna rice and short-grained Sona Masoori (also spelled Sona Masuri). In the state of Tamil Nadu, the most prized cultivar is *ponni* which is primarily grown in the delta regions of Kaveri River. Kaveri is also referred to as *ponni* in the South and the name reflects the geographic region where it is grown. In the Western Indian state of Maharashtra, a short grain variety called Ambemohar is very popular. This rice has a characteristic fragrance of Mango blossom.

Aromatic rices have definite aromas and flavours; the most noted cultivars are Thai fragrant rice, *Basmati*, Patna rice, Vietnamese fragrant rice, and a hybrid cultivar from America sold under the trade name, Texmati. Both Basmati and Texmati have a mild popcorn-like aroma and flavour. In Indonesia there are also *red* and *black* cultivars.

High-yield cultivars of rice suitable for cultivation in Africa and other dry ecosystems called the new rice for Africa (NERICA) cultivars have been developed. It is hoped that their cultivation will improve food security in West Africa.

Draft genomes for the two most common rice cultivars, *indica* and *japonica*, were published in April 2002. Rice was chosen as a model organism for the biology of grasses because of its relatively small genome (~430 megabase pairs). Rice was the first crop with a complete genome sequence.

On December 16, 2002, the UN General Assembly declared the year 2004 the International Year of Rice. The declaration was sponsored by more than 40 countries.

The High Yielding Varieties are a group of crops created intentionally during the Green Revolution to increase global food production. Rice, like corn and wheat, was genetically manipulated to increase its yield. This project enabled labor markets in Asia to shift away from agriculture, and into industrial sectors. The first 'Rice Car", IR8 was produced in 1966 at the International Rice Research Institute which is based in the Philippines at the University of the Philippines' Los Baños site. IR8 was created through a cross between an Indonesian variety named 'Peta' and a Chinese variety named 'Dee Geo Woo Gen'.

Scientists have identified and cloned many genes involved in the gibberellin signaling pathway, including GAI1 (Gibberellin Insensitive) and SLR1 (Slender Rice). Disruption of gibberellin signaling can lead to significantly reduced stem growth leading to a dwarf phenotype. Photosynthetic investment in the stem is reduced dramatically as the shorter plants are inherently more stable mechanically. Assimilates become redirected to grain production, amplifying in particular the effect of chemical fertilizers on commercial yield. In the presence of nitrogen fertilizers, and intensive crop management, these varieties increase their yield two to three times.

Future Potential

As the UN Millennium Development project seeks to spread global economic development to Africa, the 'Green Revolution' is cited as the model for economic development. With the intent of replicating the successful Asian boom in agronomic productivity, groups like the Earth Institute are doing research on African agricultural systems, hoping to increase productivity. An important way this can happen is the production of 'New Rices for Africa' (NERICA). These rices, selected to tolerate the low input and harsh growing conditions of African agriculture are produced by the African Rice Center, and billed as technology "from Africa, for Africa". The NERICA have appeared in *The New York Times* and *International Herald Tribune*, trumpeted as miracle crops that will dramatically increase rice yield in Africa and enable an economic resurgence. Ongoing research in China to develop perennial rice could result in enhanced sustainability and food security.

Rice kernels do not contain vitamin A, so people who obtain most of their calories from rice are at risk of vitamin A deficiency. German and Swiss researchers have genetically engineered rice to produce beta-carotene, the precursor to vitamin A, in the rice kernel. The beta-carotene turns the processed (white) rice a 'gold' colour, hence the name 'golden rice'. The beta-carotene is converted to vitamin A in humans who consume the rice. Although some rice strains produce beta-carotene in the hull, no non-genetically engineered strains have been found that produce beta-carotene in the kernel, despite the testing of thousands of strains. Additional efforts are being made to improve the quantity and quality of other nutrients in golden rice.

Ventria Bioscience has genetically modified rice to express lactoferrin, lysozyme, and human serum albumin which are proteins usually found in breast milk. These proteins have antiviral, antibacterial, and antifungal effects.

Rice containing these added proteins can be used as a component in oral rehydration solutions which are used to treat diarrheal diseases, thereby shortening their duration and reducing recurrence. Such supplements may also help reverse anemia.

2

Golden Rice

Golden rice is a variety of *Oryza sativa* rice produced through genetic engineering to biosynthesize beta-carotene, a precursor of pro-vitamin A in the edible parts of rice. The scientific details of the rice were first published in *Science* in 2000. Golden rice was developed as a fortified food to be used in areas where there is a shortage of dietary vitamin A. In 2005 a new variety called *Golden Rice 2* was announced which produces up to 23 times more beta-carotene than the original variety of golden rice. Neither variety is currently available for human consumption. Although golden rice was developed as a humanitarian tool, it has met with significant opposition from environmental and anti-globalization activists.

Golden rice was created by Ingo Potrykus of the Institute of Plant Sciences at the Swiss Federal Institute of Technology, working with Peter Beyer of the University of Freiburg. The project started in 1992, and at the time of publication in 2000, golden rice was considered a significant breakthrough in biotechnology, as the researchers had engineered an entire biosynthetic pathway.

Golden rice was designed to produce beta-carotene, a precursor of vitamin A, in the part of rice that people eat, the endosperm. The rice plant can naturally produce beta-carotene, which is a carotenoid pigment that occurs in the leaves and is involved in photosynthesis. However, the plant does not normally produce the pigment in the endosperm, since photosynthesis does not occur in the endosperm.

Golden rice was created by transforming rice with two beta-carotene biosynthesis genes:

- *psy* (phytoene synthase) from daffodil (*Narcissus pseudonarcissus*)
- *crtl* from the soil bacterium *Erwinia uredovora*

The insertion of a *lyc* (lycopene cyclase) gene was thought to be needed, but further research showed it is already being produced in wild-type rice endosperm.

The *psy* and *crt1* genes were transformed into the rice nuclear genome and placed under the control of an endosperm-specific promoter, so they are only expressed in the endosperm. The exogenous *lyc* gene has a transit peptide sequence attached so it is targeted to the plastid, where geranylgeranyl diphosphate formation occurs. The bacterial *crt1* gene was an important inclusion to complete the pathway, since it can catalyze multiple steps in the synthesis of carotenoids, while these steps require more than one enzyme in plants.

The end product of the engineered pathway is lycopene, but if the plant accumulated lycopene, the rice would be red. Recent analysis has shown the plant's endogenous enzymes process the lycopene to beta-carotene in the endosperm, giving the rice the distinctive yellow colour for which it is named. The original golden rice was called SGR1, and under greenhouse conditions it produced 1.6 µg/g of carotenoids.

Golden rice has been bred with local rice cultivars in the Philippines, Taiwan and with the American rice cultivar 'Cocodrie'. The first field trials of these golden rice cultivars were conducted by Louisiana State University Agricultural Centre in 2004.

Field testing will allow a more accurate measurement of the nutritional value of golden rice, and will enable feeding tests to be performed. Preliminary results from the field tests have shown field-grown golden rice produces 4 to 5 times more beta-carotene than golden rice grown under greenhouse conditions.

In 2005, a team of researchers at biotechnology company, Syngenta, produced a variety of golden rice called 'Golden Rice 2'. They combined the phytoene synthase gene from maize with *crt1* from the original golden rice. Golden rice 2 produces 23 times more carotenoids than golden rice (up to 37 µg/g), and preferentially accumulates beta-carotene (up to 31 µg/g of the 37 µg/g of carotenoids).

To receive the Recommended Dietary Allowance (RDA), it is estimated that 144 g of the most high-yielding strain would have to be eaten. Bioavailability of the carotene from either variety has not been tested in any model.

In June 2005, researcher Peter Beyer received funding from the Bill and Melinda Gates Foundation to further improve golden rice by increasing the levels of or the bioavailability of pro-vitamin A, vitamin E, iron, and zinc, and to improve protein quality through genetic modification.

A 2010 article forecast that golden rice would clear final regulatory hurdles and reach the market in 2012. The International Rice Research Institute (IRRI) is currently coordinating the Golden Rice Network with other partners who have expertise in agriculture and nutrition to research and develop Golden Rice.

In 2011, IRRI announced that Helen Keller International (HKI) a leading global health organisation that reduces blindness and prevents malnutrition worldwide, was joining their Golden Rice project to further develop and evaluate Golden Rice.

The research that led to golden rice was conducted with the goal of helping children who suffer from vitamin A deficiency (VAD). At the beginning of the 21st century, 124 million people, in 118 countries in Africa and South East Asia, were estimated to be affected by VAD. VAD is responsible for 1-2 million deaths, 500,000 cases of irreversible blindness and millions of cases of xerophthalmia annually. Children and pregnant women are at highest risk.

Vitamin A is supplemented orally and by injection in areas where the diet is deficient in vitamin A. As of 1999, there were 43 countries that had vitamin A supplementation programs for children under 5; in 10 of these countries, two high dose supplements are available per year, which, according to UNICEF, could effectively eliminate VAD. However, UNICEF and a number of NGOs involved in supplementation note more frequent low-dose supplementation should be a goal where feasible.

Because many children in countries where there is a dietary deficiency in vitamin A rely on rice as a staple food, the genetic modification to make rice produce provitamin A (beta-carotene) is seen as a simple and less expensive alternative to vitamin supplements or an increase in the consumption of green vegetables or animal products. It can be considered as the genetically engineered equivalent of fluoridated water or iodized salt.

Initial analyses of the potential nutritional benefits of golden rice suggested consumption of golden rice would not eliminate the problems of vitamin A deficiency, but should be seen as a complement to other methods of vitamin A supplementation. Since then, improved strains of golden rice have been developed containing sufficient provitamin A to provide the entire dietary requirement of this nutrient to people who eat about 75g of golden rice per day.

In particular, since carotenes are hydrophobic, there needs to be a sufficient amount of fat present in the diet for golden rice (or most other vitamin A supplements) to be able to alleviate vitamin A deficiency.

In that respect, it is significant that vitamin A deficiency is rarely an isolated phenomenon, but usually coupled to a general lack of a balanced diet. Hence, assuming a bioavailability on par with other natural sources of provitamin A, Greenpeace estimated adult humans would need to eat about 9 kilograms of cooked golden rice of the first breed to receive their RDA of beta-carotene, while a breast-feeding woman would need twice the amount; the effects of an unbalanced (fat-deficient) diet were not fully accounted for.

In other words, it would probably have been both physically impossible to grow enough as well as to eat enough of the original golden rice meet the RDA levels accepted in developed countries. (Note, however, that the RDA levels accepted in developed countries are far in excess of the amounts needed to prevent blindness.) Moreover, this claim referred to a prototype cultivar of golden rice; more recent versions have considerably higher quantities of vitamin A in them.

Intellectual Property Issues

Potrykus has spearheaded an effort to have golden rice distributed for free to subsistence farmers. This required several companies which had intellectual property rights to the results of Beyer's research to license it for free. Beyer had received funding from the European Commissions 'Carotene Plus' research program, and by accepting those funds, he was required by law to give the rights to his discovery to the corporate sponsors of that programme, Zeneca (now Syngenta). Beyer and Potrykus made use of 70 intellectual property rights belonging to 32 different companies and universities in the making of golden rice.

They needed to establish free licences for all of these, so Syngenta and humanitarian partners in the project could use golden rice in breeding programs and to develop new crops.

Free licenses, so called Humanitarian Use Licenses, were granted quickly due to the positive publicity that golden rice received, particularly in TIME magazine in July 2000. Golden rice was said to be the first genetically modified crop that was inarguably beneficial, and thus met with widespread approval. Monsanto Company was one of the first companies to grant the group free licences.

The group also had to define the cutoff between humanitarian and commercial use. This figure was set at US$10,000. Therefore, as long as a farmer or subsequent user of golden rice genetics does not make more than $10,000 per year, no royalties need be paid to Syngenta for commercial use. There is no fee for the humanitarian use of golden rice, and farmers are permitted to keep and replant seed.

Opposition

Critics of genetically engineered crops have raised various concerns. One of these is that golden rice originally did not have sufficient vitamin A. This problem was solved by the development of new strains of rice. However, there are still doubts about the speed at which vitamin A degrades once the plant is harvested, and how much would remain after cooking. A 2009 study of boiled golden rice fed to volunteers concluded that Golden Rice is effectively converted into vitamin A in humans.

Greenpeace opposes the release of any genetically modified organisms into the environment, and is concerned that golden rice is a Trojan horse that will open the door to more widespread use of GMOs.

Vandana Shiva, an Indian anti-GMO activist, argued the problem was not that the crop had any particular deficiencies, but that there were potential problems with poverty and loss of biodiversity in food crops. These problems are aggravated by the corporate control of agriculture based on genetically modified foods. By focusing on a narrow problem (vitamin A deficiency), Shiva argued, the golden rice proponents were obscuring the larger issue of a lack of broad availability of diverse and nutritionally adequate sources of food. Other groups have argued a varied diet containing foods rich in vitamin A such as sweet potato, leafy green vegetables and fruit would provide children with sufficient vitamin A.

Because of lacking real-world studies and uncertainty about how many people will use golden rice, WHO malnutrition expert Francesco Branca concludes "giving out supplements, fortifying existing foods with vitamin A, and teaching people to grow carrots or certain leafy vegetables are, for now, more promising ways to fight the problem".

Basmati

Basmati is a variety of long grain rice grown in India and Pakistan, notable for its fragrance and delicate, nuanced flavour. Its name means 'the fragrant one' in Sanskrit, but it can also mean 'the soft rice', and the word coincidently means 'my smile' in Arabic. India is the largest cultivator and exporter of this rice, followed by Pakistan; it is primarily grown through paddy field farming in the Punjab region.

The grains of basmati rice are longer than most other types of rice. Cooked grains of Basmati rice are characteristically free flowing rather than sticky, as with most long-grain rice. Cooked basmati rice can be uniquely identified by its fragrance. Basmati rice is available in two varieties: white and brown.

A number of varieties of basmati rice exist. Traditional types include Basmati-370, Basmati-385 and Basmati-Ranbirsinghpura (R.S.Pura), while hybrid basmati varieties include Pusa Basmati 1 (also called 'Todal', because the flower has awns). Fragrant rices that are derived from basmati stock but are not considered true basmati varieties include PB2 (also called sugandh-2), PB3 and RH-10.

Scientists at Indian Agricultural Research Institute (IARI), Delhi took the traditional basmati and genetically modified it to produce a hybrid which had most of the good features of traditional basmati (grain elongation, fragrance, alkali content) and the plant was a semi-dwarf type. This basmati was called Pusa Basmati-1. PB1 crop yield is higher than the traditional varieties (up to twice as much).

List of Approved Varieties

Punjab, Kernel Basmati (Pakistan), Dehradun, Safidon, Haryana, Super basmati, Kasturi (Baran, Rajasthan), Basmati 198, basmati 217, basmati 370, basmati 385, basmati 386, Bihar, Kasturi, Mahi Suganda, Pusa, Ranbir, Taraori. Some non-traditional aromatic crosses with basmati characteristics are marketed under a Sugandh designation.

Detection of Adulterated Strains

Difficulty in differentiating genuine traditional basmati from pretenders and the significant price difference between them has led fraudulent traders to adulterate traditional basmati. To protect the interests of consumers and trade, a PCR-based assay similar to DNA fingerprinting in humans allows for the detection of adulterated and non-basmati strains. Its detection limit for adulteration is from 1 per cent upwards with an error rate of ±1.5 per cent. Exporters of basmati rice use 'purity certificates' based on DNA tests for their basmati rice consignments. Based on this protocol, which was developed at the Centre for DNA Fingerprinting and Diagnostics, Labindia, an Indian company has released kits to detect basmati adulteration.

In September 1997, a Texas company called RiceTec won a patent (U.S. Patent No. 5,663,484) on 'basmati rice lines and grains'. The patent secures lines of basmati and basmati-like rice and ways of analyzing that rice. RiceTec, owned by Prince Hans-Adam of Liechtenstein, faced international outrage over allegations of biopiracy. It had also caused a brief diplomatic crisis between India and United States with India threatening to take the matter to WTO as a violation of TRIPS which could have resulted in a major embarrassment for the United States. Both voluntarily and due to review decisions by the United States Patent and Trademark Office, RiceTec lost or withdrew most of the claims of the patent, including, most importantly, the right to call their rice lines "basmati." A more limited varietal patent was granted to RiceTec in 2001 on claims dealing with three strains of the rice developed by the company.

Glycemic Index

According to the Canadian Diabetes Association, basmati rice has a 'medium' glycemic index (between 56 and 69), thus making it more suitable for diabetics as compared to certain other grains and products made from white flour.

3

Flattened Rice

Flattened rice (also called beaten rice) is a dehusked rice which is flattened into flat light dry flakes. These flakes of rice swell when added to liquid, whether hot or cold, as they absorb water, milk or any other liquids. The thicknesses of these flakes vary between almost translucently thin (the more expensive varieties) to nearly four times thicker than a normal rice grain.

This easily digestible form of raw rice is very popular across Nepal, North East India and Bangladesh, and is normally used to prepare snacks or light and easy fast food in a variety of Indian cuisine styles, some even for long-term consumption of a week or more. It is known by a variety of names: *Poha* or *Pauwa* in Hindi, *Baji* in Newari, *Pohe* in Marathi, *Chindé* in Bengali, *Chira* in Assamese, *Phovu* in Konkani, *Chudaa* in Oriya and parts of Bihar and Jharkhand, *Atukulu* in Telugu, *Bajeel* or *Bajil* in Tulu, *Chudwey* in Urdu(Dakkani), *Aval* in Malayalam and Tamil, *Avalakki* in Kannada, *Pauaa/Paunva* in Gujarati, and *Chiura* in Nepali, Bhojpuri and Chhattisgarhi.

Flattened rice can be eaten raw by immersing it in plain water or milk, with salt and sugar to taste, or lightly fried in oil with nuts, raisins, cardamoms, and other spices. The lightly fried variety is a standard breakfast in Malvaa region (surrounding Indore) of Madhya Pradesh. It can be reconstituted with hot water to make a porridge or paste, depending on the proportion of water added. In villages, particularly in Chhattisgarh, *Poha* or *Chiura* is also eaten raw by mixing with jaggery.

In Bhopal, *poha* is cooked with lightly frying mustard seeds, tumeric, chili powder, finely chopped onions and then moistened poha is added to the spicy mix and steamed for a few minutes. *Jalebi* is often eaten with *poha*.

Flattened rice is also a convenience food and very similar to instant mashed potatoes in uses and spirit.

Dishes made from Beaten Rice

- *Dhau Baji* (Newari): A dish where beaten rice is dry roasted in a pan, then mixed with yogurt and sugar.
- *Chindé'r pulao*: A snack prepared by immersing the rice flakes in cold water, drying them, and then preparing *pilaf*-style with nuts, raisins, black pepper, green chillies, and salt and sugar to taste. This is very popular as a breakfast or evening dish in families, and may not be available in any stores or restaurants.
- *Chindé bheja*: Some flakes are immersed in a bowl of usually cold water, flavoured with lime juice, salt, sugar, and a little black pepper.
- *Bajeel Ogarne*: Here beaten rice is seasoned with mustard seeds, coconut oil, and red chillies.
- *Beaten rice with curds*: Here beaten rice is soaked in water and then sieved. Curd is added with table salt, preferably eaten with mango or lemon pickle.
- *Kanda Pohe* In this dish, beaten rice is soaked and sieved. Small pieces of boiled potato, onion, mustard seeds, turmeric and red chilli are seasoned and mixed with beaten rice and served hot.
- *Dadpe Pohe*: Thin or medium beaten rice is mixed with fresh coconut, grated green mangos, chili powder, and coriander. It is then seasoned with salt and a tadka (fried mixture) of peanut oil, mustard seeds, turmeric and finely chopped onions.

- *Sweet Bajil* Beaten rice is mixed with jaggery and grated coconut.
- *Khara Bajeel*: The beaten rice is mixed with red chilli powder, salt and coconut. Sometimes seasoned.
- *Sajjige Bajeel*: Combination of upma and Khara bajeel.
- *Chudaa Dahi (Orissa)*: Combination of yogurt, sugar and flattened rice, often with banana.
- *Aval Nanachathu (Kerala)*: Combination of grated coconut, sugar, a little water, and beaten rice. Keep for 2-3 hours so rice puffs up.

Black Rice

Black rice is one of several black-coloured heirloom plants producing rice variants such as Indonesian black rice and Thai Jasmine Black Rice. Black rice is high in nutritional value including iron. Unlike other rice from Asia, it is not glutinous or rough. This grain has a similar amount of fibre to brown rice and like brown rice, has a mild, nutty taste.

Black 'forbidden rice' is so named because originally, in China, it was considered the Emperor's rice and it was forbidden for anyone else to eat it.

It is a deep black colour and turns deep purple when cooked. Its dark purple colour is primarily due to its high anthocyanin content. It has a relatively high mineral content (including iron) and, like most rice, supplies several important amino acids.

In China, noodles made from black rice have recently begun to be produced. At least one United States bread company has also begun producing 'Chinese Black Rice' bread. It shares the deep tyrian colour of cooked black rice.

The thai jasmine black rice is grown in Thailand. Jasmine rice gets its name for the fragrant jasmine scent it produces while being cooked. Black jasmine rice, while not as prevalent as the white and brown varieties, adds more vibrant colour to meals, but it also provides additional health benefits, as well.

White Rice

White rice is the name given to milled rice that has had its husk, bran, and germ removed. This is done largely to prevent spoilage and to extend the storage life of the grain. After milling, the rice is polished, resulting in a seed with a bright, white, shiny appearance.

The polishing process removes important nutrients. A diet based on unenriched white rice leaves people vulnerable to the neurological disease beriberi, due to a deficiency of thiamine (vitamin B_1). White rice is often enriched with some of the nutrients stripped from it during its processing. Enrichment of white rice with B_1, B_3, and iron is required by law in the United States.

At various times, starting in the 19th century, brown rice and wild rice have been advocated as healthier alternatives. The bran in brown rice contains significant dietary fiber and the germ contains many vitamins and minerals.

As with all natural foods, the precise nutritional composition of rice varies slightly depending on the variety, soil conditions, environmental conditions and types of fertilizers.

Typically 100 g of uncooked rice produces around 240-260 g of cooked grains.

4

List of Rice Varieties

Worldwide there are more than 40,000 different varieties of rice, species name *Oryza sativa*. Here are some of the common and popular varieties.

There are four major categories of rice worldwide: Indica, japonica, aromatic and glutinous.

African Varieties

- African rice (not Oryza sativa but a different species, known as Oryza glaberrima.)
- New Rice for Africa

Australian Varieties

- Amaroo - semi-dwarf medium grain
- Reiziq - semi-dwarf medium grain
- Jarrah - semi-dwarf medium grain
- Koshihikari - tall short grain *Japonica* style
- Opus semi-dwarf short grain *Japonica* style
- Illabong - semi-dwarf arborio style
- Langi semi-dwarf long grain, soft cooking (low amylose)
- Doongara - semi-dwarf long grain, hard cooking (high amylose)
- Kyeema - tall long grain, fragrant

Bangladeshi Varieties

- Chinigura rice

- Kalijira rice - similar to basmati and jasmine rice but with very tiny, short grains, resembling sushi rice
- Kataribhog rice
- Paijam rice
- Najirshail rice
- Balam rice
- Binni rice
- Brri Dhan - This is a group of high yielding rice varieties developed by Bangladesh Rice Research Institute.
- Hori Dhan
- Irri rice
- Miniket rice
- Hamim

Bhutanese Varieties

- Bhutanese red rice
- Brown rice but semi-milled

Cambodian Varieties

- Phka Malis similar to fragrant Thai Jasmine rice
- Neang Khon
- Phka Khnei another fragrant variety, phka meaning 'flower'
- Neang Minh long grain rice
- Phka Romdul
- Bonla Pdao
- Sen Kro Ob
- Sen Pi Dao

Canadian Varieties

- Wild rice

Chinese Varieties

- Forbidden rice

Dominican Varieties

- Prosequisa 4
- Prosequisa 5

- Prosequisa 10
- Juma 57
- Juma 58
- Juma 66
- Juma 67
- Idiaf 1
- Yocahú CFX-18
- Cristal 100
- Toño Brea
- Inglés Corto
- Inglés Largo

Indian Varieties

- Basmati
- Ambemohar
- Dubraj rice
- Aizon rice
- Champaa rice
- Clearfield rice
- Hasan serai
- HMT rice
- Jay Shrirama rice
- Joha rice
- Rosematta rice
- Navara rice
- Raja Hansa rice
- Molakolukulu
- Patna rice
- Pusa rice
- Idly rice - Short grain
- Sona Masuri
- Ranjit rice
- Katta sambar
- Hansraj
- Jyothi

- Annapoornna
- Poreiton chakhau - aromatic dark red rice from Manipur

Iranian Varieties

Many varieties of rice are cultivated in Iran. A few of them are listed below:

- Domsiah
- Binam
- Hasani
- Salari
- Ambarboo
- Sang Tarom
- Hasan Sarai

Italian Varieties

- Arborio
- Ariete
- Baldo
- Carnaroli
- Lido
- Originario
- Padano
- Ribe
- Roma
- Sant'Andrea
- Thaibonnet
- Venere
- Vialone Nano

Japanese Varieties

- Koshihikari
- Hitomebore
- Hinohikari
- Kinuhikari
- Nihonbare
- Sasanishiki

- Kirara397
- Hoshinoyume
- Domannaka
- Akitakomachi
- Haenuki
- Hanaechizen
- Akebono (rice)
- Asahi (rice)

Nepalese Varieties

- Pokhareli
- Jire Masino
- Mansooli

Lao/Thai Varieties

- Sticky Rice
- Rice biodiversity in Laos

Pakistani Varieties

- PK-385 Basmati Rice
- PK-386 Basmati Rice
- PK-198 Basmati Rice
- D-98 Basmati Rice
- KS-282
- Irri-9
- Irri-6

Rice Varieties of Karnataka

- Jaya
- Thanu
- Tunga
- IR-30864, BR-2655 (Produced in SFPP Project, VC Farm, Mandya, Karnataka, India)

Traditional Kerala Rice Varieties

- Chitteni Thavalakkannan
- Vattan
- Wayanad Kayamma

Assamese Rice Varieties

- Bora
- Malbhog
- Manuhar
- Bahadur
- Kushal
- Maniram IR-8, etc.

Tamil Nadu Rice Varieties

- IR-20,IR-50
- Aduthurai (ADT)-36
- Ambai-16
- BPT 5204
- ADT 43
- Improved white ponni
- Co-43 etc.

Indonesian Rice Varieties/Landraces

- Cianjur Pandanwangi (aromatic)
- Rajalele (semi-aromatic)
- Peta

Many Deep Swamp Rice Varieties of Kalimantan (Borneo)

- dryland rice landraces of Java
- Temanggung black rice
- Mandel Handayani
- Segreng Handayani
- Gunung Kidul red rice
- Yogyakarta

Philippine Varieties

- Baysilanon
- Dinorado
- Ifugao Rice
- Maharlika
- Milagrosa pino
- Segadis Milagrosa

- Kalinayan
- Sinandomeng
- IR-841
- IR-64
- Angelika
- Azucena
- Malagkit
- Wagwag

Other varieties which include:

- Red
- Brown
- Black
- White
- Glutinous rice

Sri Lankan Varieties

- Samba
- Sri Lankan Red Rice
- Keeri Samba
- Supiri Samba
- Supiri Nadu
- Nadu Rice
- Badhabath

Spanish Varieties

- Bomba rice
- Bahia
- Bomba
- Calasparra
- Senia

Thai Varieties

- Jasmine rice
- White rice
- White Glutinous rice
- Black Glutinous rice

- Red Cargo rice
- Brown rice

United States Varieties

- Long grain rice
- Medium grain rice
- Short grain rice
- Sweet/waxy/glutinous rice
- Aromatic rices
- Arborio rice

California Varieties

- Akitakomachi rice
- California New Variety rice
- Calmochi rice
- Calrose rice
- Wehani rice

Louisiana Varieties

- Pecan rice
- Popcorn rice

Vietnamese Varieties

- D Huong rice
- Nàng Thom Ch Đào Rice - from M L commune, C n Đu c district, Long An province
- N p cái hoa vàng from Nam Dinh province
- N p c m Rice
- N p Tú L
- Tài Nguyên Rice - from Long An province
- Tám Xoan Rice - from H i H u district, Nam Dinh province

5

Parboiled Rice

Parboiled rice is rice that has been boiled in the husk. Parboiling makes rice easier to process by hand, improves its nutritional profile (excepting its vitamin-B content, which is denatured in the process), and changes its texture.

Polishing rice by hand, that is, removing the bran layer, is easier if the rice has been parboiled. It is, however, somewhat more difficult to process mechanically. The bran of parboiled rice is somewhat oily, and tends to clog machinery. Most parboiled rice is milled in the same way as white rice.

Parboiling rice drives nutrients, especially thiamine, from the bran into the grain, so that parboiled white rice is 80 per cent nutritionally similar to brown rice. Because of this, parboiling was adopted by North American rice growers in the early 20th century.

The starches in parboiled rice become gelatinized, making it harder and glassier than other rice. Parboiled rice usually has small amounts of milk added to it to prevent the grain from over hardening. Parboiled rice takes more time to cook, and the cooked rice is firmer and less sticky. In North America, parboiled rice is generally partially or fully precooked by the processor.

Parboiling is a hydrothermal treatment of paddy. Parboiled rice is 'par'-tially 'boiled' (i.e. partially cooked rice).

In other words parboiling means precooking of rice within the husk. Paddy is first hydrated, then heated to cook the rice and finally dried.

In the 1910s, the German-British scientist invented a form of parboiling designed to retain more of the nutrients in rice, now known as the Huzenlaub Process. It involves first vacuum drying of the whole grain, then steaming, and finally vacuum drying and husking. Besides increasing rice's nutritional value, it also made it resistant to weevils and reduced cooking time.

Congee

Congee is a type of rice porridge popular in many Asian countries. It can be eaten or served with a side dish. Names for congee are as varied as the style of its preparation. Despite its many variations it can be recognised by its thick texture. It can be considered as a porridge or thick soup.

To prepare the dish, rice is boiled in large amounts of water until it softens significantly. Congee can be made in a pot or in a rice cooker. Some rice cookers have a 'congee' setting, allowing congee to be cooked overnight. The rice used can either be sticky or regular depending on the country's common practice. Culture also often dictates the way congee is cooked and eaten.

In many Asian cultures, it is also called *Kanji* (Tamil/ Malayalam/Tulu), *Ganji* (Kannada/Hindi), *Ghanji* (Telugu), *juk* (Cantonese, Korean), *chao* (Vietnamese), *jok* (Thai), kayu (Japanese), *lúgaw* (Filipino), or *jaou* (Bengali) which is derived directly from the Chinese character *zhou* (which means gruel in Mandarin).

In some cultures, congee is eaten primarily as a breakfast food or late supper; in others it is eaten as a substitute for rice at other meals. It is often considered particularly suitable for the sick as a mild, easily digestible food.

In Bangladesh, Congee-known as *Konji Jaou* or *Kanji Jaou* (depending on pronunciation)- along with Panta Bhat, is popular throughout the whole country, more so in rural areas than urban. It is made by repeatedly boiling rice in large quantities of water. The result is a thick white broth. Its consistency and colour is dictated by the water-to-rice ratio (which can be from 5:1 to 13:1) and the various types of rice used. Glutinous rice is often used in Sylhet and Khulna which makes the broth quite distinct from other types in the country. In parts of the country it is smoked while cooking-giving a unique aroma. It is usually served for breakfast with lime, salt, chilli and fried shallot. On its own, it is fed to the unwell as it is believed to be beneficial to the digestive system.

Burma

In Burma, rice congee is called *san byohk*: literally 'rice boiled'. It is very thin and plain, often made with just rice and water but sometimes with chicken or pork stock and served with a simple garnish of chopped spring onions and crispy fried onions. As in other Asian countries, *san byohk* is considered *lu ma mar zar* ('food for the unwell'), and given to people who are sick.

Cambodia

In Cambodia, rice congee (babaw) is widely eaten for breakfast. Plain congee is typically eaten with salted eggs, pickled vegetables, or dried fish. Chicken congee and seafood congee are also commonly eaten.

There are many regional variations of Chinese congees (Chinese: pinyin: *zhou*). For example, to make Cantonese congee, white rice is boiled in many times its weight of water for a long time until the rice breaks down and becomes a fairly thick white porridge (Pinyin: *báizhou*). Congees made in other regions may use different types of rice with different quantities of water, producing congees of different consistency.

Congee is often eaten with *zhacai*, salted duck eggs, lettuce and dace (*Cirrhinus chinensis*) paste, bamboo shoots, *youtiao*, *rousong*, pickled tofu, wheat gluten, with other condiments, meat or century eggs.

Other seasonings, such as white pepper and soy sauce, may be added. Grilled fish may be mixed in to provide a different texture.

Congee is often eaten with fried bread sticks known as *youtiao*. Congee with *youtiao* is commonly eaten as breakfast in many areas in China. Congee can be left watery, or can be drained so that it has a texture similar to Western oatmeal porridge. Congee can also be made from brown rice, although this is less common and takes longer to cook.

Besides being an everyday meal, congee is considered to be food therapy for the unwell. Ingredients can be determined by their supposed therapeutic value as well as flavour.

The origin of congee is unknown, but from many historical accounts it was usually served during times of famine, or when numerous patrons visited the temples, as a way to stretch the rice supply to feed more people.

In China, congee has also been used to feed young infants. However, the cooking time is much longer than for *okayu* and, because it is for infants, the congee is not seasoned with salt or any other flavouring. Often it is mixed with pre-steamed and deboned fish.

Congee can also be made from other grains like cornmeal, millet, barley, and sorghum. These are common in the north of China where rice does not grow as well as other grains suited for a colder climate. Multigrain congee mixes are sold in the health food sections of Chinese supermarkets. Congee with mung beans is usually eaten with sugar, like red bean congee.

India

In Tamil Nadu, a plain rice porridge, or the thick supernatant water on overcooked rice, is known as Kanji. The people of Kerala also call this preparation of rice in a watery state *kanji* and it is eaten as a porridge with green lentils or chutney.

Udupi and Mangalore districts people usually eat rice *ganji* in a variant manner made by Kannada-speaking, Tulu-speaking or Konkani people in and around Udupi and Mangalore (Karnataka, South India). Here parboiled rice (*Kocheel akki* in Kannada, *oorpel aari* black rice *bulenta aari* white rice in Tulu or *ukadey tandool* in Konkani) is steamed with a large amount of water. Jain Ganji Matt are famous in these districts. Usually simple Ganji with pickle & milk are served, in Jain matts. Fresh coconut is grated and the resulting milk skimmed and added to the *ganji* (called *pej* in Konkani), which is served hot with fish curry, coconut chutney, or Indian pickles.

In the state of Andhra Pradesh, it is called *ganji* in Telugu and mostly eaten by the very poor.

In Indonesia, congee is called 'bubur'. It is a favourite breakfast food, and many food vendors pass through the streets at dawn, calling 'bubur', to sell it to householders. A popular version is 'bubur ayam', which is congee with shredded chicken meat. It is also served with many condiments, such as green onion, crispy fried shallot, fried soybean, Chinese crullers (You tiao, known as cakwe in Indonesia), both salty and sweet soy sauce, and sometimes it is topped with yellow chicken broth and kerupuk (Indonesian style crackers). Unlike many other Indonesian dishes, it is not spicy; sambal or chili paste is served separately.

The food hawkers sometimes have sate to go with it, made from quail egg or chicken intestine, liver, gizzard, or heart.

In another region of Indonesia, Manado, it is very popular with Tinutuan or bubur Manado (Manadonese porridge), another porridge with ample vegetables. It is a bit different from the one which is sold in Java island. It is made from rice porridge and enhanced with water spinach or kangkung, corn kernels, yam or sweet potato, dried salty fish, lemon basil or kemangi leaves, and melinjo or *gnetum gnemon* leaves.

Sago flour is made to porridge in eastern Indonesian, as the staple food of Maluku and Papuan people. The sago congee is called Papeda and usually eaten with yellow soup made from tuna or mubara fish spiced with turmeric and lime.

Japan

Nanakusa-gayu, Simple saltiness.

Okayu (also *kayu* – is the name for the type of congee eaten in Japan, which is considerably thicker than congee produced in other cultures. For example, a Cantonese-style congee typically uses a water-to-rice ratio of 12:1, but *okayu* typically uses ratios of 5:1 (*zen-gayu*) or 7:1 (*shichibu-gayu*). Also, its cooking time is shorter than other types of congee: *okayu* is cooked for about 30 minutes, while Cantonese congees cook for an hour or more.

Okayu may be made with just rice and water, and is often seasoned with salt. Beaten eggs could be beaten into it to thicken it into gruel. Toppings may be added to enhance flavour; *negi* (a type of green onion), salmon, roe, ginger, and *umeboshi* (pickled *ume* fruit) are among the most common. *Miso* or chicken stock may be used to flavour the broth. Most Japanese electric rice cookers have a setting for *okayu*.

In Japan, *okayu* is popularly known as a food served to the ill. Because it is soft and easily digestible, *okayu* is the first solid food served to Japanese infants; it is used to help with the transition from liquids to the thicker rice dishes which constitute much of the Japanese diet. It is also commonly eaten by the elderly for the same reasons.

A type of *okayu* called *nanakusa-gayu* 'Seven Herb Porridge') is traditionally eaten on 7 January with special herbs that protect against evils and invite good luck and longevity in the new year. As a simple, light dish, *nanakusagayu* serves as a break from the many heavy dishes eaten over the Japanese New Year.

Zosui is a similar dish, which uses already cooked rice, rather than cooking the rice in the soup.

In Korea, the dish goes by the name *juk* derived from the Chinese language in which *juk [jook]* means the same thing. There are more than forty varieties of *juk* mentioned in old documents. Depending on the ingredients and consistency, *juk* can be considered as a food for recuperation (much like chicken soup in modern American culture), a delicacy, or food during famine and war.

The most general form of *juk* is simply called *heen juk* (white *juk*), which is made from plain white rice. Other varieties include different ingredients such as milk, vegetables, seafood, nuts and other grains. Being largely unflavoured, it is served together with a number of more flavourful side dishes such as jeotgal, various types of kimchi, pickled cuttlefish, spicy octopus, and other side-dishes.

Notable varieties include *jatjuk* made from finely-ground pine nuts, *jeonbokjuk* made with abalones, *yulmujuk* made from Job's Tears, and *patjuk* made from red beans.

Juk is considered the ideal choice of food for babies, the ill or elderly as it is easily eaten and digested. It is sold commercially by many *juk* chain stores in South Korea and is a common take-out dish.

Philippines

Lúgaw (alternately spelled 'lugao' or 'lugau') is the Filipino name for congee. Otherwise similar to Cantonese-style congee, *lúgaw* is typically thicker, retaining the shape of the rice but with a similar texture. It is boiled with strips of fresh ginger. Other flavours may be added according to taste. Most often it is topped with scallions and served with crispy fried garlic. As with *okayu*, fish or chicken stock may be used to flavour the broth. *Lúgaw* can also be served with *tokwa't baboy* (diced tofu and pork), *goto* (beef tripe), *utak* (brain [of pig]), *dilâ* (tongue [of pig]), *litid* ([beef] ligaments), and with *calamansi*, *patís*, and soy sauce. It is often served to the ill and the elderly, and is favoured among Filipinos living abroad in colder climates because it is warm, soft, and easily digestible.

Some provinces prefer the Spanish-influenced *arroz caldo* (literally 'broth rice'), which is often thought to be a European dish because of its name. *Arroz caldo* is actually a Chinese congee that was adapted to the tastes of the Spanish colonial settlers who patronised Chinese restaurants in the Philippines.

Arroz caldo is usually spiced with saffron and black pepper in place of or in addition to the more traditional ginger and scallion. *Arroz caldo* more closely resembles risotto than congee, from which it can be distinguished by its bright yellow saffron colour and the relatively larger pieces of meat. *Arroz caldo* is more popular among people of Ilokano heritage, although those of other provinces such as Cebu often eat it with the addition of prawns, olive oil, bay leaf, and Chinese sausage.

Portugal

In Portugal, there is a traditional soup made of rice and chicken meat that is named *Canja* (very similar pronunciation to congee). The rice is not cooked for as long as in Asian congee, so it is very soft but not disintegrated. Traditionally, a boiling fowl containing small immature eggs is used; the eggs are carefully boiled and served in the *canja*. This soup is sometimes served with a fresh mint leaf on top. Canja is traditionally given to people recovering from disease, as in Asia, and is strongly valued as comfort food. In some regions of Portugal; there is even an ancient custom of feeding the mother a strict diet of canja in the first weeks after childbirth. Canja is also eaten traditionally in Brasil and Cabo Verde, formerly Portuguese colonies.

Sri Lanka

In Sri Lanka, rice congee is known as *kola kanda* in Sinhalese and tends to have various local indigenous herbs and plants mixed in with it. It is traditionally eaten for breakfast and consists of rice, water and local herbs (*Gotu Kola*). It is also eaten by Sri Lankan Muslims for *iftar* during Ramadan. It is also occasionally made with oats. Tamils and Muslims in Sri Lanka call it *Aarisi kanji* (rice *kanji*) and use chicken or beef for it. It is sometimes made with milk (*paal kanji*), and there are many other combinations with appropriate prefixes in Tamil.

Taiwan

In Taiwan, congee is prepared in the same way as in Fujian Province, China, and consists of rice and water, with few other ingredients. Sweet potato is often added for taste, and eggs are sometimes beaten into it to thicken it to a gruel. As with most Chinese styles, congee is often served to the ill and those with difficulty chewing. A variety of side dishes are often served with congee as well.

Thailand

In Thailand, rice congee is known as 'jok' (IPA: and is often served as breakfast with a raw or partially-cooked egg added. Minced pork or beef is usually added, and the dish is usually topped with a small version of youtiao (known as *pathongko* by Thais), garlic, slivered ginger, and spicy pickles such as pickled radish and chopped spring onions. Although it is more popular as a breakfast dish, many stores specializing in congee sell it throughout the day. Variations in the meat and toppings are also frequently found. It is especially popular during Thailand's cool season.

Vietnam

In Vietnam, rice congee is called *cháo*. It is sometimes cooked with pandan leaves or Asian green beans. In its simplest form (plain rice porridge) it is a food for times of famine and hardship, when rice is not abundant. Or, as is especially common among Buddhist monks, nuns and lay people, it can be a simple breakfast food eaten with pickled vegetables or fermented tofu. Despite its humble ubiquity among the poor, it is also popular as a main entré when cooked with a variety of meats. For example, *Cháo gà* is a variety of *cháo* cooked with chicken, garlic, and ginger. The rice porridge is cooked in the broth in which a whole chicken had been boiled, and once the chicken is cooked, the meat is sliced and layered on a bed of shredded uncooked cabbage, sliced onions and drizzled with a vinegar-based sauce, to be eaten as a side dish to the porridge. Other combinations include duck porridge which is cooked in the same fashion as the chicken porridge, but with duck. *Cháo lòng heo* is made with *lòng heo* (a variety of pork entrails, including sliced cakes of congealed pork blood). It is also common to eat *cháo* during an illness, as it is believed the porridge is easy to digest while being fortifying. For such purposes, the *cháo* is sometimes cooked with roasted white rice, giving the porridge broth a more nuanced body and a subtle nutty flavour. On a related note, in some parts of Vietnam local customs call for making *cháo* for death anniversary ceremonies, during which it is offered to fortify the spirits of the dead. (This tradition, however, is not widely practiced and seems to contradict the general principle of providing only the best food for one's ancestors.)

Steamed Rice

Steamed rice refers to rice that has been cooked either by steaming or boiling.

It is a staple in Japan, China, Korea, Thailand, Philippines, Brazil and numerous other Latin American and Asian countries. It is also used as a main ingredient in many dishes.

Steamed rice is traditionally prepared in one of two ways. Actual steaming is done by placing a bowl or pot containing dry rice into a food steamer, and cooking it until done. Steamed rice is normally cooked by adding dry rice and a small amount of salt to water and boiling it in a covered pot. Today, most rice is prepared in electric rice cookers, that work the same way. During cooking, the rice absorbs the water, increasing in volume and mass. The rice is considered cooked when it has absorbed all the water.

In China, steamed rice is most commonly served in individual bowls, with each diner receiving one. Food from communal dishes is placed upon the rice, and is then eaten.

Steamed or boiled rice is used as an ingredient in many dishes. In China, leftover steamed rice is used to make porridge eaten the following morning. Some other dishes include:

- Fried rice.
- Sushi.
- Bamboo rice is a Chinese dish where rice is steamed inside a segment of bamboo.
- Kralan is a Cambodian version of bamboo rice, using beans and grated coconut, with coconut milk added to the water. It is cooked over a dry heat to steam the ingredients within.
- Nga pyaw douk.

- Zongzi is a traditional Chinese dish using glutinous rice steamed inside a leaf or bamboo.
- Puto is Philippine steamed rice cake.
- Dal bhat is a traditional India and Nepali staple dish.
- Tteok, a type of Korean rice cake
- Rice and beans
- Red beans and rice

Most common is plain, steamed white rice, however a number of varieties and are served, many with specific cooking methods. Some varieties include:

- Thai steamed rice
- Sticky rice
- Sushi rice (cooked with the addition of Japanese rice vinegar and sugar)
- Basmati rice

6

Rice and Beans

Rice and beans (called *arroz y habas, arroz con habichuelas, arroz con frijoles* or similar in Spanish, *arroz e feijão* or *feijão com arroz,* in Portuguese, *diri ak pwa* in Haitian Creole, *Avas kon arroz* or *Avikas kon arroz* in Judaeo-Spanish etc.) is a very popular dish in Latin America, the Caribbean, and in communities of Latino, Caribbean or Sephardic people elsewhere. Given the basic nature of its ingredients, rice and bean dishes exists in many regions of the world. This article, however, is primarily concerned with the Americas.

The dish usually consists of white rice accompanied by brown, red or black, dry beans (typically *Phaseolus vulgaris* or *Vigna unguiculata*) and seasoned in various ways. Different regions have different preferences. In Brazil, for example, black beans are more popular in Rio de Janeiro, Rio Grande do Sul and Santa Catarina, while in most other parts of the country these are mostly only used in feijoadas. The New Orleans specialty known as 'red beans and rice' is often accompanied by a side of smoked sausage or a fried pork chop.

In many areas, rice and beans are often served side by side rather than mixed together. Either way, they may be considered a meal, frequently with a topping of meat or chicken. Meat or other ingredients are sometimes placed atop rice and beans or (less often) mixed into it.

History

Unlike certain varieties of bean, rice is not native to the Americas. Rice was introduced to the Caribbean and South America by European colonizers at an early date with Spanish colonizers introducing Asian rice to Mexico in the 1520s at Veracruz and the Portuguese and their African slaves introducing it at about the same time to Colonial Brazil. More recent scholarship suggests that African slaves played a more active role in the establishment of rice in the New World and that African rice was an important crop from an early period.

In either case, varieties of rice and bean dishes were a staple dish among the peoples of West Africa, and they remained a staple among their descendants subjected to slavery in the Spanish New World colonies and elsewhere in the Americas.

Importance

While simple, the dish is very nutritious. Rice is rich in starch, an excellent source of energy. Rice also has iron, vitamin B and protein. Beans are also protein-rich, and contain a good amount of iron and other necessary minerals, and the consumption of the two in tandem provides all the essential amino acids. Researcher writes:

Rice and beans are an inseparable pair of staple foods for millions of Latin Americans, parts of Central America, the Caribbean, and the Andean Mountain zone. Whether consumed separately or together, these crops figure importantly in the human diet and in national economies across the entire region, and trends in their production are a matter of immediate relevance to practically all of its inhabitants.

In addition, rice and beans are common and affordable ingredients, often available even when times are hard. A Nicaraguan explained life after Hurricane Mitch by saying:

For breakfast, we have beans and rice. For lunch, we have rice and beans. For supper, we have rice and beans mixed together.

In Brazil, rice and beans are commonly eaten as everyday lunch, along with a different variety of meats and vegetables.

It is also common to prepare dinner using the lunch leftovers. Brazil is the world leader in dry beans production and Latin American leader in rice consumption.

Culture

In discussing Puerto Rican cuisine, food critic researcher wrote:

> Rice and beans are sacred They are our 'daily bread', our comfort food. When you mess with someone's rice & beans, you mess with their mind. Rice & beans are soul food I ordered *Arroz con habichuelas* and when they arrived, I poured the entire bowl of beans over the plate of rice and mixed them thoroughly to absorb the gravy. I mention mixing because rice & beans are eaten together in the same bite and not, as I saw the uninitiated do, eaten separately in isolated mouthfuls. It's a synergistic dish and makes a deliciously healthy block of complete protein when combined together.

Today, the term 'rice and beans' is used as a metonym for basic needs of food and phrases such as 'the poor can't afford their rice and beans' are frequent. It is also used more generally for anything that is basic, fundamental, or simple in phrases like "just do the rice and beans and you'll succeed". The term is also used to describe any pairing that works together well, such as "they're like rice and beans".

Seed

A seed is a small embryonic plant enclosed in a covering called the seed coat, usually with some stored food. It is the product of the ripened ovule of gymnosperm and angiosperm plants which occurs after fertilization and some growth within the mother plant. The formation of the seed completes the process of reproduction in seed plants (started with the development of flowers and pollination), with the embryo developed from the zygote and the seed coat from the integuments of the ovule.

Seeds have been an important development in the reproduction and spread of flowering plants, relative to more primitive plants like mosses, ferns and liverworts, which do not have seeds and use other means to propagate themselves. This can be seen by the success of seed plants (both gymnosperms and angiosperms) in dominating biological niches on land, from forests to grasslands both in hot and cold climates.

The term *seed* also has a general meaning that predates the above — anything that can be sown, e.g. 'seed' potatoes, 'seeds' of corn or sunflower 'seeds'. In the case of sunflower and corn 'seeds', what is sown is the seed enclosed in a shell or hull, and the potato is a tuber.

A typical seed includes three basic parts:

1. an embryo;
2. a supply of nutrients for the embryo; and
3. a seed coat.

The embryo is an immature plant from which a new plant will grow under proper conditions. The embryo has one cotyledon or seed leaf in monocotyledons, two cotyledons in almost all dicotyledons and two or more in gymnosperms. The radicle is the embryonic root. The plumule is the embryonic shoot. The embryonic stem above the point of attachment of the cotyledon(s) is the epicotyl. The embryonic stem below the point of attachment is the hypocotyl.

Within the seed, there usually is a store of nutrients for the seedling that will grow from the embryo. The form of the stored nutrition varies depending on the kind of plant. In angiosperms, the stored food begins as a tissue called the endosperm, which is derived from the parent plant via double fertilization. The usually triploid endosperm is rich in oil or starch and protein. In gymnosperms, such as conifers, the food storage tissue is part of the female gametophyte, a haploid tissue. In some species, the embryo is embedded in the endosperm or female gametophyte, which the seedling will use upon germination. In others, the endosperm is absorbed by the embryo as the latter grows within the developing seed, and the cotyledons of the embryo become filled with this stored food. At maturity, seeds of these species have no endosperm and are termed exalbuminous seeds. Some exalbuminous seeds are bean, pea, oak, walnut, squash, sunflower, and radish. Seeds with an endosperm at maturity are termed albuminous seeds. Most monocots (e.g. grasses and palms) and many dicots (e.g. brazil nut and castor bean) have albuminous seeds. All gymnosperm seeds are albuminous.

The seed coat (or *testa*) develops from the tissue, the integument, originally surrounding the ovule. The seed coat in the mature seed can be a paper-thin layer (e.g. peanut) or something more substantial (e.g. thick and hard in honey locust and coconut). The seed coat helps protect the embryo from mechanical injury and from drying out.

In addition to the three basic seed parts, some seeds have an appendage on the seed coat such an aril (as in yew and nutmeg) or an elaiosome (as in Corydalis) or hairs (as in cotton). There may also be a scar on the seed coat, called the hilum; it is where the seed was attached to the ovary wall by the funiculus.

Kinds of Seeds

Many structures commonly referred to as 'seeds' are actually dry fruits. Sunflower seeds are sold commercially while still enclosed within the hard wall of the fruit, which must be split open to reach the seed. Different groups of plants have other modifications, the so-called *stone* fruits (such as the peach) have a hardened fruit layer (the endocarp) fused to and surrounding the actual seed. Nuts are the one-seeded, hard shelled fruit, of some plants, with an indehiscent seed, such as an acorn or hazelnut.

Seed Production

Seeds are produced in several related groups of plants, and their manner of production distinguishes the angiosperms ('enclosed seeds') from the gymnosperms ('naked seeds'). Angiosperm seeds are produced in a hard or fleshy structure called a fruit that encloses the seeds, hence the name. (Some fruits have layers of both hard and fleshy material). In gymnosperms, no special structure develops to enclose the seeds, which begin their development 'naked' on the bracts of cones. However, the seeds do become covered by the cone scales as they develop in some species of conifer.

Seed production in natural plant populations vary widely from year-to-year in response to weather variables, insects and diseases, and internal cycles within the plants themselves. Over a 20-year period, for example, forests composed of loblolly pine and shortleaf pine produced from 0 to nearly 5 million sound pine seeds per hectare. Over this period, there were six bumper seeds, five poor seeds crops, and nine good seed crops, when evaluated in regard to producing adequate seedlings for natural forest reproduction.

Seed Development

The inside of a *Ginkgo* seed, showing a well-developed embryo, nutritive tissue (megagametophyte), and a bit of the surrounding seed coat.

The internal structure of a dicot seed and embryo:

(a) seed coat;

(b) endosperm;

(c) cotyledon; and

(d) hypocotyl.

The seed, which is an embryo with two points of growth (one of which forms the stems the other the roots) is enclosed in a seed coat with some food reserves. Angiosperm seeds consist of three genetically distinct constituents:

1. the embryo formed from the zygote;
2. the endosperm, which is normally triploid;
3. the seed coat from tissue derived frcm the maternal tissue of the ovule.

In angiosperms, the process of seed development begins with double fertilization and involves the fusion of the egg and sperm nuclei into a zygote. The second part of this process is the fusion of the polar nuclei with a second sperm cell nucleus, thus forming a primary endosperm. Right after fertilization, the zygote is mostly inactive but the primary endosperm divides rapidly to form the endosperm tissue. This tissue becomes the food that the young plant will consume until the roots have developed after germination or it develops into a hard seed coat. The seed coat forms from the two integuments or outer layers of cells of the ovule, which derive from tissue from the mother plant, the inner integument forms the tegmen and the outer forms the testa. When the seed coat forms from only one layer it is also called the testa, though not all such testa are homologous from one species to the next.

In gymnosperms, the two sperm cells transferred from the pollen do not develop seed by double fertilization but one sperm nucleus unites with the egg nucleus and the other sperm is not used. Sometimes each sperm fertilizes an egg cell and one zygote is then aborted or absorbed during early development. The seed is composed of the embryo (the result of fertilization) and tissue from the mother plant, which also form a cone around the seed in coniferous plants like Pine and Spruce.

The ovules after fertilization develop into the seeds; the main parts of the ovule are the funicle; which attaches the ovule to the placenta, the nucellus; the main region of the ovule were the embryo sac develops, the micropyle; A small pore or opening in the ovule where the pollen tube usually enters during the process of fertilization, and the chalaza; the base of the ovule opposite the micropyle, where integument and nucellus are joined together.

The shape of the ovules as they develop often affects the finale shape of the seeds. Plants generally produce ovules of four shapes: the most common shape is called anatropous, with a curved shape. Orthotropous ovules are straight with all the parts of the ovule lined up in a long row producing an uncurved seed. Campylotropous ovules have a curved embryo sac often giving the seed a tight 'c' shape. The last ovule shape is called amphitropous, where the ovule is partly inverted and turned back 90° on its stalk or funicle.

In the majority of flowering plants, the zygote's first division is transversely oriented in regards to the long axis, and this establishes the polarity of the embryo. The upper or chalazal pole becomes the main area of growth of the embryo, while the lower or micropylar pole produces the stalk-like suspensor that attaches to the micropyle. The suspensor absorbs and manufacturers nutrients from the endosperm that are utilized during the embryos growth.

The embryo is composed of different parts; the epicotyle will grow into the shoot, the radicle grows into the primary root, the hypocotyl connects the epicotyle and the radicle, the cotyledons form the seed leaves, the testa or seed coat forms the outer covering of the seed. Monocotyledonous plants like corn, have other structures; instead of the hypocotyle-epicotyle, it has a coleoptile that forms the first leaf and connects to the coleorhiza that connects to the primary root and adventitious roots form from the sides. The seeds of corn are constructed with these structures; pericarp, scutellum (single large cotyledon) that absorbs nutrients from the endosperm, endosperm, plumule, radicle, coleoptile and coleorhiza - these last two structures are sheath-like and enclose the plumule and radicle, acting as a protective covering. The testa or seed coats of both monocots and dicots are often marked with patterns and textured markings, or have wings or tufts of hair.

Seed Size and Seed Set

Seeds are very diverse in size. The dust-like orchid seeds are the smallest with about one million seeds per gram; they are often embryonic seeds with immature embryos and no significant energy reserves. Orchids and a few other groups of plants are myco-heterotrophs which depend on mycorrhizal fungi for nutrition during germination and the early growth of the seedling. Some terrestrial Orchid seedlings, in fact, spend the first few years of their life deriving energy from the fungus and do not produce green leaves. At over 20 kg, the largest seed is the coco de mer. Plants that produce smaller seeds can generate many more seeds per flower, while plants with larger seeds invest more resources into those seeds and normally produce fewer seeds. Small seeds are quicker to ripen and can be dispersed sooner, so fall blooming plants often have small seeds. Many annual plants produce great quantities of smaller seeds; this helps to ensure that at least a few will end in a favourable place for growth. Herbaceous perennials and woody plants often have larger seeds, they can produce seeds over many years, and larger seeds have more energy reserves for germination and seedling growth and produce larger, more established seedlings after germination.

Seed Functions

Seeds serve several functions for the plants that produce them. Key among these functions are nourishment of the embryo, dispersal to a new location, and dormancy during unfavourable conditions. Seeds fundamentally are a means of reproduction and most seeds are the product of sexual reproduction which produces a remixing of genetic material and phenotype variability that natural selection acts on.

Embryo Nourishment

Seeds protect and nourish the embryo or young plant. Seeds usually give a seedling a faster start than a sporeling from a spore, because of the larger food reserves in the seed and the multicellularity of the enclosed embryo.

Seed Dispersal

Unlike animals, plants are limited in their ability to seek out favourable conditions for life and growth. As a result, plants have evolved many ways to disperse their offspring by dispersing their seeds. A seed must somehow 'arrive' at a location and be there at a time favourable for germination and growth. When the fruits open and release their seeds in a regular way, it is called dehiscent, which is often distinctive for related groups of plants, these fruits include; Capsules, follicles, legumes, silicles and siliques. When fruits do not open and release their seeds in a regular fashion they are called indehiscent, which include the fruits achenes, caryopsis, nuts, samaras, and utricles.

Seed dispersal is seen most obviously in fruits; however many seeds aid in their own dispersal. Some kinds of seeds are dispersed while still inside a fruit or cone, which later opens or disintegrates to release the seeds. Other seeds are expelled or released from the fruit prior to dispersal. For example, milkweeds produce a fruit type, known as a *follicle*, that splits open along one side to release the seeds. Iris capsules split into three 'valves' to release their seeds.

- By wind (anemochory)
- Dandelion seeds (achenes) can be carried long distances by the wind.
- The seed pod of milkweed (Asclepias syriaca)

Many seeds (e.g. maple, pine) have a wing that aids in wind dispersal.

The dustlike seeds of orchids are carried efficiently by the wind.

Some seeds, (e.g. dandelion, milkweed, poplar) have hairs that aid in wind dispersal.

Some winged seeds have two, and some have only one wing.

By Water (Hydrochory)

Some plants, such as *Mucuna* and *Dioclea*, produce buoyant seeds termed sea-beans or drift seeds because they float in rivers to the oceans and wash up on beaches.

By Animals (Zoochory)

Seeds (burrs) with barbs or hooks (e.g. acaena, burdock, dock) which attach to animal fur or feathers, and then drop off later.

Seeds with a fleshy covering (e.g. apple, cherry, juniper) are eaten by animals (birds, mammals, reptiles, fish) which then disperse these seeds in their droppings.

Seeds (nuts) which are an attractive long-term storable food resource for animals (e.g. acorns, hazelnut, walnut); the seeds are stored some distance from the parent plant, and some escape being eaten if the animal forgets them.

Myrmecochory

Myrmecochory is the dispersal of seeds by ants. Foraging ants disperse seeds which have appendages called elaiosomes (e.g. bloodroot, trilliums, Acacias, and many species of Proteaceae). Elaiosomes are soft, fleshy structures that contain nutrients for animals that eat them. The ants carry such seeds back to their nest, where the elaiosomes are eaten. The remainder of the seed, which is hard and inedible to the ants, then germinates either within the nest or at a removal site where the seed has been discarded by the ants. This dispersal relationship is an example of mutualism, since the plants depend upon the ants to disperse seeds, while the ants depend upon the plants seeds for food. As a result, a drop in numbers of one partner can reduce success of the other. In South Africa, the Argentine ant (*Linepithema humile*) has invaded and displaced native species of ants. Unlike the native ant species, Argentine ants do not collect the seeds of *Mimetes cucullatus* or eat the elaiosomes. In areas where these ants have invaded, the numbers of *Mimetes* seedlings have dropped.

Seed Dormancy

Seed dormancy has two main functions: the first is synchronizing germination with the optimal conditions for survival of the resulting seedling; the second is spreading germination of a batch of seeds over time so that a catastrophe after germination (e.g. late frosts, drought, herbivory) does not result in the death of all offspring of a plant (bet-hedging). Seed dormancy is defined as a seed failing to germinate under environmental conditions optimal for germination, normally when the environment is at a suitable temperature with proper soil moisture. This true dormancy or innate dormancy is therefore caused by conditions within the seed that prevent germination. Thus dormancy is a state of the seed, not of the environment. Induced dormancy, enforced dormancy or seed quiescence occurs when a seed fails to germinate because the external environmental conditions are inappropriate for germination, mostly in response to conditions being too dark or light, too cold or hot, or too dry. Seed dormancy is not the same as seed persistence in the soil or on the plant, though even in scientific publications dormancy and persistence are often confused or used as synonyms.

Often seed dormancy is divided into four major categories: exogenous; endogenous; combinational; and secondary. A more recent system distinguishes five classes of dormancy:morphological, physiological, morphophysiological, physical and combinational dormancy.

- *Exogenous dormancy* is caused by conditions outside the embryo including:
  - *Physical dormancy* or hard seed coats occurs when seeds are impermeable to water. At dormancy break a specialized structure, the 'water gap', is disrupted in response to environmental cues, especially temperature, so that water can enter the seed and germination can occur. Plant families where physical dormancy occurs include Anacardiaceae, Cannaceae, Convulvulaceae, Fabaceae and Malvaceae.
  - *Chemical dormancy* considers species that lack physiological dormancy, but where a chemical prevents germination. This chemical can be leached out of the seed by rainwater or snow melt or be deactivated somehow. Leaching of chemical inhibitors from the seed by rain water is often cited as an important cause of dormancy release in seeds of desert plants, however little evidence exists to support this claim.
- *Endogenous dormancy* is caused by conditions within the embryo itself, including:
  - *Morphological dormancy* where germination is prevented due to morphological characteristics of the embryo. In some species the embryo is just a mass of cells when seeds are dispersed, it is not differentiated. Before germination can take place both differentiation and growth of the embryo have to occur. In other species the embryo is differentiated but not fully grown (under-developed) at dispersal and embryo growth up to a species specific length is required before germination can occur. Examples of plant families where morphological dormancy occurs are Apiaceae, Cycadaceae, Liliaceae, Magnoliaceae and Ranunculaceae.

- *Morphophysiological dormancy* seeds with under-developed embryos, and which in addition have physiological components to dormancy. These seeds therefore require a dormancy-breaking treatments as well as a period of time to develop fully grown embryos. Plant families where morphophysiological dormancy occurs include Apiaceae, Aquifoliaceae, Liliaceae, Magnoliaceae, Papaveraceae and Ranunculaceae Some plants with morpho-physiological dormancy like Asarum or Trillium species have multiple types of dormancy, one affects radicle (root) growth while the other affects plumule (shoot) growth. The terms 'double dormancy' and '2-year seeds' are used for species whose seeds need two years to complete germination or at least two winters and one summer. Dormancy of the radicle (seedling root)is broken during the first winter after dispersal while dormancy of the shoot bud is broken during the second winter.
- *Physiological dormancy* means that the embryo can, due to physiological causes, not generate enough power to break through the seed coat, endosperm or other covering structures. Dormancy is typically broken at cool wet, warm wet or warm dry conditions. Abscisic acid is usually the growth inhibitor in seeds and its production can be affected by light.
- Drying; some plants including a number of grasses and those from seasonally arid regions need a period of drying before they will germinate, the seeds are released but need to have a lower moisture content before germination can begin. If the seeds remain moist after dispersal, germination can be delayed for many months or even years. Many herbaceous plants from temperate climate zones have physiological dormancy that disappears

with drying of the seeds. Other species will germinate after dispersal only under very narrow temperature ranges, but as the seeds dry they are able to germinate over a wider temperature range.

- *Combinational dormancy* In seeds with combinational dormancy the seed or fruit coat is impermeable to water and the embryo has physiological dormancy. Depending on the species physical dormancy can be broken before or after physiological dormancy is broken.
- *Secondary dormancy* is caused by conditions after the seed has been dispersed and occurs in some seeds when non-dormant seed is exposed to conditions that are not favourable to germination, very often high temperatures. The mechanisms of secondary dormancy are not yet fully understood but might involve the loss of sensitivity in receptors in the plasma membrane.

The following types of seed dormancy do not involve seed dormancy strictly spoken as lack of germination is prevented by the environment not by characteristics of the seed itself:

- *Photodormancy or light sensitivity* affects germination of some seeds. These photoblastic seeds need a period of darkness or light to germinate. In species with thin seed coats, light may be able to penetrate into the dormant embryo. The presence of light or the absence of light may trigger the germination process, inhibiting germination in some seeds buried too deeply or in others not buried in the soil.
- *Thermodormancy* is seed sensitivity to heat or cold. Some seeds including cocklebur and amaranth germinate only at high temperatures (30°C or 86°F) many plants that have seed that germinate in early to mid summer have thermodormancy and germinate only when the soil temperature is warm. Other seeds need cool soils to germinate, while others like celery are inhibited when soil temperatures are too warm. Often thermodormancy requirements disappear as the seed ages or dries.

Not all seeds undergo a period of dormancy. Seeds of some mangroves are viviparous, they begin to germinate while still attached to the parent. The large, heavy root allows the seed to penetrate into the ground when it falls. Many garden plants have seeds that will germinate readily as soon as they have water and are warm enough, though their wild ancestors may have had dormancy, these cultivated plants lack seed dormancy. After many generations of selective pressure by plant breeders and gardeners dormancy has been selected out.

For annuals, seeds are a way for the species to survive dry or cold seasons. Ephemeral plants are usually annuals that can go from seed to seed in as few as six weeks.

Seed germination is a process by which a seed embryo develops into a seedling. It involves the reactivation of the metabolic pathways that lead to growth and the emergence of the radicle or seed root and plumule or shoot. The emergence of the seedling above the soil surface is the next phase of the plants growth and is called seedling establishment.

Three fundamental conditions must exist before germination can occur:

1. The embryo must be alive, called seed viability.
2. Any dormancy requirements that prevent germination must be overcome.
3. The proper environmental conditions must exist for germination.

Seed viability is the ability of the embryo to germinate and is affected by a number of different conditions. Some plants do not produce seeds that have functional complete embryos or the seed may have no embryo at all, often called empty seeds. Predators and pathogens can damage or kill the seed while it is still in the fruit or after it is dispersed. Environmental conditions like flooding or heat can kill the seed before or during germination. The age of the seed affects its health and germination ability: since the seed has a living embryo, over time cells die and cannot be replaced. Some seeds can live for a long time before germination, while others can only survive for a short period after dispersal before they die.

Seed vigour is a measure of the quality of seed, and involves the viability of the seed, the germination percentage, germination rate and the strength of the seedlings produced.

The germination percentage is simply the proportion of seeds that germinate from all seeds subject to the right conditions for growth. The germination rate is the length of time it takes for the seeds to germinate. Germination percentages and rates are affected by seed viability, dormancy and environmental effects that impact on the seed and seedling. In agriculture and horticulture quality seeds have high viability, measured by germination percentage plus the rate of germination. This is given as a per cent of germination over a certain amount of time, 90 per cent germination in 20 days, for example.

'Dormancy' is covered above; many plants produce seeds with varying degrees of dormancy, and different seeds from the same fruit can have different degrees of dormancy. It's possible to have seeds with no dormancy if they are dispersed right away and do not dry (if the seeds dry they go into physiological dormancy). There is great variation amongst plants and a dormant seed is still a viable seed even though the germination rate might be very low.

Environmental conditions effecting seed germination include; water, oxygen, temperature and light.

Three distinct phases of seed germination occur: water imbibition; lag phase; and radicle emergence.

In order for the seed coat to split, the embryo must imbibe (soak up water), which causes it to swell, splitting the seed coat. However, the nature of the seed coat determines how rapidly water can penetrate and subsequently initiate germination. The rate of imbibition is dependent on the permeability of the seed coat, amount of water in the environment and the area of contact the seed has to the source of water. For some seeds, imbibing too much water too quickly can kill the seed. For some seeds, once water is imbibed the germination process cannot be stopped, and drying then becomes fatal. Other seeds can imbibe and lose water a few times without causing ill effects, but drying can cause secondary dormancy.

Inducing Germination

A number of different strategies are used by gardeners and horticulturists to break seed dormancy.

Scarification which allows water and gases to penetrate into the seed, include methods that physically break the hard seed coats or soften them by chemicals. Means of scarification include soaking in hot water or poking holes in the seed with a pin or rubbing them on sandpaper or cracking with a press or hammer. Soaking the seeds in solvents or acids is also effective for many seeds. Sometimes fruits are harvested while the seeds are still immature and the seed coat is not fully developed and sown right away before the seed coat become impermeable.

Under natural conditions seed coats are worn down by rodents chewing on the seed, the seeds rubbing against rocks (seeds are moved by the wind or water currents), by undergoing freezing and thawing of surface water, or passing through an animal's digestive tract. In the latter case, the seed coat protects the seed from digestion, while often weakening the seed coat such that the embryo is ready to sprout when it gets deposited (along with a bit of fertilizer) far from the parent plant. Microorganisms are often effective in breaking down hard seed coats and are sometimes used by people as a treatment, the seeds are stored in a moist warm sandy medium for several months under non-sterile conditions.

Stratification also called moist-chilling is a method to break down physiological dormancy and involves the addition of moisture to the seeds so they imbibe water and then the seeds are subject to a period of moist chilling to after-ripen the embryo. Sowing outside in late summer and fall and allowing to overwinter outside under cool conditions is an effective way to stratify seeds, some seeds respond more favourably to periods of oscillating temperatures which are part of the natural environment.

Leaching or the soaking in water removes chemical inhibitors in some seeds that prevent germination. Rain and melting snow naturally accomplish this task. For seeds planted in gardens, running water is best - if soaked in a container, 12 to 24 hours of soaking is sufficient. Soaking longer, especially in stagnant water that is not changed, can result in oxygen starvation and seed death. Seeds with hard seed coats can be soaked in hot water to break open the impermeable cell layers that prevent water intake.

Other methods used to assist in the germination of seeds that have dormancy include prechilling, predrying, daily alternation of temperature, light exposure, potassium nitrate, the use of plant growth regulators like gibberellins, cytokinins, ethylene, thiourea, sodium hypochlorite plus others. Some seeds germinate best after a fire, for some seeds fire cracks hard seed coats while in other seeds chemical dormancy is broken in reaction to the presence of smoke, liquid smoke is often used by gardeners to assist in the germination of these species.

Origin and Evolution

The origin of seed plants is a problem that still remains unsolved. However, more and more data tends to place this origin in the middle Devonian. The description in 2004 of the proto-seed *Runcaria heinzelinii* in the Givetian of Belgium is an indication of that ancient origin of seed-plants. As with modern ferns, most land plants before this time reproduced by sending spores into the air, that would land and become whole new plants.

The first 'true' seeds are described from the upper Devonian, which is probably the theater of their true first evolutionary radiation. The seed plants progressively became one of the major elements of nearly all ecosystems.

Many seeds are edible and the majority of human calories comes from seeds, especially from cereals, legumes and nuts. Seeds also provide most cooking oils, many beverages and spices and some important food additives. In different seeds the seed embryo or the endosperm dominates and provides most of the nutrients. The storage proteins of the embryo and endosperm differ in their amino acid content and physical properties. For example the gluten of wheat, important in providing the elastic property to bread dough is strictly an endosperm protein.

Seeds are used to propagate many crops such as cereals, legumes, forest trees, turfgrasses and pasture grasses. Particularly in developing countries, a major constraint faced is the inadequacy of the marketing channels to get the seed to poor farmers. Thus the use of farmer-retained seed remains quite common.

Seeds are also eaten by animals, and are fed to livestock. Many seeds are used as birdseed.

Poison and Food Safety

While some seeds are edible, others are harmful, poisonous or deadly. Plants and seeds often contain chemical compounds to discourage herbivores and seed predators. In some cases, these compounds simply taste bad (such as in mustard), but other compounds are toxic or break down into toxic compounds within the digestive system. Children, being smaller than adults, are more susceptible to poisoning by plants and seeds.

A deadly poison, ricin, comes from seeds of the castor bean. Reported lethal doses are anywhere from two to eight seeds, though only a few deaths have been reported when castor beans have been ingested by animals.

In addition, seeds containing amygdalin—apple, apricot, bitter almond, peach, plum, cherry, quince, and others—when consumed in sufficient amounts, may cause Cyanide poisoning. Other seeds that contain poisons include annona, cotton, custard apple, datura, uncooked durian, golden chain, horse-chestnut, larkspur, locoweed, lychee, nectarine, rambutan, rosary pea, sour sop, sugar apple, wisteria, and yew. The seeds of the strychnine tree are also poisonous, containing the poison strychnine.

The seeds of many legumes, including the common bean (*Phaseolus vulgaris*), contain proteins called lectins which can cause gastric distress if the beans are eaten without cooking.

The common bean and many others, including the soybean, also contain trypsin inhibitors which interfere with the action of the digestive enzyme trypsin. Normal cooking processes degrade lectins and trypsin inhibitors to harmless forms.

Flax seed oil (in bottles) and coconut oil (in jars in the middle).

Cotton fiber grows attached to cotton plant seeds. Other seed fibers are from kapok and milkweed.

Many important nonfood oils are extracted from seeds. Linseed oil is used in paints. Oil from jojoba and crambe are similar to whale oil.

Seeds are the source of some medicines including castor oil, tea tree oil and the discredited cancer drug, Laetrile.

Many seeds have been used as beads in necklaces and rosaries including Job's tears, Chinaberry, rosary pea, and castor bean. However, the latter three are also poisonous.

Other seed uses include:

- Seeds once used as weights for balances.
- Seeds used as toys by children, such as for the game Conkers.
- Resin from *Clusia rosea* seeds used to caulk boats.
- Nematicide from milkweed seeds.
- Cottonseed meal used as animal feed and fertilizer.

Seed Records

The massive fruit of the coco de mer.

The oldest viable carbon-14-dated seed that has grown into a plant was a Judean date palm seed about 2,000 years old, recovered from excavations at Herod the Great's palace on Masada in Israel. It was germinated in 2005.

The largest seed is produced by the coco de mer, or 'double coconut palm', *Lodoicea maldivica*. The entire fruit may weigh up to 23 kilograms (50 pounds) and usually contains a single seed.

The earliest fossil seeds are around 365 million years old from the Late Devonian of West Virginia. The seeds are preserved immature ovules of the plant *Elkinsia polymorpha*.

7

Rice Variety in India

Rice breeding programme in India was started by researcher, the then Economic Botanist during 1911 in undivided Bengal with headquarters at Dacca (now in Bangladesh). Subsequently, in 1912, a crop specialist was appointed exclusively for rice in Madras Province. Prior to the establishment of the Indian Council of Agricultural Research (ICAR) in 1929, Bengal and Madras were the only provinces which had specialist exclusively for rice crop. After the establishment of ICAR, it initiated rice research projects in various states of the country and by 1950, 82 research stations in 14 states of the country were established, fully devoted for rice research projects. These research stations, mainly by the pure line method of selection, released 445 improved varieties. These varieties were of various kind such as:

- Earliness
- Deep water and flood resistant
- Lodging resistant
- Drought resistant
- Non-shredding of grains
- Dormancy of seed
- Control of wild rice
- Disease resistant
- Higher response to heavy mannuring.

Thus, during the pure line period of selection from 1911-1949, the advantage of natural selection have been fully exploited and there have been varieties available for every rice ecology. During the early period of breeding research programme, varieties were developed suitable for specific stress situation or for resistant to particular disease. When, after World War II, synthetic fertilizers became popular, efforts were made to identify varieties which respond to heavy fertilization.

After the establishment of the Central Rice Research Institute (CRRI) at Cuttak in 1946 by the Govt. of India, rice research and training received an added impetus. There had been a systematic screening of exotic types from the genetic stocks. Besides, for the purpose of direct introduction in the country, many Chinese, Japanese, Taiwanese and Russian types were also tested. The Chinese types, which were first, prior to 1947, tested in Kashmir Valley, found fairly successful and the Japanese and Russian types were found unsuitable under Indian conditions due to poor yield, unacceptable grain qualities and susceptibility to blast.

Inter-racial hybridization programme between japonicas and indicas was initiated during 1950-54. The Food and Agriculture Organisation of the United Nations with a view of improving production of cereal on an international basis after the end of World-War II, launched a collaborative project japonica X indica hybridization in South-East Asian countries. The object of these project was to transfer the high yielding capacity and response to use higher dose of fertilizers into local indica varieties from japonica varieties. Indica varieties were already well adapted to the local conditions and had tolerance to diseases and pests of the region. A parallel project of japonica X indica hybridization was also started by ICAR with the same objectives. These projects could achieve very limited success. Only four varieties, viz. - *Malinja* and *Mashuri* in Malaysia, ADT-27 in Tamil Nadu, India and Circna in Australia were released from more than 700 hybrid combinations.

The Central Rice Research Institute, Cuttack also started another project in 1960 with a view to evolve high yielding fertilizer responsive varieties with japonica in 11 states. In this project remarkable success was achieved in the development of japonica × indica hybrids.

The International Rice Research Institute was established in the Philippines in 1960 and this institute helped in evolving dwarf high yielding varieties with the concept of improving the plant type in indica rices based on the use of a gene from semi-dwarf Chinese varieties. These high yielding varieties were highlighted during the International Rice Year in 1966 by ICAR through national demonstration trials. This was the beginning of moving towards self-sufficiency in rice production. Further, the ICAR launched the All-India Co-ordinated Rice Improvement Project (AICRIP) in 1965 that helped in co-ordination of interdisciplinary and inter-institutional research results on the country basis for improving the production, productivity and profitability of rice in India.

Inter-racial hybridization programme between semi-dwarf Taiwanese types/derivatives and indica was started during 1965 onwards. India operated its most intensive rice breeding programmes under the AICRIP with the development of Taichung (Native) - I from the semi-dwarf mutant and achieved remarkable success. Padma and Jaya were the first varieties that emerged from the programme. Subsequently, many semi-dwarf varieties were released by the Central Variety Release Committee and also by the different state agencies. Most of these varieties have got high yield potential.

During the period of inter-racial hybridization between semi-dwarf Taiwanese types/derivatives and indica which was started during 1965, the most significant achievement is the prolific release of high yielding varieties. Infact 123 varieties were released during this period in 12 years as compared to 51 high yielding varieties released during the four decades prior to 1965. The semi-dwarf varieties have been found superior in efficiency of grain production as compared to the tall traditional varieties.

Development of Hybrid Rice

Research programme was initiated during 1970 to develop hybrid rice variety in the country. There was no success in this programme during the subsequent two decades. However, the research programme was accelerated and intensified from 1989 with a mission mode project. With this concerted research efforts, a remarkable success was achieved within a short span of 5 years and half a dozen rice hybrid rice varieties were developed from public and private sectors. The first four hybrid rice varieties were released in the country during 1994. Subsequently, two more hybrid rice varieties were also released. By the end of 2001, a total of 19 hybrid rice varieties were released.

Variety Release Procedure

Any variety of agricultural or horticultural crops in being recommended by the Central Seed Committee constituted under the Seeds Act, 1966 for its release and notification for commercial cultivation. This committee is headed by the Secretary (A&C), Dept. of Agriculture & Co-operation, Ministry of Agriculture.

The Central Seed Committee consists of two sub-committees:

- Central Sub-Committee on Crop Standards, Notification and Release of varieties for agricultural crops, chaired by DDG (FC), ICAR.
- Central Sub-Committee on Crop Standards, Notification and Release of varieties for horticultural crops, chaired by DDG (Hort.), ICAR.

The proposal for release and notification of a particular variety is submitted by the concerned breeder through his respective Institute of ICAR or a breeder of the University through his respective State Government This proposal is scrutinized and considered by the sub-committee and if the proposal for release of variety is for more than one state, such a variety is released by the Central Seed Committee. In case proposal for release of variety is for one state or specially for a particular zone of the state, such variety is released by the State Seed Committee.

Seed Production Procedure

Under the seed production programme, the following classification of seed is in vogue.

1. Nucleus Seed The seed or the research material produced by the breeder by various selection procedure in a pure line variety or clone is known as nucleus seed.
2. Breeder Seed It is the seed or vegetative propagating material produced by the breeder who develops or evolves the particular variety. The breeder seed is also produced by other Agricultural Universities under the direct supervision of the breeder of the concerned crop. Breeder seed is the source for the production of foundation seed.
3. Foundation Seed Foundation seed is a progeny of breeder seed. It is produced from the genetically pure breeder seed. Foundation seed is produced by the National Seeds Corporation (NSC), State Farm Corporation of India (SFCI) and all States Seeds Development Corporations.
4. Certified Seed Certified seed is produced from foundation seeds. This seed is certified by the State Seed Certification Agency established under the State Governments. Certified seed is produced by the National Seeds Corporation, State Farm Corporation of India and State Seeds Development Corporations under the supervision of State Seed Certification Agencies.

Rice and Various Processed Types

Paddy Rice or Rough Rice: In most of the world and in California, the term paddy rice is used to describe the rice as it comes from the field after harvest. The rice has been threshed and each grain is separate. The grain of rice has a hard husk protecting the kernel inside. The husk (or hull) that covers rice is much thicker and tougher than most cereal grain husks. Paddy rice is also called rough rice. (Primarily in the southern growing area of the U.S.) By weight, the composition of paddy rice is approximately: 22 per cent husk (including about 2% trash), 10 per cent bran, and 68 per cent rice (2% of the rice are very small pieces, brewers rice, and fines). The rice portion can have varying percentages of broken kernels. A typical milling yield in California for medium grain would be described as 54/68. 54 per cent brokens and 68 per cent total. (14% brokens). In the southern growing area, a typical yield for long grain would be 58/68. In Japan where harvest and drying conditions are ideal a typical yield would be 67/70. Paddy rice is not as dense as milled rice and usually weighs about 37 lbs per cubic ft. Brown rice, milled rice, and brokens weigh about 52 lbs per cubic ft.

Most paddy rice is milled in the U.S. Some is exported to countries like Brazil, Mexico, and Turkey for milling. The export of paddy harms the milling industry and eventually the farmer. The U.S. is about the only country in the world that allows the export of paddy rice. It does not make sense from an economic standpoint (the unnecessary freight cost of hulls and bran). It only occurs when the importing country has some sort of duty advantage for paddy rice that allows it to occur.

Brown Rice: After the husk is removed the remaining product is called brown rice. Brown rice is more nutritious than white rice, but very little rice is consumed in the brown form. Brown rice contains a bran layer that is about 12 per cent of the brown kernel by weight. The protein in white rice is much more nutritious than most cereal grains but has a low level of the essential amino acid, lysine. The protein level in bran layer of brown rice is higher and has more lysine. The protein in brown rice has one of the most complete essential amino acid profiles of any vegetable crop. (No vegetables alone are complete.) The rice bran layer of brown rice also contains digestible fiber as well as minerals and vitamins not found in milled rice. It was learned that incidences of beriberi were dramatically reduced when diets where switched from white milled rice to brown rice or even parboiled rice which contained more thiamin. The oil content of the rice bran contains several vitamin E components and valuable nutrients. Because minerals and vitamins are lost when the bran is removed, years ago many states passed laws requiring white rice to be fortified with vitamins and minerals. Despite its nutritional value, consumption of brown rice is low because it takes almost one hour to cook and many people do not care for the taste and texture. Unfortunately, once the husk is removed from rice, the bran layer starts going rancid and this contributes to the bitter taste of brown rice.

Very little brown rice is actually consumed in the U.S. or the world for that matter. Some rice is exported in the brown form (primarily to Japan and Europe) for further processing.

Milled Rice: Milled Rice has had the hulls and bran removed. It is also called white rice or polished rice. Most milled rice sold into the domestic market has been milled very hard and has had the broken content removed to below 4 per cent. Less expensive rice sold to export markets may be milled to a lessor degree and may have higher percentages of broken kernels. State laws require that milled rice sold to U.S. consumers be enriched with vitamins to make its nutritional value similar to brown rice. For this reason, cooking directions mention that the rice should not be washed. (The enrichment is usually a powder and is easily removed with water.) Most ethnic consumers who eat a lot of rice wash the rice to improve taste and texture. Much of the Japonica rice packaged in California is not enriched and is labeled as coated with glucose (allowed by law) for these consumers who do not like the taste of enrichment and who were going to wash it away anyway.

Almost all rice is consumed in the milled form, and most rice exported from the U.S. is exported in the milled form.

Broken Rice: The kernel of rice can become cracked in the field, during the drying process, or during the milling process. Cracks are usually caused by moisture migrating too quickly within the kernel (drying too fast, or moisture being added back to a dry kernel). Often these cracks cause the kernels to break during milling and so broken rice is generated. The percentage of broken kernels (relative to total milled rice) generated during milling usually ranges from 12 per cent to 24 per cent in the U.S. Most brokens are removed during the milling process to less than 4 per cent in order to give the consumer a high quality rice. Broken rice tends to get mushy during cooking and makes a poor quality table rice. There are different sizes of broken kernels. With long grain rice in the south brokens are often separated into different sizes. From largest to small they are called; second heads, screenings, and brewers. In California, where the kernel is smaller to begin with, the brokens kernels are only separated into second heads and brewers.

In the past most broken rice in the U.S. went to the beer industry. Today, most of the rice going into beer is now whole kernel. The dog food industry uses the majority of the broken rice. They tend to start with the lower quality brewers rice and then move into the more expensive screenings and second heads as needed. The rice flour industry is growing and tends to use the higher quality sorted second heads and screenings. The beer industry still takes some of the higher quality second heads. Some brokens are now being exported to Japan out of California.

Rice Bran and Stabilized Rice Bran: The percentage of rice bran in paddy rice ranges from 10 per cent to 12 per cent. There is no clear distinction between the bran layer and endosperm. The harder the rice is milled, the more bran is generated. Obviously some of the endosperm is going into the bran and so the properties unique to rice bran are diluted as the rice is milled harder. Rice Bran is a very nutritional product. It contains a higher content of protein and its protein has a better amino acid profile that the proteins found in rice and most plant sources. Rice Bran contains about 16 per cent to 18 per cent oil. Rice bran oil is loaded with vitamin E components. It is exceptionally high in Tocopherols and Tocotreinols. Rice bran is also high in oryzanol. Studies have shown that rice bran and rice bran oil lower cholesterol levels and improve cardiovascular health. Rice bran also contains high levels of vitamin B, and other vitamins, minerals, and essential fatty acids.

Unfortunately, rice bran goes rancid soon after milling. Lipase enzyme attacks the oil once the bran structure has been destroyed, and free fatty acid levels build up very quickly. The bran quickly develops a bad taste and odor. In the mid 1980s, a USDA Research group in California developed a method to stabilize the bran. A simple dry heat extruder is used to reach a temperature of about 270° F for a short period of time. This temperature deactivates the lipase enzyme. The temperature range is critical. Too low and the lipase is not deactivated, too high and vitamin E components are destroyed. The vitamin E components prevent oxidative rancidity over a long period of time. The process is relatively simple and when done properly, the bran is safe from both enzymatic and oxidative rancidity. Unfortunately, stabilized bran does not have a particularly great taste, and has not yet become popular in the human market. Sage V Foods (when founded as Comet Rice Ingredients) was involved in the original technology and has been stabilizing bran for over ten years.

Organic Rice: The number of acres planted to organic rice in the U.S is very small, but growing. For rice to be certified organic by organisations such as CCOF, the field used must have gone for three years without use of pesticides, herbicides, fertilizers, or any chemicals. Then the crop must be grown, harvested, stored, and milled under organic conditions. The field yields for organic rice are unpredictable and average about half of conventional rice. Much of the rice is removed in the milling process because of damages due to insects and weeds. It is very difficult to store organic rice and avoid insect problems. The final cost of milled organic rice is about three times that of conventional rice.

Today in the U.S. there is no federal standard for organic rice. (This may change soon.) There are several non profit and private organisations who certify rice as organic. They have strict requirements and the public has learned to trust and respect many of their logos on organic products. Sage V Foods is certified by CCOF and other organisations.

Parboiled Rice: Parboiled rice has been through a special cooking process, called parboiling, prior to milling. While in the paddy form, the rice is soaked and then steam cooked. This process does not allow the kernel to swell during the cooking and the moisture level does not exceed 40 per cent, versus cooked table rice, which is most often cooked to a moisture level of 64 per cent. The starch granule is cooked (technically gelatinized), but not allowed to swell. The rice is then dried while still in the paddy form and then passed through a standard milling process to remove the hull and bran.

This process has been going on for centuries in many countries and is believed to have started in ancient India. Researchers learned in the early 1900's that parboiled rice retained some of the vitamins that exist in bran, but are lost in the milling of milled rice. The incidence of beriberi was reduced when diets were changed from white rice to parboiled rice because of increased levels of thiamin in parboiled rice. Uncle Ben made the process famous in the United States with its converted (same as parboiled) rice. The process may have originated to sterilize the rice and allow longer storage conditions. (All rice comes from the field with insect eggs in the germ of the rice. These eggs hatch when the temperature is warm and moisture is available.) The high temperatures occurring during parboiling kill any insect eggs in the rice and essentially sterilize it. Parboiling also mends the cracks in the rice (glues broken rice back together) and dramatically improves the milling yield of whole kernels in the rice. This improvement in milling yield, especially for poor quality paddy, can justify the cost of the process.

Parboiling changes the texture of the rice. It becomes firmer and less sticky. It is a much more durable kernel. It takes just as long to cook (actually a little longer) as white rice, but is much easier to cook. It is almost fool proof. It can be overcooked without being mushy or losing its grain shape. It does not have to be steamed. It can be cooked by blanching only. It has a long steam table life, which is important for restaurants. For these reasons, parboiled rice was adopted as the preferred rice of the restaurant industry long ago and so many consumers have become accustomed to the taste and texture parboiled rice. It is the only type of rice that can withstand the harsh treatment of most industrial processes that involve cooking and then freezing, canning, or drying. Most rice that is sold in the supermarket in some sort of cooked or partially cooked form has been parboiled.

In the U.S., some parboiled rice is sold into the consumer market, but most is sold into the food service (for use in restaurants) and industrial markets (for use in prepared meals). A great deal is exported to Saudi Arabia, South Africa, Europe and other countries.

Instant Rice: Instant Rice or Quick Cooking Rice is rice that has been precooked and then dried so that the consumers can recook the rice in a short period of time. Kraft General Food's 'Minute Rice' is instant rice. Regular white rice takes about 15 minutes to cook. Parboil Rice takes about 18 minutes to cook. Instant rice can be ready in a little as 3 minutes.

Cooking rice involves getting moisture to the center of the kernel then getting that moisture to a temperature of over about 160° F to gelatinize the starch. Raw starch in uncooked rice is tightly compacted and so it takes about 15 minutes for boiling hot water to migrate to the center of the kernel. There are several processes to make instant rice, but the one most commonly used starts much like the home cooking process. Rice is blanched in hot water, steamed, and then rinsed. Then the rice is then dried in a hot oven drier. The degree of cooking and degree of puffing in the drier determine the final cook time for the instant rice.

When the rice is cooked again by the consumer, the water migrates faster through the kernel because the starch has been gelatinized and there are many small cracks and fissures in the kernel. Quality of the final cooked rice is affected by the instantizing process. The faster the rice cooks, the lower the quality. Instant rice that cooks in 10 minutes is very close to the real thing. Instant rice that cooks in 5 minutes has a much poorer texture that rice cooked in a home rice cooker. Rice that is ready in hot water (like cup of noodles) is very mushy. All companies involved are trying to improve the process, but it is impossible to make a dry instant rice that cooks in under five minutes that is equal in quality to rice cooked in the home in a rice cooker.

Most companies that manufature instant rice sell the rice to the consumer though grocery stores.

IQF Rice: Individually Quick Frozen Rice is rice that has been fully cooked (to about 64% moisture) and then quick frozen. The rice can be thawed and heated in a microwave (in two to four minutes) and is ready to eat. Unlike instant rice, there has been no damage (cracking or fissuring of the kernel), and so the quality of this product is as good or better than rice cooked at home in a rice cooker.

The process for making this rice is very similar to the cooking process used at home. Once the rice is cooked and ready to eat, it is then quick-frozen. Sage V Foods is the leader in this new and developing industry. Most IQF rice is sold today in 1400 lb bulk totes to large industrial users who use the rice to put into frozen entrees containing rice. The IQF rice is easy to handle and can flow through conveying and portion scaling systems. Sage V Foods can flavour, mix with vegetables, and package IQF rice in small microwaveable pouches.

Worldwide there are more than 40,000 different varieties of rice, though only a small number offer the quality acceptable to be grown commercially in the U.S. In the United States. Rice types can be divided into long, medium, and short grain. Limited waxy rice and arborio is produced, as well as some aromatic and specialty varieties.

The primary differences in these rices is their cooking characteristics and, in some cases, a subtle flavour difference.

From a nutritional standpoint they are equal and indeed can often (with the exception of waxy rice or arborio) be interchanged in recipes. Long grain rice has a long, slender kernel, four to five times longer than its width.

Cooked grains are separate, light and fluffy. Medium grain rice has a shorter, wider kernel (two to three times longer than its width) than long grain rice. Cooked grains are more moist and tender, and have a greater tendency to cling together than long grain.

Short grain rice has a short, plump, almost round kernel. Cooked grains are soft and cling together U.S. sweet rice is short and plump with a chalky white, opaque kernel. When cooked, sweet rice loses its shape and is very glutinous. Sweet is more often used in commercial product formulations. The starch and flour from sweet rice is used in frozen products as a binder for gravies, sauces, and fillings because it is resistant to breakdown during freezing and thawing, unlike some corn orwheatstarches.

Aromatic rices: Aromatic rices have a flavour and aroma similar to that of roasted nuts or popcorn.

The natural compound that gives aromatic rice the characteristic aroma and flavour is present in all rice, but in the aromatic varieties it is present in much higher concentrations. The most popular domestically grown aromatic rices include: della which cooks dry, separate and fluffy; jasmine which cooks more moist and tends to cling together; and basmati which cooks into very long, slender grains which are dry, separate and fluffy.

U.S. aromatic: U.S. aromatic red rice has a deep, honey-red bran. Like brown rice, it is minimally processed to retain its bran layers and takes 45 to 50 minutes to prepare. Cooked grains have a savory, nutty flavour and are slightly chewy.

Basmati Rice: It is a long grain fragrant rice, aged to enhance aroma and reduce moisture content. Grown in India and Pakistan.

U.S. basmati: U.S. basmati rice is an aromatic long grain rice that has a distinctive aroma and flavour similar to that of popcorn or roasted nuts. When cooked, it swells only lengthwise, resulting in long slender grains that are dry, separate and fluffy.

Texmati: It is a cross between basmati rice and American long grain rice.

Black Rice: It is a black whole grain, aromatic rice usually used in desserts. Varieties include Chinese Forbidden Blak and Thai Black Sticky Rice.

U.S. black japonica: It is an aromatic rice with a dark black bran. Like brown rice, it is minimally processed to retain its bran layers and takes 45 to 50 minutes to prepare. Cooked grains are slightly chewy with a subtle sweet spiciness.

Calrose (California Rose) a medium grain rice originally developed in California for ease of mechanical harvesting and minimal water use. Numerious varieties developed from the original are the most popular rice in U.S.

U.S. Della, Delrose, and Delmont varieties combine the qualities of regular long grain rice and basmati rice. They have an aroma similar to basmati. However, cooked grains swell in both length and width, like regular long grain rice.

Jasmine Rice: It is a long grain Thai rice with a unique aroma.

U.S. jasmine rice: It is an aromatic long grain rice that has a distinctive aroma and flavour similar to that of popcorn or roasted nuts. Cooked grains are soft, moist and cling together.

Red Rice: Red rice is a fragrant reddish brown whole grain rice grown in Bhutan, France and other areas.

Wehani rice: It is an aromatic long grain reddish-brown rice developed from basmati rice by Lundbeerg Family Farms.

Arborio rice is an Italian short grain rice with high starch content, traditionally used to make Risotto.

U.S. Arborio rice is a large, bold rice with a characteristic white dot at the center of the grain. By the way of length/ width ratio and starch characteristics, it is classified as a medium grain rice. Primarily used in risotto, this rice develops a creamy texture around a chewy center and has exceptional ability to absorb flavours.

Carnaroli Rice is in the same family as Arborio rice but with a larger grain. From Piedmont and Lombardy regions of Italy, it is considered to be one of the best rices for Risotto.

Rice Forms

Rough (Paddy or Cargo) Rice Kernels still within the hull. Before the rice can be packaged or cooked, the outer hull or husk must be removed.

Brown Rice

Kernels of rice from which only the hull has been removed. Brown rice may be eaten as is or milled into white rice. Cooked brown rice has a slightly chewy texture and a nut-like flavour. The light brown colour of brown rice is caused by the presence of bran layers which are rich in minerals and vitamins, especially the B-complex group.

Regular Milled White Rice

Regular-milled white rice, often referred to as 'white' or 'polished' rice is the most common form of rice. The outer husk is removed, and the layers of bran are milled until the grain is white.

Parboiled Rice

Rough rice that has gone through a steam-pressure process before milling. This procedure gelatinizes the starch in the grain, and ensures a firmer, more separate grain. Parboiled rice is favoured by consumers and chefs who desire an extra fluffy and separate cooked rice.

Precooked Rice

White or brown rice that has been completely cooked and dehydrated after milling. This process reduces time required for cooking.

8

Rice Production in India China, Japan and in Bangladesh

Rice Production in India

India is the world's second largest producer of white rice, accounting for 20 per cent of all world rice production. Rice is India's preeminent crop, and is the staple food of the people of the eastern and southern parts of the country. Production increased from 53.6 million tons in FY 1980 to 74.6 million tons in FY 1990, a 39 per cent increase over the decade. By FY 1992, rice production had reached 111 million tons, second in the world only to China with its 182 million tons. Since 1950 the increase has been more than 350 per cent. Most of this increase was the result of an increase in yields; the number of hectares increased only 40 per cent during this period. Yields increased from 1,336 kilograms per hectare in FY 1980 to 1,751 kilograms per hectare in FY 1990. The per-hectare yield increased more than 262 per cent between 1950 and 1992.

The country's rice production declined to 89.13 million tonnes in 2009-10 crop year (July-June) from record 99.18 milli on tonnes in the previous year due to severe drought that affected almost half of the country.India could achieve a record ric- production of 100 million tonnes in 2010-11 crop year on the back of better monsoon this year.

Andhra Pradesh is the top most rice-producing State in the country.

Rice Production in China

Rice production in China is an important part of the national economy.

China is the world's largest producer of rice, and the crop makes up a little less than half of the country's total grain output. China accounts for 26 per cent of all world rice production. In a given year total rice output came from four different crops. The early rice crop grows primarily in provinces along the Chang Jiang and in provinces in the south; it is planted in February to April and harvested in June and July and contributes about 34 per cent to total rice output. Intermediate and single-crop late rice grows in the southwest and along the Chang Jiang; it is planted in March to June and harvested in October and November and also contributed about 34 per cent to total rice output in the 1980s. Double-crop late rice, planted after the early crop is reaped, is harvested in October to November and adds about 25 per cent to total rice production. Rice grown in the north is planted from April to June and harvested from September to October; it contributes about 7 per cent to total production.

All rice cultivation is highly labor intensive. Rice is generally grown as a wetland crop in fields flooded to supply water during the growing season. Transplanting seedlings requires many hours of labor, as does harvesting. Mechanization of rice cultivation is only minimally advanced. Rice cultivation also demands more of other inputs, such as fertilizer, than most other crops.

Rice is highly prized by consumers as a food grain, especially in south China, and per capita consumption has risen through the years. Also, as incomes have risen, consumers have preferred to eat more rice and less potatoes, corn, sorghum, and millet. Large production increases in the early 1980s and poor local transportation systems combined to induce farmers to feed large quantities of lower quality rice to livestock.

Rice Production in Japan

Rice production in Japan is important to the food supply in Japan, with rice being a staple part of the Japanese diet.

The most striking feature of Japanese agriculture however is the shortage of farmland. The 4.63 million hectares under cultivation in 2008 has shrunk, with most farmers over 65.

However, the land is intensively cultivated. Paddy fields occupy much of the countryside, whether on the alluvial plains, the terraced slopes, or the swamp land and coastal bays. Nonrice farm land share the terraces and lower slopes and are planted with wheat and barley in the autumn and with sweet potatoes, vegetables, and dry rice in the summer. Intercropping is common: such crops are alternated with beans and peas.

The History of rice and rice agriculture in the Japanese archipelago is not a long one. According to the accepted view, rice was introduced into Japan during the period between the Final Jomon and the Early Yayoi Period. But recent phytolith studies indicate that rice may have been in Japan as early as the Early Jomon, approximately 6000 years ago. Rice occupies an emotional place in Japanese history, society, and political economy.

Rice production is important to the food supply, with rice being a staple part of the Japanese diet. Japan is the ninth largest producer of rice in the world in rice production. The rice seasons in Northern Japan last from May-June to September-October. In central Japan, it is from April-May to August-October. In southern Japan the rice season is form April-May to August-September. About 85 per cent of the 2.3 million farms in Japan plant rice yearly. Improved varieties of japonica rice are grown in almost all prefectures in the country. The most widely planted variety is Koshihikari. Onigiri rice balls are popular.

The average rice field acreage of a Japanese farmer is very small and rice production is highly mechanized. Due to small farms, rice production is considered a part time occupation by many farmers. The number of Japanese farm households and farm population has declined in recent decades. Rice production has also declined. The decline came about because in 1969, the Ministry of Agriculture, Forestry, and Fisheries has asked farmers to reduce rice acreage; under the Staple Food Control Act of 1942 the Japanese government is formally in charge of all rice production, distribution, and sales.

Since the postwar Land Reform (1945-1949), Japanese farms have remained fragmented and small. To prevent the reconsolidation of farmland, joint-stock companies cannot own farmland; agricultural cooperatives can own farmland only if they do the actual farming. Currently the average rice farmer works only 1.65 acres (whereas the typical American farm is 160 times larger).

As part of the government's control of rice, rice imports are banned except in processed forms. Also, because of the disproportionate political power wielded by farmers, rice production is subsidized by the government. This aggravated trade frictions between Japan and the United States.

Tokyo's rationale for the ban is that self-sufficiency in rice is important for food security purposes. In addition domestic farm groups have long maintained that rice cultivation is part of Japanese culture. Researcher argued that Japanese consumers have become more tolerant of high rice prices because their food expenditure as a ratio of total expenditure has declined as their incomes rise.

Surprisingly, consumer groups have not actively supported the lifting of the ban in order to reduce the rice price. The main reason is reportedly the Japanese consumers' demand for 'high-quality' rice. Surveys do indicate that consumers believe that foreign rice tastes bad.

In the Uruguay Round of GATT (General Agreement of Tariffs and Trade) negotiations in 1990, Japan refused to give concessions in eliminating its ban on rice imports. It was estimated that without the ban, U.S. rice exports to Japan could have amounted to $656 million a year. As of 2010 free trade in connection with the Trans-Pacific Partnership is again being debated in Japan.

Rice Production in Bangladesh

Rice production in Bangladesh is a crucial part of the national economy.

The dominant food crop of Bangladesh is rice, accounting for about 75 per cent of agricultural land use (and 28% of GDP). Rice production increased every year in the 1980s (through 1987) except FY 1981, but the annual increases have generally been modest, barely keeping pace with the population. Rice production exceeded 15 million tons for the first time in FY 1986.

In the mid-1980s, Bangladesh was the fourth largest rice producer in the world, but its productivity was low compared with other Asian countries, such as Malaysia and Indonesia. It is currently the world's sixth-largest producer. Highyield varieties of seed, application of fertilizer, and irrigation have increased yields, although these inputs also raise the cost of production and chiefly benefit the richer cultivators.

The cultivation of rice in Bangladesh varies according to seasonal changes in the water supply. The largest harvest is aman, occurring in November and December and accounting for more than half of annual production. Some rice for the aman harvest is sown in the spring through the broadcast method, matures during the summer rains, and is harvested in the fall.

The higher yielding method involves starting the seeds in special beds and transplanting during the summer monsoon. The second harvest is aus, involving traditional strains but more often including high-yielding, dwarf varieties. Rice for the aus harvest is sown in March or April, benefits from April and May rains, matures during in the summer rain, and is harvested during the summer. With the increasing use of irrigation, there has been a growing focus on another rice-growing season extending during the dry season from October to March. The production of this boro rice, including high-yield varieties, expanded rapidly until the mid-1980s, when production leveled off at just below 4 million tons.

Where irrigation is feasible, it is normal for fields throughout Bangladesh to produce rice for two harvests annually. Between rice-growing seasons, farmers will do everything possible to prevent the land from lying fallow and will grow vegetables, peanuts, pulses, or oilseeds if water and fertilizer are available.

9

Rice Cultivation

Rice crosses all cultural boundaries and is a food that many people count on for their daily meals. It is easy enough to just head to the grocery store and buy rice. However, in order to have a true appreciation for this diet staple it is important to understand how rice is planted and grown.

Rice is generally grown in warmer regions. It will not survive if the temperature is too low. Rice requires a minimum of 10° C. Yet there are varieties of rice that can be grown at high altitudes, and it is not uncommon in some regions to see rice paddies terraced up the sides of hills and mountains.

It is possible, but generally not efficient to grow rice in a green house. It usually done on an experimental basis in order to minimize variables in the growing process. Rice seeds are placed in a pot and covered with compost. The pots are kept very warm and slightly damp. This is done to ease the process of germination, which may take a few weeks to a month.

When the seeds germinate (can take two weeks to several months) it is time for them to go into a larger pot. If they do not have a large enough environment then the rice planting will fail. They should be placed deep down into the soil to ensure that the roots can take hold and become strong and vital.

Green house growth requires plenty of water and sunlight. It should also receive a moderate amount of fertilizer - too much will burn the plant and too little will result in poor quality plants. The plants should be supported by twigs or stakes. The grass stems grow to be over three feet (a meter) high. Tiny flowers on the plant indicate healthy rice. Since there is no wind inside a greenhouse, it is important make sure pollen spreads from one plant to another. This can be done by running your fingers through the flowers on successive batches of plants.

The rice pots should continue to be well-watered until the grains begin to mature, when they should be kept much drier in order to help the grains to ripen more quickly. Harvest the grains when ripe.

Rice farming is done on a subsistence basis in some countries and on a huge scale in other. In the U.S. most rice is grown in the Southeast and in California. In developed countries rice production is highly automated. In the New South Wales Riverina area the land is leveled using laser guided bulldozers. With leveled fields water use can be minimized and production maximized. The seed is cast in the rice bays by air planes using satellite guidance technologies. The seed is soaked for 24 hours and then dried. When cast over the wet beds it settles to the bottom and takes hold of the soil. Within ten days it is shooting through the water's surface. Plants are sown to produce 300 plants per square meter in 5-20 centimetres of water.

Chemical insecticides and herbicides are used up until the last 100 days of growth. This insures the maximum yield but virtually no exposure to chemicals by humans. The plants continue to grow for several months. They have hairy roots, strong central stems, and tillers on which the flowers grow. In the fall, March and April in Australia, the beds are drained and dried out and the grains are harvested using huge machines built specifically for the purpose.

Subsistence farmers have to take somewhat of a different approach. The first step is to prepare the soil. This means tilling the land so that the soil is very loose. When the soil is loose it allows for the roots of the rice plants to grow and expand. Once the soil is tilled, rice farmers then spread manure or other fertilizer. This gives the plants the nutrients they need to grow large and healthy.

When the soil is ready, farmers start to plant the rice seedlings. This is usually done in 'paddies' where the water is no more than ankle deep. These seedlings are usually allowed to germinate in other environments before they are planted on the farmland. The plants are kept under water for several months using irrigation techniques. If these rice seedlings are healthy and will spread their roots far until they are very strong rice plants. In regions where rice has been cultivated for centuries pest and weed control can be a difficult process without the help of chemicals. Much of this is done by hand and is very labour intensive.

When flowering is complete and the grains have grown, water is drained from the rice paddies in order to let the rice grains mature. The maturing process is speeded up by the stress put on the plant by the lack of water. When the grains have matured the farmer can begin to harvest them. Once cut, the rice is threshed to separate it from its hull. Then it is winnowed by tossing it in the air above a sheet or mat in a light breeze. It can then be stored for later use or brought to market.

Rice, like many starches, is an enjoyable food because it is versatile. It is commonly eaten with many different spices and used in literally thousands of recipes. Before adding it to your menu or including it in a dish it is important to learn how to properly prepare rice.

Before choosing a preparation method consider the best method for the dish. The different ways of cooking rice create a significant difference in the outcome. A good cook will experiment and become knowledgeable in the various methods.

As rice cooks it expands by absorbing water. To do this, boil water, and add a touch of salt. When the rice is tender, stop boiling and pour out the water. When the water is gone, cover the pot so that the rice can steam cook until it is ready.

If the correct amount of water is used, there will be no water to pour off. (Ed. - I have found through experimentation that 4 cups of boiling water with 1¾ cups rice makes the best rice without having to pour off any water. The instructions say not to remove the lid during cooking, but I frequently stir rice during the steaming process, when I see that there is no water left I turn off the heat and allow the rice to set while other dishes finish cooking.) Simply bring water to a boil, turn down to simmer, add rice, a bit of butter or oil, put lid on pan, and steam for about 20-30 minutes.

Steam cookers make this process even easier. Add water to the steam cooker. The rice is poured into a special compartment. The rest is automated, and may even 'ding' to signal that the rice is ready. This is a quick a simple way to cook rice!

Another way to prepare rice is to saute it. This is great for certain recipes and is usually done in a mixture containing many different ingredients. Fried rice is a favorite, but not quite as healthy as when other methods are used. But even rices cooked in this manner require the addition of water after the rice has been fried in butter or oil.

Some more helpful hints when preparing rice:

- A typical serving of rice is about $^{1}/_{3}$ cup.
- Rinse rice before cooking it to remove any dust.
- A sauteed rice is generally less soggy than a steamed rice.
- Cook rice in a ratio of 2 $^{1}/_{8}$ parts water to one part rice.
- Steam rice at a very low setting.

Though the process is fairly simple, things can occasionally go wrong with rice preparation. If there is water left, it may be cooked off by turning up the heat and removing the lid, or by simply pouring it off.

It the rice is a bit crunchy adding a bit of water and cooking longer should solve the problem. Over-cooked rice will turn starchy and mushy. It is best to use the rice for dessert recipes like rice pudding. It is pretty much impossible at this point to bring it back to its preferred consistency.

Ultimately, rice has many advantages at the table. It is fairly simple to prepare. It complements other dishes, and can be a filling ingredient in many recipes. By its nature it lends itself to experimentation in the kitchen.

Rice is a filling ingredient for any recipe. Yet, with a small pad of butter, and a bit of salt and pepper it stands out on its own as a mouth-watering dish. Rice is an appealing ingredient because it is versatile. So much so that it can be used in both savory and sweet recipes (rice pudding).

Some recipes (such as pig-in-the-blanket or stuffed peppers) call for the rice to be cooked first. In others (Spanish rice), the ingredients are all cooked together. There are many brands of prepared rice, from Uncle Bens, to Rice-a-Roni, to Zatarain's. All of which provide delicious, easy-to-make dishes out of a box.

Nevertheless, people get excited about recipes made from scratch for a very good reason. Scratch recipes provide original flavours and give the cook a degree of flexibility in spice selection impossible from a packet of prepared spices. Our editors have put together a few recipes to demonstrate the versatility and appeal of rice.

10

Paddy Field

A paddy field is a flooded parcel of arable land used for growing rice and other semiaquatic crops. Paddy fields are a typical feature of rice farming in east, south and southeast Asia. Paddies can be built into steep hillsides as terraces and adjacent to depressed or steeply sloped features such as rivers or marshes. They can require a great deal of labour and materials to create, and need large quantities of water for irrigation. Flooded paddies provide an ideal environment for rice cultivation and discourage the growth of many weeds. The water buffalo is one of the most important working animals adapted for life in wetlands, and is used extensively in paddy fields.

During the twentieth century, paddy field farming became the dominant form of growing rice. Paddy field farming is practiced in Cambodia, Bangladesh, China, Taiwan, India, Indonesia, Japan, North Korea, South Korea, Malaysia, Myanmar, Nepal, Pakistan, the Philippines, Sri Lanka, Thailand, Vietnam, and Laos, as well as Piedmont in Italy, the Camargue in France, the Artibonite Valley in Haiti, and Sacramento Valley in California. Paddy fields are a major source of atmospheric methane and have been estimated to contribute in the range of 50 to 100 million tonnes of the gas per annum. Recent studies have shown that this can be significantly reduced while also boosting crop yield by draining the paddies to allow the soil to aerate to interrupt methane production.

The word 'paddy' is derived from the Malay word *padi,* rice plant.

Archaeologists generally accept that wet-field cultivation originated in China. At Caoxieshan, a site of the Neolithic Majiabang culture, archaeologists excavated paddy fields. Some archaeologists claim that Caoxieshan may date to 4000-3000 BC, but as of now the oldest excavated rice paddy field dated by absolute scientific dating techniques are from Korea. There is archaeological evidence that unhusked rice was stored for the military and for burial with the deceased from the Neolithic period to the Han Dynasty in China.

Paddy field farming goes back thousands of years in Korea. A pit-house at the Daecheon-ni site yielded carbonized rice grains and radiocarbon dates indicating that rice cultivation in dry-fields may have begun as early as the Middle Jeulmun Pottery Period (c. 3500-2000 BC) in the Korean Peninsula. Ancient paddy fields have been carefully unearthed in Korea by institutes such as Kyungnam University Museum (KUM) of Masan. They excavated paddy field features at the Geumcheon-ni Site near Miryang, South Gyeongsang Province. The paddy field feature was found next to a pit-house that is dated to the latter part of the Early Mumun Pottery Period (c. 1100-850 BC). KUM has conducted excavations that have revealed similarly dated paddy field features at Yaeum-dong and Okhyeon in modern-day Ulsan.

The earliest Mumun features were usually located in low-lying narrow gullies that were naturally swampy and fed by the local stream system. Some Mumun paddy fields in flat areas were made of a series of squares and rectangles separated by bunds approximately 10 cm in height, while terraced paddy fields consisted of long irregular shapes that followed natural contours of the land at various levels.

Mumun Period rice farmers used all of the elements that are present in today's paddy fields such terracing, bunds, canals, and small reservoirs. We can grasp some paddy-field farming techniques of the Middle Mumun (c. 850-550 BC) from the well-preserved wooden tools excavated from archaeological rice fields at the Majeon-ni Site. However, iron tools for paddy-field farming were not introduced until sometime after 200 BC. The spatial scale of paddy-fields increased with the regular use of iron tools in the Three Kingdoms of Korea Period (c. AD 300/400-668).

The first paddy fields in Japan date to the Early Yayoi period. The Early Yayoi has been re-dated and thus it appears that wet-field agriculture developed at approximately the same time as in the Korean peninsula.

In the Philippines, the use of rice paddies can be traced to prehistoric times, as evidenced in the names of towns such as Pila, Laguna, whose name can be traced to the straight mounds of dirt that form the boundaries of the rice paddy, or 'Pilapil'.

Wet rice cultivation in Vietnam dates back to the Neolithic Hoa Binh culture and Bac Son culture.

Although China's agricultural output is the largest in the world, only about 15 per cent of its total land area can be cultivated. About 75 per cent of the cultivated area is used for food crops. Rice is China's most important crop, raised on about 25 per cent of the cultivated area. The majority of rice is grown south of the Huai River, in the Yangtze valley, the Zhu Jiang delta, and in Yunnan, Guizhou, and Sichuan provinces.

Rice appears to have been used by the Early Neolithic populations of Lijiacun and Yunchanyan in China. Evidence of possible rice cultivation from ca. 11,500 BP has been found, however it is still questioned whether the rice was indeed being cultivated, or instead being gathered as wild rice. Bruce Smith, an archaeologist at the Smithsonian Institution in Washington, D.C., who has written on the origins of agriculture, says that evidence has been mounting that the Yangtze was probably the site of the earliest rice cultivation. In 1998, Crawford & Shen reported that the earliest of 14

AMS or radiocarbon dates on rice from at least nine Early to Middle Neolithic sides is no older than 7000 BC, that rice from the Hemudu and Luojiajiao sites indicates that rice domestication likely began before 5000 BC, but that most sites in China from which rice remains have been recovered are younger than 5000 BC.

During the Spring and Autumn Period (722-481 BC), two revolutionary improvements in farming technology took place. One was the use of cast iron tools and beasts of burden to pull plows, and the other was the large-scale harnessing of rivers and development of water conservation projects. The engineer Sunshu Ao of the 6th century BC and Ximen Bao of the 5th century BC are two of the oldest hydraulic engineers from China, and their works were focused upon improving irrigation systems. These developments were widely spread during the ensuing Warring States Period (403-221 BC), culminating in the enormous Du Jiang Yan Irrigation System engineered by Li Bing by 256 BC for the State of Qin in ancient Sichuan. During the Eastern Jin (317-420) and the Northern and Southern Dynasties (420-589), land-use became more intensive and efficient, rice was grown twice a year and cattle began to be used for plowing and fertilization. It should be noted that in circa 750, 75 per cent of China's population lived north of the river Yangtse, but by 1250, 75 per cent of China's population lived south of the river Yangtse. Such large-scale internal migration was possible due to introduction of quick-ripening strains of rice from Vietnam suitable for multi-cropping.

Localities in China which are famous for their spectacular rice paddies are Yuanyang County, Yunnan, and Longsheng County, Guangxi.

India

India has the largest paddy output in the world and is also the second largest exporter of rice in the world. Paddy fields are a common sight throughout India, be they be northern gangetic plains or southern peninsular plateaus. Paddy is cultivated at least twice a year in most parts of India, the two seasons being known as *Rabi* and *Kharif* respectively. The former cultivation is dependent on irrigation, while the latter depends on Monsoon. The paddy cultivation plays a major role in socio-cultural life of rural India. Many festivals such as *Onam* in Kerala, *Bihu* in Assam, *Sankranthi* in Andhra Pradesh *Thai Pongal* in Tamil Nadu, *Makara Sankranthi* in Karnataka, *Nabanna* in West Bengal celebrates harvest of Paddy. Andhra Pradesh is historically known as the 'Rice Bowl of India', while Thanjavur is historically known as the 'Granary of South India' and the *Rice bowl of Tamil Nadu*. Nanchinadu was known as the rice bowl of the former Kingdom of Travancore. In Kerala there is a place (which spreads into three districts) called Kuttanadu, which is famous for paddy cultivation. Kuttanadu is called the rice bowl of Kerala.

Indonesia

Prime Javanese paddy yields roughly 6 metric tons of unmilled rice (2.5 metric tons of milled rice) per hectare. When irrigation is available, rice farmers typically plant Green Revolution rice varieties allowing three growing seasons per year. Since fertilizer and pesticide are relatively expensive inputs, farmers typically plant seeds in a very small plot. Three weeks following germination, the 6-8 inch stalks are picked and replanted at greater separation, in a backbreaking manual procedure.

Rice harvesting in Central Java is often performed not by owners or sharecroppers of paddy, but rather by itinerant middlemen, whose small firms specialize in harvesting, transport, milling, and distribution to markets.

The fertile volcanic soil of much of the Indonesian archipelago—and particularly the islands of Java and Bali—has made rice a central dietary staple. Steep terrain on Bali resulted in an intricate cooperation systems, locally called *subak*, to manage water storage and drainage for rice terraces.

Italy

Rice is grown in northern Italy, especially in the valley of the river Po. The paddy fields are irrigated by fast-flowing streams descending from the Alps. Risotto, a rice dish flavoured with saffron is a typical dish from the rice-growing area near Milan that has now travelled around the world.

Japan

The acidic soil conditions common in Japan due to volcanic eruptions have made the paddy field the most productive farming method. Paddy fields are represented by the kanji ? (commonly read as *ta*) that has had a strong influence on Japanese culture. In fact, the character which originally meant 'field' in general, is used in Japan exclusively to convey the meaning 'rice paddy field'. One of the oldest samples of writing in Japan is widely credited to the kanji ? found on pottery at the archaeological site of Matsusaka, Mie that dates to the late 2nd century. *Ta* is used as a part of many place names as well as in many family names. Most of these places are somehow related to the paddy field and in many cases, are based on the history of a particular location. For example, where a river runs through a village, the place east of river may be called *Higashida* , literally 'east paddy field'. A place with a newly irrigated paddy field, especially those during or later than Edo period, may be called *Nitta* or *Shinden* (both), 'new paddy field'. In some places, lakes and marshes were likened to a paddy field and were named with *ta*, like *Hakkoda*.

Today, many family names have *ta* as a component, a practice which can be largely attributed to a government edict in the early Meiji Period requiring all Japanese people to have a family name. Many chose a name based on or near the place they lived or the job they had, and with nearly three fourths of population being farmers, many made family names using *ta*. Some common examples are *Tanaka* , literally meaning 'middle of paddy field'; *Nakata*, 'rice field in the middle'; *Kawada*, 'paddy field by a river' and *Furuta*, 'old paddy field'.

In recent years rice consumption in Japan has fallen and many rice farmers are increasingly elderly. The government has subsidized rice production since the 1970s, and is protectionist regarding cheaper imported rice.

Korea

Arable land in small alluvial flats of most rural river valleys in South Korea are dedicated to paddy-field farming. Farmers assess paddy fields for any necessary repairs in February. Fields may be rebuilt, and bund breaches are repaired. This work is carried out until mid-March, when warmer spring weather allows the farmer to buy or grow rice seedlings. They are transplanted (usually by rice transplanter) from the indoors into freshly flooded paddy fields in May. Farmers tend and weed their paddy fields through the summer until around the time of Chuseok, a traditional holiday held on August 15 of the Lunar Calendar (circa mid-September by Solar Calendar). The harvest begins in October. Coordinating the harvest can be challenging because many Korean farmers have small paddy fields in a number of locations around their villages, and modern harvesting machines are sometimes shared between extended family members. Farmers usually dry the harvested grains in the sun before bringing them to market.

The Chinese (or Sino-Korean) character for 'field', *jeon*, is found in some place names, especially small farming townships and villages. However, the specific Korean term for 'paddy' is a purely Korean word, 'non' (Hangeul).

Madagascar

In Madagascar, the average annual consumption of rice is 130 kg per person, one of the largest in the world.

According to a 1999 study of UPDRS/FAO:

The majority of rice is related to irrigation (1,054,381 ha). The choice of methods conditioning performance is determined by the variety and quality control of water.

The 'Tavy', is traditionally the culture of flooded upland rice on burning of cleared natural rain forest (135,966 ha). Criticized as being the cause of deforestation, 'Tavy' is still widely practiced by farmers in Madagascar, who find a good compromise between climate risks, availability of labour and food security.

'Tanety' means hill. By extension, the 'tanety' is also growing upland rice, carried out on the grassy slopes have been deforested for the operation of charcoal. (139,337 ha)

Among the many varieties, rice of Madagascar include: 'Vary lava' is a translucent long and large grain rice. It is a luxury ricer. Vary Makalioka, is translucent long and thin grain rice. 'Vary Rojofotsy' is a -half long.grain rice 'Vary mena' or red rice, is exclusive to Madagascar.

They are sought-after rice, so that the Malagasy prefer often to export them and import in return foreign rice for lower quality.

Myanmar

Rice is grown primarily in three areas - the Irrawaddy Delta, the area along and the delta of the Kaladan River, and the Central plains around Mandalay. Up until the later 1960s, Myanmar was the main exporter of rice. Termed the rice basket of South East Asia, much of the rice grown in Myanmar does not rely on fertilizers and pesticides, thus, although 'organic' in a sense, it has been unable to cope with population growth and other rice economies which utilized fertilizers.

Rice is now grown in all the three seasons of Myanmar, though primarily in the Monsoon season - from June to October. Rice grown in the delta areas rely heavily on the river water and sedimented minerals from the northern mountains, whilst the rice grown in the central regions require irrigation from the Ayeryarwaddy River.

The fields are tilled when the first rains arrive - traditionally measured at 40 days after Thingyan, the Burmese New Year - around the beginning of June. In modern times, tractors are used, but traditionally, buffalos were employed. The rice plants are planted in nurseries and then transplanted by hand into the prepared fields. The rice is then harvested in late November - 'when the rice bends with age'. Most of the rice planting and harvesting are done by hand. The rice is then threshed and stored, ready for the mills.

Philippines

Paddy fields are a common sight in the Philippines. Several vast paddy fields exist in the provinces of Nueva Ecija, Isabela, Cagayan, Bulacan, etc. Nueva Ecija produces the biggest share of rice for national food security.

Banaue Rice Terraces

The Banaue Rice Terraces are located in Northern Luzon and were built by the Ifugaos 2000 years ago. Streams and springs found in the mountains were tapped and channeled into irrigation canals that run downhill through the rice terraces. Other notable Philippine paddy fields are the Batad Rice Terraces, the Bangaan Rice Terraces, the Mayoyao Rice Terraces and the Hapao Rice Terraces.

Located at Barangay Batad in Banaue, the Batad Rice Terraces are shaped like an amphitheatre, and can be reached by a 12-kilometre ride from Banaue Hotel and a 2-hour hike uphill through mountain trails. The Bangaan Rice Terraces portray the typical Ifugao community, where the livelihood activities are within the village and its surroundings. The Bangaan Rice Terraces is accessible in a one-hour ride from Poblacion, Banaue, then a 20-minute trek down to the village. It can be viewed best from the road to Mayoyao. The Mayoyao Rice Terraces is located at Mayoyao, 44 kilometres away from Poblacion, Banaue. The town of Mayoyao lies in the midst of these rice terraces. All dikes are tiered with flat stones. The Hapao Rice Terraces can be reached within 55 kilometres from the capital town of Lagawe. Other Ifugao stone-walled rice terraces are located in the municipality of Hungduan.

Sri Lanka

Agriculture in Sri Lanka mainly depends on rice production. Sri Lanka sometimes exports rice but not in recent years. Around 1.5 million hectares of land is cultivated in Sri Lanka for paddy in 2008/2009 maha: 64 per cent of which is cultivated during the dry season and 35 per cent cultivated during the wet season. Around 879,000 farmer families are engaged in paddy cultivation in Sri Lanka. They make up 20 per cent of the country's population and 32 per cent of the employment.

Thailand

Rice production in Thailand represents a significant portion of the Thai economy. It uses over half of the farmable land area and labour force in Thailand.

Thailand has a strong tradition of rice production. It has the fifth-largest amount of land under rice cultivation in the world and is the world's largest exporter of rice. Thailand has plans to further increase its land available for rice production, with a goal of adding 500,000 hectares to its already 9.2 million hectares of rice-growing areas. The Thai Ministry of Agriculture expects rice production to yield around 30 million tons of rice for 2008. The most produced strain of rice in Thailand is jasmine rice, which is a higher quality type of rice. However, jasmine has a significantly lower yield rate than other types of rice, but it also normally fetches more than double the price of other strains in a global market.

Vietnam

Rice fields in Vietnam are the predominant land use in the valley of the Red River and the Mekong Delta. In the Red River Delta of northern Vietnam, farmers must dam up (nowadays 3000 km long) against the annual flood, and it is also the necessary condition to form an alliance among Vietnamese ancient tribals to found Vietnamese people's first state. In the Mekong Delta of southern Vietnam, there is an interlacing drainage and irrigation canal system that has become the symbol of this area and impacts on the lifestyle of local people. In Northwestern Vietnam, Thai people built their *"valley culture"* based on the economic foundation of glutinous rice upland fields.

The primary festival related to rice fields is (Vietnamese) (Tay language) in the first day of every crop wishing for yield more than usual. In the past, this was the official national ceremony that the King would make the first plough and people would worship Than Nong (god of agriculture), *th d a* (god of the soil), *thành hoàng làng* (god of the village), and *th?n lúa* (god of rice plants).

During the Tr N Dynasty, there were three kinds of rice field: *ru ng qu c kh* and *ru ng ao* of the common people.

In Vietnamese literature, a rice field is described as wide enough for a flock of storks to span their wings across: *'d ng lúa th ng cánh cò bay'* and the sway of rice plants in the wind is compared to waves of the sea and called *'sóng lúa'*. These images are very common phrases describing the beauty of the Vietnamese landscape.

11

Paddy Cultivation

Since early times, paddy cultivation has been the main supplier of food in many Asian countries. The basic aim food of security could not be achieved in any other way. At the same time, however, many paddy farmers are poor by national standards. Apart from hard work, they are becoming exposed to new challenges such as lower trade barriers; competition; new demands; and a reduced water availability.

In future, revenues of the agricultural sector will increase, but a large part of the value will be generated by crops other than rice, as well as meat, and, quite likely, biofuel. Less labour-intensive production systems will prevail. Competition will benefit the more efficient production systems at the cost of less efficient ones.

The transition between today and the future is a major challenge. If conducted smoothly, the sector will emerge as prosperous and competitive, well placed to generate income for the farmers and food for the population. If conducted less smoothly, there is a risk of unemployment and low incomes.

Since early times, paddy cultivation has been the main supplier of food in many Asian countries. The basic aim food of security could not be achieved in any other way. Also, paddy cultivation provides the livelihood for many people - in several countries the majority of the labour force.

At the same time, however, many paddy farmers are poor by national standards. Apart from hard work, they are now exposed to new challenges such as lower trade barriers; competition from abroad; new demands; and a reduced water availability.

Many countries see their agricultural sectors lagging behind industries and services in terms of technology and revenue. agriculture being much higher than the sector's contribution to the tional economy. This means that there is less revenue to share than it is the case within industry and the service sector.

Of course there is no rule saying that each sector should generate an equal value - in terms of money - per employee. (Rather, in an economic perspective, the sectors should contribute to the best of their potential, and in a social perspective, food is important in its own right). On the other hand, the imbalance seems consistent with the fact that paddy cultivation can be a hard way to earn a living.

Paddy Cultivation Today and in the Future

In a strongly generalised way, and with a particular view to SE Asia, a simple distinction can be made between three stages of the paddy cultivation sector.

Traditional production units are household-based and small. Some household members may seek a living off the farm, and bring back cash. A few cows and buffaloes can make a visible difference to the household economy, and so can a bit of seasonal fishing. Paddy cultivation is labour intensive, but typically the peak demands of labour, for transplanting and harvesting, are extreme, short and synchronised. If the cultivation is rainfed, without reliable access to irrigation water, it becomes vulnerable to weather irregularities. In some places, the yield is low (but the quality can be high). Access to markets can be impeded by a variety of physical and structural (market-related) constraints.

Irrigated paddy cultivation is (and will remain) the predominant off-stream water use.

A Transition Process

Many Asian countries are in this stage. The process of structural change is important, because it will affect many households over a time span of decades.

The agricultural sector will diversify, and the thrust of its development may occur for production systems other than rice. Food production will increase, but the process will see a big loss of employment in traditional paddy cultivation. The production unit - the farm size - will increase, driven by new technology that requires less labour but more capital, combined with a need of higher production efficiencies - more output and higher value per unit of input. Labour-intensive production systems - such as the System of Rice Intensification (SRI) - will be marginal.

The changes are driven by a combination of circumstances. Lower trade barriers will increase the exposure to competitive pressure, reflecting comparative advantages and disadvantages, as well as exposure to global price fluctuations - a tendency that will interact, in an unpredictable way, with escalating weather irregularities caused by a global climate change. New lifestyles will affect the demand of many commodities, including food (and energy) - for example if people consume more meat. A new demand of biofuel is a distinct possibility.

The recent tendency of large-scale international acquisition of agricultural land (and water) will affect the availability of production factors and have an explicit purpose of increasing the supply of food and other agricultural products - although perhaps in distant countries.

The use of pesticides (and fertilisers) will escalate, partly necessitated by the diversification. Pesticides can end up in the environment and can contaminate edible fish and water used for drinking.

Higher revenue per ha will make agricultural lands an investment object - a bit like it occurred during the green revolution, and as it is clearly seen when an area is supplied with irrigation infrastructure. Small-scale land owners risk to lose their land in connection with irregular weather or in case of social shocks, such as illness in the family.

Rice will remain the favoured staple food. Revenues of the agricultural sector will increase, but a large part of the value will be generated by crops other than rice, as well as meat, and, quite likely, biofuel. Less labour-intensive production systems will prevail. The technological development will proceed in the direction of further diversification and continued efficiency improvements, covering primary production, livestock and processing.

Lower trade barriers will increase the exposure to price fluctuations. Also, there will be a much higher exposure to competition, which will benefit the more efficient production systems at the cost of less efficient ones.

Stormy Weather Over the Paddy Fields

The transition between today and the future is a major challenge. If conducted smoothly, the sector will emerge as prosperous and competitive, well placed to generate income for the farmers and food for the population. If conducted less smoothly, there is a risk of unemployment, and farm incomes that are even lower than today. This can happen if the changes take place too fast, or without appropriate support.

The transition will take place on a background of increased demand of water for households and industries. The figure below shows that the population of Asia as a whole is estimated to grow by a factor of more than 3 between 1950 and 2050 - whilethe population of Viet Nam is estimated to grow by a factor of more than 4 in the same period. The household demand is the population multiplied by the per capita demand, both of which are growing - the latter more than the former. The required larger amounts of food must be produced with less water.

Policy Implications

Between them, the various challenges clearly indicate a need of change. Below are listed some policy implications, in random order, as applicable from case to case. Efficiency improvement is a general aim, considering the need to improve the income of the farmers, in an increasingly competitive environment, while, at the same time, producing more food with less water. This comprises the water efficiency - ton per m^3 of water output - as well as the economic efficiency - value generated per m^3 of water.

Another important aim is livelihood generation, expectedly mainly outside the farms, but preferably including rural livelihoods, in order to reduce the rate of (an unavoidable and possibly eventually beneficial) urban migration. Towns must grow, and will, but best at a rate that allows for facilities, infrastructure and services to grow accordingly.

A value chain perspective can support generation of revenue and livelihoods, for example by encouragement of agro-processing, including innovative products, and partly undertaken de-centrally by small and medium enterprises.

Branding of products and related marketing can, sometimes, add attractive value at a moderate cost.

Gentle, pro-poor market regulation can be applied in support of shifting to new products (perhaps biofuel), and in support of a common national aim of affordable food prices while at the same time maintaining an income of the farmers that at least exceeds their production cost. A high predictability will support the intended outcome and reduce the risk of adverse effects.

Credit, including (but not limited to) micro-credit, is a general precondition for investment and innovation. Some kind of risk insurance can make it possible for the farmers to keep their land in case of emergencies. Water uses must be regulated. There is a particular scope for strict regulation of new, water-dependent industries, because these can adapt more easily than existing ones with older technology - and sometimes even saving water, energy and money at the same time. The regulation must cover both surface water and groundwater.

Disaster preparedness (for floods, drought and pests) must be in place. Organisation of farmers (like in water user groups) can facilitate efficiency improvements, other kinds of technological development, and access to markets. Interaction must be maintained between development of irrigation and cultivation. Upgrading one without upgrading the other is not optimal. An integrated (IWRM) approach can highly increase the returns on the efforts.

Soil management will become more important (and the benefits more visible) when water is sparse and in connection with diversifying the cultivation on lands that are not well suited crops other than rice. Use of pesticides must be kept at acceptable levels, supported by education and awareness campaigns and supportive extension and weather forecast services.

Continued research is required, including international networking, knowledge- sharing and active collaboration. Results must be made available to the end users by pilot and demonstration activities, well functional extension services, and networking among farmers - possibly across borders.

Agricultural development must be cautious and gradual. There is always a risk of unforeseen adverse side effects when implementing new technologies, and even when implementing existing and well proven technologies in new places. If everyone grew water melons the market would fail.

1. Cadmium in Asian countries.
2. Cadmium can be supplied layers) polished rice) to the paddy fields by wastewater, sludge, phosphate fertilizer, and sometimes by mine tailings Command area.

The area that can receive water via an irrigation scheme crop intensity. The part of an area that is actually cultivated. If the whole area is cultivated in the wet season, and half of it is cultivated in the dry season (due to water shortage), the crop intensity becomes 150 per cent.

Crop Water Requirement

The amount of water required for cultivation of a crop, as available to the crop in the field where it grows (mm/day, mm/ month or mm/crop). The crop requirement equals the evapotranspiration of the crop in question. The crop requirement is supplied by rainfall, soil moisture variation and irrigation. Irrigation water requirement (in FAO terminology) is the part of the crop requirement that is not supplied by rainfall or by soil moisture variation.

Demand Management

Intervention in order to reduce the consumption of water, in order to meet a water shortage, or a shortage of funds for infrastructural development, or to improve the water efficiency. Demand management can comprise improved operation and maintenance of distribution systems (including reduction of water losses), green taxes to reduce the demand,awareness campaigns to change consumer habits, introduction of new crops or cultivation routines, etc.

Demand Satisfaction

The ratio between the water that is available (at the intake from a river or a gate of a reservoir) and the withdrawal demand, at a given time for a given purpose (for example a given crop and a given cultivation routine). The demand satisfaction is 100 per cent if there is enough water to serve the demand Drought: 'A period with an extraordinary water shortage' (due to the rainfall being less than normal).

Efficiency

1. The ratio between output (for example food or money) and input (for example land, water, labour, or energy);
2. The 'economic efficiency' is the ratio between value generated and water used/allocated;
3. The 'scheme efficiency' or the 'irrigation water efficiency' is the ratio between the crop water requirement and the irrigation demand evapotranspiration. The loss of water from the ground to the atmosphere by evaporation and by transpiration (of plants).

Potential evapotranspiration is the capacity of the atmosphere to remove water from the ground, if water is abundantly available. Reference evapotranspiration (ETO) is the evapotranspiration of a well-defined vegetation cover, measured by a standard routine, and used for calculating the evapotranspiration for a given crop during its cultivation cycle (by multiplication with a time-varying crop coefficient) FAO: United Nations Food and Agriculture Organisation Husk (or chaff): The outer cover of a grain of paddy, removed by thrashing and winnowing. Can be used for fuel (but contains little energy and a lot of ash) Irrigable area: The area that can actually be irrigated with a specific (present or future) infrastructure (disregarding the finite availability of water).

Irrigation

Artificial supply of water (other than rainwater) for cultivation, from groundwater, or by diversion of surface water, or by distribution or retention of flood water, or from a storage tank or reservoir. FAO makes a distinction between 5 possible sources of irrigation water: Surface water, renewable groundwater, fossil water, treated wastewater and desalinated water. Please compare with 'water-managed area' Irrigation demand (or withdrawal demand for irrigation) .

The required gross amount of water needed to be abstracted (from the river or reservoir) to cultivate a crop (mm/month or mm/crop). Irrigation demand = crop requirement, plus the return flow from the field to the river, plus miscellaneous losses (distribution, conveyance, and percolation out of the root zone) Losses of water.

At scheme level, losses take place via evaporation, seepage, percolation, and release of return flows; but at the basin level, the 'lost' volumes can often be utilized at a different time and place Manageable water resources.

According to researcher:

The part of the water resources which is considered to be available for development under specific economic and environmental conditions. This figure considers factors such as the dependability of the flow, extractable groundwater, minimum flow required for non consumptive use, etc. Also called water development potential Moisture content.

Paddy is best milled with a moisture content of 14 per cent. Many rice buyers apply an upper limit of 12-12.5 per cent for milled rice. The official upper limit for Thai Hom Mali rice is 14 per cent Paddy:

1. a field where rice is grown;
2. rice in its husk (also called rough rice) parboiled rice is soaked, cooked and dried before it is milled.

As compared with ordinary white rice, the milling efficiency is higher. Parboiled rice has a different taste and texture, and needs a somewhat longer cooking time. Some countries have a traditional preference for parboiled rice Percolation, seepage: Flow through a porous material. Some authors distinguish between seepage ('horizontal' leakage through a bund) and percolation ('vertical' leakage through the soil layers to the groundwater).

Precipitation

Rainfall and snow reaching the ground Puddling (of paddy fields): Softening (by various operations) of the top soil layer before transplanting, at the same time levelling the soil surface and destroying weeds, while maintaining a low permeability of the sub-soil (to reduce percolation losses) Rice species: Rice (Oryza) is one of around 600 members of the grass (Poacea) family of plants.

Two species (of about 22) are cultivated. *Oryza glaberrima* (African rice) is native to Sub-Saharan frica, where it was domesticated in the upper Niger River Basin some 2-3,000 years ago. *Oryza sativa,* (Asian rice), domesticated 10-15,000 years ago, is by far the prevalent cultivated species. Long-grain rice (*indicas*) and short-grain rice (*japonicas*) are groups of varieties. Well-known varieties are (the aromatic) *basmati* rice (from India and Pakistan) and (the aromatic) Thai jasmine rice (Thai Hom Mali).

Straw is used for animal feed, fuel, and fertilizer. Roughly, 2 tons of straw are produced for each ton of paddy 4 Transplanting 5: Traditional lowland cultivation often comprises sowing the rice in nursery beds, and transplanting the seedlings after a period of 12 days to 6 weeks. Transplanting requires intensive labour within a short period of the cropping calendar. Depending on site-specific conditions, this can give a higher yield (but a longer cultivation period, and hereby a higher risk of drought exposure), ascompared with direct seeding (or broadcasting) Virtual water: Water represented by a traded commodity (for example rice). (1 kg of milled rice may represent 3-6 m^3 of water). (If so, for example, Thailand would export some 30 km^3 of virtual water per year, represented by the country's rice export).

The opinion is offered that this line of thinking is not entirely fruitful - the comparative value of the traded commodity may be quite different from the comparative value of the 'virtual water' Water-managed area. According to researcher an area on which water, other than direct rainfall, is used for the purpose of agricultural production. The term irrigation refers to that part of the water managed areas that is equipped to provide water to the crops White rice (or milled rice or polished rice): The inner rice grain, consisting mainly of starch. Milling increases the storage time and reduces the cooking time, but removes the protein, fibre, vitamins and minerals.

Withdrawal demand: Same as irrigation demand Yield (of rice): Production (in t/ha/crop or t/ha/year). In the Lower Mekong Basin, the annual yield is 1.9 t/ha/year (Cambodia 2000), 2.0 t/ha/year (NE Thailand 2001), 2.9 t/ha/year (Laos 1999) and 4.1t/ha/year (Viet Nam, Mekong Delta 1999). In SE Asia, yields are higher in the dry season than in the wet season, because the solar radiation from the clear sky is higher in the dry season, even if the day length is shorter 7 Rice is the traditional stable food in Southeast Asia, and can assure food security (at the family level, as well as at the national level) Agriculture, and mainly paddy cultivation and related occupations, provides the livelihood for some 75 per cent of the people living in the Lower Mekong Basin Rice can grow on soil types that are not well suited for other crops.

Rice can grow in areas that are waterlogged or inundated Rice can be stored for years The commercial demand of rice is relatively stable (but prices are low) Rice is relatively robust towards pests, and lowland rice is very robust towards weeds One crop of rice can be raised in 3-4 months, well within the period of the monsoon rainfall Traditional Southeast-Asian cultivation systems comprise: Upland (or aerobic) rice, grown in dry fields; lowland (wet) (rainfed or irrigated) rice, grown in fields that are inundated for the major part of the cultivation period. Lowland rice can be transplanted or direct seeded; and deepwater/floating rice, growing in water depths between 0.5 m and 4-5 m. Among these, lowland rice is by far the most important in terms of production and occupation.

Rice can be transplanted or direct seeded (or broadcast) Transplanted rice gives a higher yield, and a somewhat better control of the cultivation cycle (relative to the rainfall), because the transplanting can be postponed by some weeks, if need be. In return, the maturation period is 5-7 days longer than for direct seeded rice - and the risk of faulty weather is related to the length of the cultivation period. Transplanting is labour-intensive (around 10 person-days per hectare, or more) Lowland rice does not grow well in stagnant water. Either, a slow flow must be maintained, orthe field must be drained and re-flooded at intervals. This generates a return flow of excess water, of the same magnitude as the crop water requirement.

Regarding the water supply, there is a broad scale between fully irrigated and fully rainfed crops. In most cases, irrigated crops are partly rainfed. Supplementary irrigation (for example during the onset of the wet season) can be important for orderly cultivation, whereby it can represent a high added value per m3 of water used.

Irrigation can comprise a variety of operations, alone or in a combination.

Storage of Water in a Reservoir

Pumping (large-scale or small-scale) (from a river, lake, canal or reservoir); diversion of water from a river, by a control structure (weir), into a network of canals; retention of surface runoff (towards the end of the wet season), by dams, canals and gates; and retention of return flows from upstream paddy fields, by canals and gates.

Groundwater irrigation is hardly economically feasible for paddy cultivation, due to high operation costs and low value produced. To some extent, however, the same can be said about surface water irrigation, unless weather conditions and the topography are favourable. Operation of irrigation schemes can be complex, and sometimes very much so. Good operation is supported by thorough professional insight, access to historical data, real-time data and reliable forecasts.

Due to the losses, the irrigation demand is much higher than the crop water requirement. It is seen, however, that much of the water that is 'lost' goes to groundwater recharge or can be usedfor other purposes downstream.

Both the crop water requirement and the rainfall depend on the location. The crop water requirement varies during the cultivation period, and the rainfall varies with an annual cycle.

Therefore, the water balance is made on a monthly or daily basis for the entire cultivation period. A suitable basic unit is mm/day.

For over-all water resources management purposes it is convenient to know the irrigation demand for an entire crop, expressed in mm/crop or m^3/crop/ha. Obviously, this value depends on the time, place and duration of the actual cultivation period, and it will highly depend on how much of the crop requirement that is served by irrigation and how much by rainfall.

Water Efficiencies

The scheme efficiency is the over-all ratio between the water needed by the crop and the water that needs to be withdrawn for irrigated cultivation. Scheme efficiencies are often low in places where water is by tradition abundantly available.

The conveyance efficiency (the extent to which the water reaches its destination) depends on whether the canal is lined, and on the canal length and soil type. Also, the state of maintenance is important.

The field application efficiency for irrigated paddy cultivation depends on the system layout, the management of the system, and the skills and coordination between the farmers.

Irrigation Demand and Crop Requirement

In an example from Thailand, the crop requirement was determined to 3.6 and 5.0 mm/day for rainfed and irrigated rice, respectively 18. Assuming a 120 days cultivation period, this equals 4,300 - 6,100 m^3/crop/ha. The efficiency is the part of the water that is used for its intended purpose. If a scheme efficiency is 30 per cent it means that 30 per cent of the water is used by the crops, while 70 per cent is lost on the way to the crops or are subsequently released as return flows.

- Land preparation 150-250 mm/crop Restoring soil moisture
- Ploughing and puddling
- Evapotranspiration 500-1200
- 4-10 mm/crop mm/day
- Crop requirement
- Seepage and percolation 200-700
- 2-6 mm/crop mm/day
- Maintaining water pounding
- Mid-season drainage 50-100 mm/crop Refilling after drainage
- Total average over a 120 days cultivation period 900-2250
- 7.5-20 mm/crop mm/day
- Total water utilization from rainfall + irrigation, excluding return flows

Water Used per kg Rice

As shown by the following examples, it requires a lot of water to produce rice - in particular where the traditional cultivation systems are based on abundance of water. As a rule of thumb, it requires 5 m^3 of water to produce 1 kg of rice.

For a given crop at a given time and place, the yield depends on many factors, including the continuous water supply, the crop variety, weed management, and the use of fertilizer. Within limits, each kilogram of nitrogen fertilizer can produce 10-15 kg more rice 20. Assume a specific crop water requirement of (for example) around 4 m^3/kg paddy. If so, 1 kg of fertilizer can replace 40-60 m^3 of water.

In the Mekong Delta, the irrigation demand (for fully irrigated paddy) has been reported at 1 l/s/ha21 or 8.6 mm/day. The yield of (dry season) rice is 5.0 t/ha 22. Assuming a 120 days cultivation period, this is 2.1 m^3 of water per kg dry season paddy rice. Assuming post-harvest losses of 10 per cent and a milling rate of 65 per cent, this becomes 3.5 m^3 of water per kg milled rice.

In Northeast Thailand, the irrigation demand (for fully irrigated paddy) has been reported at 12,000 m^3/ha/crop 23 (or 1200 mm/crop or 10 mm/day).

The yield of (dry season) rice is 3.3 t/ha24. This is 3.6 m^3 of water per kg dry season paddy rice.

Assuming post-harvest losses of 10 per cent and a milling rate of 65 per cent, this becomes 6.2 m^3 of water per kg milled rice.

- Banana 970 m^3/ton
- Groundnut 1880 m^3/ton
- Maize 780 m^3/ton
- Soybean 3050 m^3/ton
- Sugarcane 200 m^3/ton
- Watermelon 270 m^3/ton
- Onion (dry) 490 m^3/ton
- Rice 4050 m^3/ton

Note: Various irrigation losses not included.

Post-harvest losses are not included.

Record yields - 'China cultivates record high-yield super rice'

Chinese agronomists have cultivated a new species of 'super rice', the Super Rice II YOU 28, with average yield reaching a record high of 18,400 kilograms per hectare.

The figure broke the records set in 2004 of 18,300 kilograms per hectare, setting a new world record, said Shi

Changjun, leader of the super rice acceptance test. Experts from the China Rice Research Institute, Yunnan Agricultural University and the Yunnan Provincial Academy of Agriculture conducted on-the-spot acceptance check over harvest of the super rice.

The new species of high-yield hybrid rice was sown in March, planted in May and harvested on September 10 in Taoyuan Village, Yongsheng County of south China's Yunnan Province, with fertility period lasting 192 days.

Like other water-dependent production systems, paddy cultivation requires a certain quality standard of the consumed water on the one hand, and represents a certain environmental pressure on the other.

Production systems based on paddy cultivation in combination with paddy field fisheries can be economically attractive - the income from the fish can exceed the income from the cultivationbut require water that is uncontaminated to a standard where fish can survive.

Example from Thailand (2003 figures):

- Import of fertilizers: 3,840,000 tonnes/year.
- Import of pesticides: 50,331 tonnes/year.

These figures relate to the entire agricultural sector of Thailand, which comprises a variety of crops other than rice.

If the irrigation tailwater carry 'hard' pollutants (like bio-accumulating and slowly decaying pesticide residuals), the consequences to the fisheries sector and the public health can be severe. Paddy cultivation in itself is robust to pesticide residues in the irrigation water, but is sensitive to salinity, which is a problem in downstream areas of the river basin that are exposed to sea water intrusion.

Water Resources Management

A fruitful distinction can be made between basin level management, for a river basin or sub-basin; and scheme level management (or system level management), for a single irrigation scheme.

These two levels differ widely in terms of agenda, management options, and needs of knowledge and data.

Also, the water balances are different at the two levels. At the basin level, percolation losses and return flows at the scheme level are (typically) not 'losses' but rather 're-allocations'. The third level of management, the farm level, is not covered by this lecture note.

Basin Level Management

The purpose of water resources management at the basin level is to establish and maintain some harmony between:

1. the over-all water availability; and
2. the potential demand of water.

This exercise must be carried out in time and space. That there is enough water on the average is of little practical interest. In the Lower Mekong Basin, the average water availability is 19 m^3/person/day, or 7,100 m^3/person/year 28, but still, there are severe seasonal water shortages - and a strong need of water resources management.

For a given area, the availability is largely determined by the rainfall (and by large-scale storage facilities), while the demand is determined by the crops, the cultivation routines, and the applied technology. The availability and the demand are linked by prevailing, traditional production system modalities, but are otherwise largely unrelated.

The irrigation demand may be the largest item in the budget in terms of volume, but not in terms of significance. The domestic demand is much smaller in terms of volume, but much higher in terms of significance. In terms of value generated, paddy irrigation comes low on a long list of industrial and agricultural water uses.

A balance must be maintained between consumptive (or 'off-stream') water uses and non-consumptive (or 'in-stream' water uses). The former comprise domestic, industrial and agricultural demands. The latter represent the needs of the fisheries and navigation sectors, as well as the ecological demand of water (to maintain a desired state of aquatic and floodplain ecosystems and other wetlands). Hydropower reservoirs fall somewhat in between, but are important, as they can re-distribute the water availability over the year.

In some rivers, for example the Mekong, the lower parts are only slightly elevated above sea level, and with no control structures to keep the saline sea water out. If so, a certain minimum flow must be maintained to prevent saline intrusion.

For planning purposes and feasibility analyses, knowledge is required about the over-all, 'reliable' water availability (which can for example be 'the water available in 4 out of 5 years').

At the basin level, the return flows are not really losses - quite often, they can be used further downstream in the basin, at a later time. Similarly, percolation is regarded as groundwater recharge, rather than a loss. Still, these flows must be taken into account, since they need to be removed from the river or the reservoir in the first place.

Water management at the basin level is not always based on win-win-solutions. Development initiatives that benefit some people in some areas can have adverse consequences to other people living in adjacent areas. Many irrigation schemes with an undisputed over-all positive 'bottom line' can deprive some people of land and/or water.

Scheme Level Management.

The purpose of scheme level management is to serve the crop water requirement.

Scheme level management requires real-time information about storage volumes and/or river stages and/or flow rates; good forecasts of rainfall and river stage over as long a period of time as possible; knowledge about normal rainfall and stage, and typical variation intervals, as a function of time; and knowledge about optimal and critical crop requirements. In some places, scheme level management can also comprise operational protection againstfloods, or operational protection against salt water intrusion, by means of control gates or flow regulation. An important feature of scheme level management is the coordination among the water users.

This must take place either in a close dialogue, or by the water users themselves. Scientific research related to rice cultivation is carried out by International Rice Research Institute (IRRI), International Water Management Institute (IWMI), and many otherinternational and national research centres and programmes. FAO maintains a major knowledge base and develops tools for agricultural management and related water resources management.

Increased water efficiency (tons per m^3) increased nutrient efficiency (tons per ton fertilizer used) improved drought tolerance integrated pest management golden rice 35 Recent breakthroughs in scientific technology have made it possible to enhance the nutritional value of rice through modifying the genetic code.

The best-known example of this technology is 'golden rice', which contains carotenoids (precursors to vitamin A) from daffodil genes.

Yield Gaps

The yield gap is the (often significant) difference between an actual and a potential yield. A distinction can be made between:

1. the gap between the potential theoretical yield and the experiment station yield;
2. the gap between the experiment station yield and the potential farm yield; and
3. the gap between the potential and the actual farm yield.

Factors causing yield gaps include:

1. *Biophysical:* Climate/weather, soils, water, pest pressure, weeds.
2. *Technical/management:* Tillage, variety/seed selection, water, nutrients, weeds, pests, and postharvest management.
3. *Socio-economic:* Socio-economic status, farmer's traditions and knowledge, family size, household income/expenses/investment.
4. *Institutional/policy:* Government policy, rice prices, credit, input supply, land tenure, market, research, development, extension.

5. *Technology transfer and linkages:* The competence and facilities of extension staff; integration among research, development and extension; farmers' resistance to new technology; knowledge and skills; weak linkages among public, private and non-governmental extension staffs.

Social and Economic Aspects

In Southeast Asia, paddy cultivation is of decisive importance in terms of employment and food.

It is not a very profitable livelihood, however: In NE Thailand (1996/97), the net profit of paddy cultivation was estimated from minus 49 to plus 21 USD/ha/crop for irrigated HYV rice in the wet and dry season, respectively, and at minus 44 USD/ha/crop for the traditional wet season rainfed local variety rice (family labour valued at 2.5 USD/day). In Cambodia, the net profit of paddy cultivation was estimated at 2 USD/ha/crop for rainfed wet season rice and 2 USD/ha/crop for irrigated dry season rice (family labour valued at 1 USD/day). The average income of people in the farm sector (2002) was two times lower than in non-farm sectors, and 3.8 times lower than the income of skilled labour workers. Most of the 6.2 million people living below the poverty line were in the farm sector.

Slow progress (towards sustainable agriculture) was attributed to lack of land ownership documents, lack of water, lack of labour, lack of investment, and debt. Farmers themselves also lacked the 'inspiration', patience and diligence to succeed. A farmer who wants to shift from paddy to other crops faces various obstacles, including the following: Whether the soil is suited for other crops; new needs of capital, technology and knowledge (and hereby, perhaps, new dependencies on suppliers); whether the alternative crops require more fertilizer and more pesticides (and hereby additional expenses, occupational safety risks, and pollution that can impede local fisheries and cause other harm); unfamiliar (and possibly risky) distribution and marketing systems (and hereby, perhaps, new dependencies on buyers); and social risks in general - illness in the family, natural disasters - and how to cover them.

Between them, these obstacles can point towards contract farming, with its variety of pros and cons. Also, the obstacles can point towards land ownership concentration.

Management Aspects

At the basin level, water-related management can be supported by developments towards: Supportive water allocation within the basin, and, possibly, among basins (subject to careful analysis of benefits and side effects); coordinated operational flow management of retention, release, and diversion of water, using existing or new infrastructure; coordinated, basin-level flood and drought preparedness, including forecast services and contingency planning; coordinated hydropower development in a multi-disciplinary perspective (subject to careful analysis of benefits and side effects); salinity control measures (that can reduce the required minimum flow while protecting downstream irrigation systems and ecosystems) (subject to careful analysis of benefitsand side effects); coordinated, basin-level ground-water management (mapping, protection, regulation, monitoring) (to prevent contamination and assure prudent utilization); coordinated, basin-level morphological management (to protect infrastructure, waterways and ecosystems); awareness of the proper use of fertilizers and pesticides, with supportive regulation; coordinated management of wetlands and headwater areas; support in many ways to a partial crop diversification, combining paddy with other crops (and/or livestock and/or fish cultivation) (for example learning from experience achieved in Thailand, Viet Nam and elsewhere); support in many ways to enhancing the water efficiency and the economic efficiency of the primary production (involving extension services and bridging institutions) support in many ways to enhancing the added value of the primary production (within post-processing, distribution and marketing); and networking and knowledge-sharing among river basin organisations.

At the scheme level, water-related management of paddy cultivation can be supported by development comprising

Making operational data and information readily available; scheme-level flood and drought preparedness and contingency planning; networking and knowledge-sharing between scheme operators and water users; credit facilities for investment and disaster mitigation; and awareness of technological opportunities within crops, cultivation routines, water management and soil management.

The over-all water efficiency and the economic efficiency of water utilization can be enhanced by general measures such asSupportive land ownership structure; de-centralization of ownership and decision-making, as practical from case to case (considering the size of the scheme; its technological complexity; water sharing with other schemes; and various other site-specific circumstances) scientific research, international networking, bridging institutions and extension services; broad capacity-building; and holistic development of farming, post-processing, distribution and marketing (for example learning from experience achieved in Thailand and elsewhere).

Social risk management is an important companion to water management. Without one, the other can fail, or initial achievements can eventually become undermined. This can happen if intended beneficiaries of an irrigation development lose their land due to floods, drought, crop or livestock diseases, illness in the family, market failure, or other social shocks CGIAR (Consultative Group on International Agricultural Research) Three CGIAR research centers focus on rice research:

(a) The International Rice Research Institute (IRRI) in the Philippines

(b) The West Afri ca Rice Development Association (WARDA) in Cote d'Ivoire

(c) The Centro Internacional de Agricultura Tropical (CIAT) in Colombia.

Top producers (2003/04 data from US Department of Agriculture).

1. China 118,000,000 t
2. India 89,000,000 t
3. Indonesia 33,300,000 t
4. Bangladesh 26,000,000 t
5. Vietnam 21,000,000 t
6. Thailand 17,800,000 t
7. Burma 10,440,000 t
8. Philippines 8,500,000 t
9. Brazil 7,300,000 t
10. Japan 7,100,000 t

Top producers per capita (2003/04 data from US Department of Agriculture)

1. Thailand 277 kg/person
2. Vietnam 257 kg/person
3. Burma 246 kg/person
4. Bangladesh 188 kg/person
5. Indonesia 142 kg/person
6. Philippines 100 kg/person
7. South Korea 93 kg/person
8. China 92 kg/person
9. India 85 kg/person
10. Japan 56 kg/person

Top exporters (2003/04 data from US Department of Agriculture)

1. Thailand 8,000,000 t
2. Vietnam 4,000,000 t
3. India 3,000,000 t
4. United States 2,900,000 t
5. China 2,500,000 t
6. Pakistan 1,600,000 t
7. Uruguay 750,000 t
8. Egypt 700,000 t
9. Burma 500,000 t

Water

Only a minimum of water is applied during the vegetative growth period, and then only a thin layer of water is maintained on the field during the flowering and grain filling stage. Alternatively, to save labour time, some farmers flood and drain (dry) their fields in 3-5 day cycles with good results. Best water management practices depend on soil type, labour availability and other factors, so farmers should experiment on how best to apply the principle of having moist but well-drained soil while thier rice plants are growing.

Nutrients

Soil nutrient supplies should be augmented, preferably with compost, made from any available biomass. Better quality compost such as with manure can give additional yield advantages. Chemical fertilizer can be used and gives better results than with no nutrient amendments, but it contributes less to good soil structure and active microbial communities in the rhizosphere than does organic matter. At least initially, nutrient amendments may not be necessary to achieve higher yields with the other SRI practices, but it is desirable to build up soil fertility over time. Rice-root exudation, greater with SRI, enhances soil fertility.

Weeds

Since weeds become a problem in fields that are not kept flooded, weeding is necessary at least once or twice, starting 10-12 days after transplanting, and preferably 3 or 4 times before the canopy closes. Using a rotary hoe — a simple, inexpensive, mechanical push-weeder has the advantage of aerating the soil at the same time that weeds are eliminated. (They are left in the soil to decompose so their nutrients are not lost.) Additional weedings beyond two increase yield more than enough under most conditions to justify the added labour costs.

Increasing the productivity per unit of water consumed Changing crop varieties to ne crop varieties that can provide increased yields for each unit of water consumed, or the same yields with fewer units of water consumed. Crop substitution by switching from high- to less-water-consuming crops, or switching to cropswith higher economic or physical productivity per unit of water consumed. Deficit, supplemental, or precision irrigation. With sufficient water control, higher productivity can be achieved using irrigation strategies that increase the returns per unit of water consumed. Improved water management to provide better timing of supplies to reduce stress at critical crop growth stages leading to increased yields or by increasing water supply reliability so that farmers invest more in other agricultural inputs leading to higher output per unit of water.

Optimizing non-water inputs. In association with irrigation strategies that increase the yield per unit of water consumed, agronomic practices such as land preparation and fertilization can increase the return per unit of water.

Reducing Non-beneficial Depletion

Lessening of non-beneficial evaporation - by reducing: evaporation from water applied to irrigated fields through specific irrigation technologies such as drip irrigation, or agronomic practices such as mulching, or changing crop planting dates to match periods of less-evaporative demand. evaporation from fallow land, decreasing the area of free water surfaces, decreasing non- or less-beneficial vegetation and controlling weeds.

Reducing water flows to sinks - by interventions that reduce irrecoverable deep percolation and surface runoff. Minimizing salinization of return flows - by minimizing flows through saline soils or through saline groundwater to reduce contamination of recoverable irrigation return flows.

Shunting polluted water to sinks - to avoid the need to dilute with freshwater, saline or otherwise polluted water should be shunted directly to sinks.

Reusing Return Flows

Reallocating water among uses Reallocating water from lower- to higher-value uses. Reallocation will generally not result in any direct water savings, but it can dramatically increase the economic productivity of water. Because downstream commitments may change, reallocation of water can have serious legal, equity and other social considerations that must be addressed.

Tapping Uncommitted Outflows

Improving management of existing facilities to obtain more beneficial use from existing water supplies. A number of policy, design, management and institutional interventions may allow for anexpansion of irrigated area, increased cropping intensity or increased yields within the service areas. Possible interventions are reducing delivery requirements by improved application efficiency, water pricing, and improved allocation and distribution practices.

Reusing return flows through gravity and pump diversions to increase irrigated area. Adding storage facilities so that more water is available for release during drier periods. Storage takes many forms including reservoir impoundments, groundwater aquifers, small tanks and ponds on farmers' fields.

Varieties Use early varietes of local, photoperiod sensitive varieties. Local and photoperiod sensitive varieties are grouped as early variety (120 days) medium variety (150 days) and late variety (180 days) Use high yield varieties, the production can be doubled with the same amount of water consumption. Growing season Cultivate in the rainy season and harvest at the end of the season. For non photoperiod sensitive varieties (110 to 120 days) the harvesting date should be planned at the end of rainy season in order to set the growing date. Cropping calendar should be planned suitable to wet and dry season.

Cultivation practice Good land preparation with smooth level of each field plot. Do not plough so deep that hard pan will be broken. Compact field boundary (dike) to avoid seepage loss.

Irrigation system Concrete lining in irrigation system. Construct on-farm system (extensive or intensive on-farm development work) Water application and management Irrigate water according to crop water requirement Keep water level in paddy field about 6 cm deep Introduce rotation irrigation Stop irrigation in the tillering stage for some time. Besides, the water saving oxygen can also be brought the soil. Stop irrigation 20 days before harvesting.

12

Importance of Agriculture

Agriculture is the cultivation of animals, plants, fungi and other life forms for food, fiber, and other products used to sustain life. Agriculture was the key implement in the rise of sedentary human civilization, whereby farming of domesticated species created food surpluses that nurtured the development of civilization. The study of agriculture is known as agricultural science. Agriculture is also observed in certain species of ant and termite, but generally speaking refers to human activities.

The history of agriculture dates back thousands of years, and its development has been driven and defined by greatly different climates, cultures, and technologies. However, all farming generally relies on techniques to expand and maintain the lands suitable for raising domesticated species. For plants, this usually requires some form of irrigation, although there are methods of dryland farming; pastoral herding on rangeland is still the most common means of raising livestock. In the developed world, industrial agriculture based on large-scale monoculture has become the dominant system of modern farming, although there is growing support for sustainable agriculture (e.g. permaculture or organic agriculture).

Modern agronomy, plant breeding, pesticides and fertilizers, and technological improvements have sharply increased yields from cultivation, but at the same time have caused widespread ecological damage and negative human health effects. Selective breeding and modern practices in animal husbandry such as intensive pig farming have similarly increased the output of meat, but have raised concerns about animal cruelty and the health effects of the antibiotics, growth hormones, and other chemicals commonly used in industrial meat production.

The major agricultural products can be broadly grouped into foods, fibers, fuels, and raw materials. In the 21st century, plants have been used to grow biofuels, biopharmaceuticals, bioplastics, and pharmaceuticals. Specific foods include cereals, vegetables, fruits, and meat. Fibers include cotton, wool, hemp, silk and flax. Raw materials include lumber and bamboo. Other useful materials are produced by plants, such as resins. Biofuels include methane from biomass, ethanol, and biodiesel. Cut flowers, nursery plants, tropical fish and birds for the pet trade are some of the ornamental products.

In 2007, one third of the world's workers were employed in agriculture. The services sector has overtaken agriculture as the economic sector employing the most people worldwide. Despite the size of its workforce, agricultural production accounts for less than five per cent of the gross world product (an aggregate of all gross domestic products).

The word *agriculture* is the English adaptation of Latin *agricultura*, from *ager*, 'a field', and *cultura*, 'cultivation' in the strict sense of 'tillage of the soil'. Thus, a literal reading of the word yields 'tillage of a field/of fields'.

Agriculture has played a key role in the development of human civilization. Until the Industrial Revolution, the vast majority of the human population laboured in agriculture. The type of agriculture they developed was typically subsistence agriculture in which farmers raised most of their crops for consumption on farm, and there was only a small portion left over for the payment of taxes, dues, or trade. In subsistence agriculture cropping decisions are made with an eye to what the family needs for food, and to make clothing, and not the world marketplace. Development of agricultural techniques has steadily increased agricultural productivity, and the widespread diffusion of these techniques during a time period is often called an agricultural revolution. A remarkable shift in agricultural practices has occurred over the past century in response to new technologies, and the development of world markets. This also led to technological improvements in agricultural techniques, such as the Haber-Bosch method for synthesizing ammonium nitrate which made the traditional practice of recycling nutrients with crop rotation and animal manure less necessary.

Synthetic nitrogen, along with mined rock phosphate, pesticides and mechanization, have greatly increased crop yields in the early 20th century. Increased supply of grains has led to cheaper livestock as well. Further, global yield increases were experienced later in the 20th century when high-yield varieties of common staple grains such as rice, wheat, and corn (maize) were introduced as a part of the Green Revolution. The Green Revolution exported the technologies (including pesticides and synthetic nitrogen) of the developed world to the developing world. Thomas Malthus famously predicted that the Earth would not be able to support its growing population, but technologies such as the Green Revolution have allowed the world to produce a surplus of food.

Many governments have subsidized agriculture to ensure an adequate food supply. These agricultural subsidies are often linked to the production of certain commodities such as wheat, corn (maize), rice, soybeans, and milk. These subsidies, especially when instituted by developed countries have been noted as protectionist, inefficient, and environmentally damaging.

In the past century agriculture has been characterized by enhanced productivity, the use of synthetic fertilizers and pesticides, selective breeding, mechanization, water contamination, and farm subsidies. Proponents of organic farming such as Sir Albert Howard argued in the early 20th century that the overuse of pesticides and synthetic fertilizers damages the long-term fertility of the soil. While this feeling lay dormant for decades, as environmental awareness has increased in the 21st century there has been a movement towards sustainable agriculture by some farmers, consumers, and policymakers.

In recent years there has been a backlash against perceived external environmental effects of mainstream agriculture, particularly regarding water pollution, resulting in the organic movement. One of the major forces behind this movement has been the European Union, which first certified organic food in 1991 and began reform of its Common Agricultural Policy (CAP) in 2005 to phase out commodity-linked farm subsidies, also known as decoupling. The growth of organic farming has renewed research in alternative technologies such as integrated pest management and selective breeding. Recent mainstream technological developments include genetically modified food.

In late 2007, several factors pushed up the price of grains consumed by humans as well as used to feed poultry and dairy cows and other cattle, causing higher prices of wheat (up 58%), soybean (up 32%), and maize (up 11%) over the year. Food riots took place in several countries across the world. Contributing factors included drought in Australia and elsewhere, increasing demand for grain-fed animal products from the growing middle classes of countries such as China and India, diversion of foodgrain to biofuel production and trade restrictions imposed by several countries.

An epidemic of stem rust on wheat caused by race Ug99 is currently spreading across Africa and into Asia and is causing major concern. Approximately 40 per cent of the world's agricultural land is seriously degraded. In Africa, if current trends of soil degradation continue, the continent might be able to feed just 25 per cent of its population by 2025, according to UNU's Ghana-based Institute for Natural Resources in Africa.

Agricultural practices such as irrigation, crop rotation, fertilizers, and pesticides were developed long ago, but have made great strides in the past century. The history of agriculture has played a major role in human history, as agricultural progress has been a crucial factor in worldwide socio-economic change. Division of labour in agricultural societies made commonplace specializations rarely seen in hunter-gatherer cultures. So, too, are arts such as epic literature and monumental architecture, as well as codified legal systems. When farmers became capable of producing food beyond the needs of their own families, others in their society were freed to devote themselves to projects other than food acquisition. Historians and anthropologists have long argued that the development of agriculture made civilization possible. The total world population probably never exceeded 15 million inhabitants before the invention of agriculture.

The Fertile Crescent of Western Asia, Egypt, and India were sites of the earliest planned sowing and harvesting of plants that had previously been gathered in the wild. Independent development of agriculture occurred in northern and southern China, Africa's Sahel, New Guinea and several regions of the Americas. The eight so-called Neolithic founder crops of agriculture appear: first emmer wheat and einkorn wheat, then hulled barley, peas, lentils, bitter vetch, chick peas and flax.

By 7000 BC, small-scale agriculture reached Egypt. From at least 7000 BC the Indian subcontinent saw farming of wheat and barley, as attested by archaeological excavation at Mehrgarh in Balochistan in what is present day Pakistan. By 6000 BC, mid-scale farming was entrenched on the banks of the Nile. This, as irrigation had not yet matured sufficiently. About this time, agriculture was developed independently in the Far East, with rice, rather than wheat, as the primary crop. Chinese and Indonesian farmers went on to domesticate taro and beans including mung, soy and azuki. To complement these new sources of carbohydrates, highly organized net fishing of rivers, lakes and ocean shores in these areas brought in great volumes of essential protein. Collectively, these new methods of farming and fishing inaugurated a human population boom that dwarfed all previous expansions and continues today.

By 5000 BC, the Sumerians had developed core agricultural techniques including large-scale intensive cultivation of land, monocropping, organized irrigation, and the use of a specialized labour force, particularly along the waterway now known as the Shatt al-Arab, from its Persian Gulf delta to the confluence of the Tigris and Euphrates. Domestication of wild aurochs and mouflon into cattle and sheep, respectively, ushered in the large-scale use of animals for food/fibre and as beasts of burden. The shepherd joined the farmer as an essential provider for sedentary and seminomadic societies. Maize, manioc, and arrowroot were first domesticated in the Americas as far back as 5200 BC.

The potato, tomato, pepper, squash, several varieties of bean, tobacco, and several other plants were also developed in the Americas, as was extensive terracing of steep hillsides in much of Andean South America. The Greeks and Romans built on techniques pioneered by the Sumerians, but made few fundamentally new advances. Southern Greeks struggled with very poor soils, yet managed to become a dominant society for years. The Romans were noted for an emphasis on the cultivation of crops for trade.

In the same region, a parallel agricultural revolution occurred, resulting in some of the most important crops grown today. In Mesoamerica wild teosinte was transformed through human selection into the ancestor of modern maize, more than 6000 years ago. It gradually spread across North America and was the major crop of Native Americans at the time of European exploration. Other Mesoamerican crops include hundreds of varieties of squash and beans. Cocoa was also a major crop in domesticated Mexico and Central America. The turkey, one of the most important meat birds, was probably domesticated in Mexico or the U.S. Southwest. In the Andes region of South America the major domesticated crop was potatoes, domesticated perhaps 5000 years ago. Large varieties of beans were domesticated, in South America, as well as animals, including llamas, alpacas, and guinea pigs. Coca, still a major crop, was also domesticated in the Andes.

A minor center of domestication, the indigenous people of the Eastern U.S. appear to have domesticated numerous crops. Sunflowers, tobacco, varieties of squash and Chenopodium, as well as crops no longer grown, including marshelder and little barley were domesticated. Other wild foods may have undergone some selective cultivation, including wild rice and maple sugar. The most common varieties of strawberry were domesticated from Eastern North America.

By 3500 BC, the simplest form of the plough was developed, called the ard. Before this period, simple digging sticks or hoes were used. These tools would have also been easier to transport, which was a benefit as people only stayed until the soil's nutrients were depleted. However, through excavations in Mexico it has been found that the continuous cultivating of smaller pieces of land would also have been a sustaining practice. Additional research in central Europe later revealed that agriculture was indeed practiced at this method. For this method, ards were thus much more efficient than digging sticks.

During the Middle Ages, farmers in North Africa, the Near East, and Europe began making use of agricultural technologies including irrigation systems based on hydraulic and hydrostatic principles, machines such as norias, water-raising machines, dams, and reservoirs. This combined with the invention of a three-field system of crop rotation and the moldboard plow greatly improved agricultural efficiency.

In the European medieval period, agriculture was considered part of the set of *seven mechanical arts*.

After 1492, a global exchange of previously local crops and livestock breeds occurred. Key crops involved in this exchange included the tomato, maize, potato, manioc, cocoa bean and tobacco going from the New World to the Old, and several varieties of wheat, spices, coffee, and sugar cane going from the Old World to the New. The most important animal exportation from the Old World to the New were those of the horse and dog (dogs were already present in the pre-Columbian Americas but not in the numbers and breeds suited to farm work). Although not usually food animals, the horse (including donkeys and ponies) and dog quickly filled essential production roles on western-hemisphere farms.

The potato became an important staple crop in northern Europe. Since being introduced by Portuguese in the 16th century, maize and manioc have replaced traditional African crops as the continent's most important staple food crops.

By the early 19th century, agricultural techniques, implements, seed stocks and cultivar had so improved that yield per land unit was many times that seen in the Middle Ages. Although there is a vast and interesting history of crop cultivation before the dawn of the 20th century, there is little question that the work of Charles Darwin and Gregor Mendel created the scientific foundation for plant breeding that led to its explosive impact over the past 150 years.

With the rapid rise of mechanization in the late 19th century and the 20th century, particularly in the form of the tractor, farming tasks could be done with a speed and on a scale previously impossible. These advances have led to efficiencies enabling certain modern farms in the United States, Argentina, Israel, Germany, and a few other nations to output volumes of high-quality produce per land unit at what may be the practical limit.

The Haber-Bosch method for synthesizing ammonium nitrate represented a major breakthrough and allowed crop yields to overcome previous constraints. In the past century agriculture has been characterized by enhanced productivity, the substitution of synthetic fertilizers and pesticides for labour, water pollution, and farm subsidies. In recent years there has been a backlash against the external environmental effects of conventional agriculture, resulting in the organic movement.

The cereals rice, corn, and wheat provide 60 per cent of human food supply. Between 1700 and 1980, 'the total area of cultivated land worldwide increased 466 per cent' and yields increased dramatically, particularly because of selectively bred high-yielding varieties, fertilizers, pesticides, irrigation, and machinery. For example, irrigation increased corn yields in eastern Colorado by 400 to 500 per cent from 1940 to 1997.

However, concerns have been raised over the sustainability of intensive agriculture. Intensive agriculture has become associated with decreased soil quality in India and Asia, and there has been increased concern over the effects of fertilizers and pesticides on the environment, particularly as population increases and food demand expands. The monocultures typically used in intensive agriculture increase the number of pests, which are controlled through pesticides. Integrated pest management (IPM), which "has been promoted for decades and has had some notable successes" has not significantly affected the use of pesticides because policies encourage the use of pesticides and IPM is knowledge-intensive.

Although the 'Green Revolution' significantly increased rice yields in Asia, yield increases have not occurred in the past 15-20 years. The genetic 'yield potential' has increased for wheat, but the yield potential for rice has not increased since 1966, and the yield potential for maize has 'barely increased in 35 years'. It takes a decade or two for herbicide-resistant weeds to emerge, and insects become resistant to insecticides within about a decade. Crop rotation helps to prevent resistances.

Agricultural exploration expeditions, since the late 19th century, have been mounted to find new species and new agricultural practices in different areas of the world. Two early examples of expeditions include Frank N. Meyer's fruit- and nut-collecting trip to China and Japan from 1916-1918 and the Dorsett-Morse Oriental Agricultural Exploration Expedition to China, Japan, and Korea from 1929-1931 to collect soybean germplasm to support the rise in soybean agriculture in the United States.

In 2009, the agricultural output of China was the largest in the world, followed by the European Union, India and the United States, according to the International Monetary Fund. Economists measure the total factor productivity of agriculture and by this measure agriculture in the United States is roughly 2.6 times more productive than it was in 1948.

Six countries – the U.S., Canada, France, Australia, Argentina and Thailand - supply 90 per cent of grain exports. Water deficits, which are already spurring heavy grain imports in numerous middle-sized countries, including Algeria, Iran, Egypt, and Mexico, may soon do the same in larger countries, such as China or India.

Cropping systems vary among farms depending on the available resources and constraints; geography and climate of the farm; government policy; economic, social and political pressures; and the philosophy and culture of the farmer. Shifting cultivation (or slash and burn) is a system in which forests are burnt, releasing nutrients to support cultivation of annual and then perennial crops for a period of several years.

Then the plot is left fallow to regrow forest, and the farmer moves to a new plot, returning after many more years (10-20). This fallow period is shortened if population density grows, requiring the input of nutrients (fertilizer or manure) and some manual pest control. Annual cultivation is the next phase of intensity in which there is no fallow period. This requires even greater nutrient and pest control inputs.

Further industrialization lead to the use of monocultures, when one cultivar is planted on a large acreage. Because of the low biodiversity, nutrient use is uniform and pests tend to build up, necessitating the greater use of pesticides and fertilizers. Multiple cropping, in which several crops are grown sequentially in one year, and intercropping, when several crops are grown at the same time are other kinds of annual cropping systems known as polycultures.

In tropical environments, all of these cropping systems are practiced. In subtropical and arid environments, the timing and extent of agriculture may be limited by rainfall, either not allowing multiple annual crops in a year, or requiring irrigation. In all of these environments perennial crops are grown (coffee, chocolate) and systems are practiced such as agroforestry. In temperate environments, where ecosystems were predominantly grassland or prairie, highly productive annual cropping is the dominant farming system.

The last century has seen the intensification, concentration and specialization of agriculture, relying upon new technologies of agricultural chemicals (fertilizers and pesticides), mechanization, and plant breeding (hybrids and GMO's). In the past few decades, a move towards sustainability in agriculture has also developed, integrating ideas of socio-economic justice and conservation of resources and the environment within a farming system. This has led to the development of many responses to the conventional agriculture approach, including organic agriculture, urban agriculture, community supported agriculture, ecological or biological agriculture, integrated farming and holistic management, as well as an increased trend towards agricultural diversification.

Animals, including horses, mules, oxen, camels, llamas, alpacas, and dogs, are often used to help cultivate fields, harvest crops, wrangle other animals, and transport farm products to buyers. Animal husbandry not only refers to the breeding and raising of animals for meat or to harvest animal products (like milk, eggs, or wool) on a continual basis, but also to the breeding and care of species for work and companionship. Livestock production systems can be defined based on feed source, as grassland - based, mixed, and landless.

Grassland based livestock production relies upon plant material such as shrubland, rangeland, and pastures for feeding ruminant animals. Outside nutrient inputs may be used, however manure is returned directly to the grassland as a major nutrient source. This system is particularly important in areas where crop production is not feasible because of climate or soil, representing 30-40 million pastoralists. Mixed production systems use grassland, fodder crops and grain feed crops as feed for ruminant and monogastic (one stomach; mainly chickens and pigs) livestock. Manure is typically recycled in mixed systems as a fertilizer for crops. Approximately 68 per cent of all agricultural land is permanent pastures used in the production of livestock.

Landless systems rely upon feed from outside the farm, representing the de-linking of crop and livestock production found more prevalently in OECD member countries. In the U.S., 70 per cent of the grain grown is fed to animals on feedlots. Synthetic fertilizers are more heavily relied upon for crop production and manure utilization becomes a challenge as well as a source for pollution.

Tillage is the practice of plowing soil to prepare for planting or for nutrient incorporation or for pest control. Tillage varies in intensity from conventional to no-till. It may improve productivity by warming the soil, incorporating fertilizer and controlling weeds, but also renders soil more prone to erosion, triggers the decomposition of organic matter releasing CO_2, and reduces the abundance and diversity of soil organisms.

Pest control includes the management of weeds, insects/mites, and diseases. Chemical (pesticides), biological (biocontrol), mechanical (tillage), and cultural practices are used. Cultural practices include crop rotation, culling, cover crops, intercropping, composting, avoidance, and resistance. Integrated pest management attempts to use all of these methods to keep pest populations below the number which would cause economic loss, and recommends pesticides as a last resort.

Nutrient management includes both the source of nutrient inputs for crop and livestock production, and the method of utilization of manure produced by livestock. Nutrient inputs can be chemical inorganic fertilizers, manure, green manure, compost and mined minerals. Crop nutrient use may also be managed using cultural techniques such as crop rotation or a fallow period. Manure is used either by holding livestock where the feed crop is growing, such as in managed intensive rotational grazing, or by spreading either dry or liquid formulations of manure on cropland or pastures.

Water management is where rainfall is insufficient or variable, which occurs to some degree in most regions of the world. Some farmers use irrigation to supplement rainfall. In other areas such as the Great Plains in the U.S. and Canada, farmers use a fallow year to conserve soil moisture to use for growing a crop in the following year. Agriculture represents 70 per cent of freshwater use worldwide.

In the United States, food costs attributed to processing, distribution, and marketing have risen while the costs attributed to farming have declined. This is related to the greater efficiency of farming, combined with the increased level of value addition (e.g. more highly processed products) provided by the supply chain. From 1960 to 1980 the farm share was around 40 per cent, but by 1990 it had declined to 30 per cent and by 1998, 22.2 per cent. Market concentration has increased in the sector as well, with the top 20 food manufacturers accounting for half the food-processing value in 1995, over double that produced in 1954. As of 2000 the top six US supermarket groups had 50 per cent of sales compared to 32 per cent in 1992. Although the total effect of the increased market concentration is likely increased efficiency, the changes redistribute economic surplus from producers (farmers) and consumers, and may have negative implications for rural communities.

Crop alteration has been practiced by humankind for thousands of years, since the beginning of civilization. Altering crops through breeding practices changes the genetic make-up of a plant to develop crops with more beneficial characteristics for humans, for example, larger fruits or seeds, drought-tolerance, or resistance to pests. Significant advances in plant breeding ensued after the work of geneticist Gregor Mendel. His work on dominant and recessive alleles gave plant breeders a better understanding of genetics and brought great insights to the techniques utilized by plant breeders. Crop breeding includes techniques such as plant selection with desirable traits, self-pollination and cross-pollination, and molecular techniques that genetically modify the organism.

Domestication of plants has, over the centuries increased yield, improved disease resistance and drought tolerance, eased harvest and improved the taste and nutritional value of crop plants. Careful selection and breeding have had enormous effects on the characteristics of crop plants. Plant selection and breeding in the 1920s and 1930s improved pasture (grasses and clover) in New Zealand. Extensive X-ray an ultraviolet induced mutagenesis efforts (i.e. primitive genetic engineering) during the 1950s produced the modern commercial varieties of grains such as wheat, corn (maize) and barley.

The Green Revolution popularized the use of conventional hybridization to increase yield many folds by creating 'high-yielding varieties'. For example, average yields of corn (maize) in the USA have increased from around 2.5 tons per hectare (t/ha) (40 bushels per acre) in 1900 to about 9.4 t/ha (150 bushels per acre) in 2001. Similarly, worldwide average wheat yields have increased from less than 1 t/ha in 1900 to more than 2.5 t/ha in 1990. South American average wheat yields are around 2 t/ha, African under 1 t/ha, Egypt and Arabia up to 3.5 to 4 t/ha with irrigation. In contrast, the average wheat yield in countries such as France is over 8 t/ha. Variations in yields are due mainly to variation in climate, genetics, and the level of intensive farming techniques (use of fertilizers, chemical pest control, growth control to avoid lodging).

Genetically Modified Organisms (GMO) are organisms whose genetic material has been altered by genetic engineering techniques generally known as recombinant DNA technology. Genetic engineering has expanded the genes available to breeders to utilize in creating desired germlines for new crops. After mechanical tomato-harvesters were developed in the early 1960s, agricultural scientists genetically modified tomatoes to be more resistant to mechanical handling. More recently, genetic engineering is being employed in various parts of the world, to create crops with other beneficial traits. New research on woodland strawberry genome was found to be short and easy to manipulate. Researchers now have tools to improve strawberry flavours and aromas of cultivated strawberries as stated in a publication by Nature Genetics.

Herbicide-tolerant GMO Crops

Roundup Ready seed has a herbicide resistant gene implanted into its genome that allows the plants to tolerate exposure to glyphosate.

Roundup is a trade name for a glyphosate-based product, which is a systemic, nonselective herbicide used to kill weeds.

Roundup Ready seeds allow the farmer to grow a crop that can be sprayed with glyphosate to control weeds without harming the resistant crop.

Herbicide-tolerant crops are used by farmers worldwide. Today, 92 per cent of soybean acreage in the US is planted with genetically modified herbicide-tolerant plants.

With the increasing use of herbicide-tolerant crops, comes an increase in the use of glyphosate-based herbicide sprays. In some areas glyphosate resistant weeds have developed, causing farmers to switch to other herbicides. Some studies also link widespread glyphosate usage to iron deficiencies in some crops, which is both a crop production and a nutritional quality concern, with potential economic and health implications.

Insect-resistant GMO Crops

Other GMO crops used by growers include insect-resistant crops, which have a gene from the soil bacterium *Bacillus thuringiensis* (Bt), which produces a toxin specific to insects. These crops protect plants from damage by insects; one such crop is Starlink. Another is cotton, which accounts for 63 per cent of US cotton acreage.

Some believe that similar or better pest-resistance traits can be acquired through traditional breeding practices, and resistance to various pests can be gained through hybridization or cross-pollination with wild species. In some cases, wild species are the primary source of resistance traits; some tomato cultivars that have gained resistance to at least 19 diseases did so through crossing with wild populations of tomatoes.

Costs and Benefits of GMOs

Genetic engineers may someday develop transgenic plants which would allow for irrigation, drainage, conservation, sanitary engineering, and maintaining or increasing yields while requiring fewer fossil fuel derived inputs than conventional crops. Such developments would be particularly important in areas which are normally arid and rely upon constant irrigation, and on large scale farms. However, genetic engineering of plants has proven to be controversial. Many issues surrounding food security and environmental impacts have risen regarding GMO practices. For example, GMOs are questioned by some ecologists and economists concerned with GMO practices such as terminator seeds, which is a genetic modification that creates sterile seeds. Terminator seeds are currently under strong international opposition and face continual efforts of global bans.

Another controversial issue is the patent protection given to companies that develop new types of seed using genetic engineering. Since companies have intellectual ownership of their seeds, they have the power to dictate terms and conditions of their patented product. Currently, ten seed companies control over two-thirds of the global seed sales. Vandana Shiva argues that these companies are guilty of biopiracy by patenting life and exploiting organisms for profit Farmers using patented seed are restricted from saving seed for subsequent plantings, which forces farmers to buy new seed every year. Since seed saving is a traditional practice for many farmers in both developing and developed countries, GMO seeds legally bind farmers to change their seed saving practices to buying new seed every year.

Locally adapted seeds are an essential heritage that has the potential to be lost with current hybridized crops and

GMOs. Locally adapted seeds, also called land races or crop eco-types, are important because they have adapted over time to the specific microclimates, soils, other environmental conditions, field designs, and ethnic preference indigenous to the exact area of cultivation. Introducing GMOs and hybridized commercial seed to an area brings the risk of cross-pollination with local land races Therefore, GMOs pose a threat to the sustainability of land races and the ethnic heritage of cultures. Once seed contains transgenic material, it becomes subject to the conditions of the seed company that owns the patent of the transgenic material.

Modern agriculture is a term used to describe the wide majority of production practices employed by America's farmers. The term depicts the push for innovation, stewardship and advancements continually made by growers to sustainably produce higher-quality products with a reduced environmental impact. Intensive scientific research and robust investment in modern agriculture during the past 50 years has helped farmers double food production.

Safety

The agriculture industry works with government agencies and other organisations to ensure that farmers have access to the technologies required to support modern agriculture practices. Farmers are supported by education and certification programmes that ensure they apply agricultural practices with care and only when required.

Sustainability

Technological advancements help provide farmers with tools and resources to make farming more sustainable.

New technologies have given rise to innovations like conservation tillage, a farming process which helps prevent land loss to erosion, water pollution and enhances carbon sequestration.

Affordability

The goal of modern agriculture practices is to help farmers provide an affordable supply of food to meet the demands of a growing population. With modern agriculture, more crops can be grown on less land allowing farmers to provide an increased supply of food at an affordable price.

Food Safety, Labelling and Regulation

Food security issues also coincide with food safety and food labeling concerns. Currently a global treaty, the BioSafety Protocol, regulates the trade of GMOs. The EU currently requires all GMO foods to be labeled, whereas the US does not require transparent labeling of GMO foods. Since there are still questions regarding the safety and risks associated with GMO foods, some believe the public should have the freedom to choose and know what they are eating and require all GMO products to be labeled.

The Food and Agriculture Organisation (FAO) of the United Nations leads international efforts to defeat hunger and provides a neutral forum where nations meet as equals to negotiate agreements and debate food policy and the regulation of agriculture. According to Dr. Samuel Jutzi, director of FAO's animal production and health division, lobbying by "powerful" big food corporations has stopped reforms that would improve human health and the environment. The "real, true issues are not being addressed by the political process because of the influence of lobbyists, of the true powerful entities", he said, speaking at the Compassion in World Farming annual forum. For example, recent proposals for a voluntary code of conduct for the livestock industry that would have provided incentives for improving standards for health, and environmental regulations, such as the number of animals an area of land can support without long-term damage, were successfully defeated due to large food company pressure.

Environmental impact Agriculture imposes external costs upon society through pesticides, nutrient runoff, excessive water usage, and assorted other problems. A 2000 assessment of agriculture in the UK determined total external costs for 1996 of £2,343 million, or £208 per hectare. A 2005 analysis of these costs in the USA concluded that cropland imposes approximately $5 to 16 billion ($30 to $96 per hectare), while livestock production imposes $714 million. Both studies concluded that more should be done to internalize external costs, and neither included subsidies in their analysis, but noted that subsidies also influence the cost of agriculture to society. Both focused on purely fiscal impacts. The 2000 review included reported pesticide poisonings but did not include speculative chronic effects of pesticides, and the 2004 review relied on a 1992 estimate of the total impact of pesticides.

Agriculture accounts for 70 per cent of withdrawals of freshwater resources. However, increasing pressure being placed on water resources by industry, cities and the involving biofuels industry means that water scarcity is increasing and agriculture is facing the challenge of producing more food for the world's growing population with fewer water resources. Scientists are also realising that water resources need to be allocated to maintain natural environmental services, such as protecting towns from flooding, cleaning ecosystems and supporting fish stocks. In the book *Out of Water: From abundance to scarcity and how to solve the world's water problems*, researchers of the International Water Management Institute lay down a six-point plan of action for addressing the global challenge of producing sufficient food for the world with dwindling water resources. One of the actions they say is required is to ensure all water systems, such as lakes and rivers, have water allocated to environmental flow.

A key player who is credited to saving billions of lives because of his revolutionary work in developing new agricultural techniques is Norman Borlaug. His transformative work brought high-yield crop varieties to developing countries and earned him an unofficial title as the father of the Green Revolution.

Livestock Issues

A senior UN official and co-author of a UN report detailing this problem, Henning Steinfeld, said 'Livestock are one of the most significant contributors to today's most serious environmental problems'. Livestock production occupies 70 per cent of all land used for agriculture, or 30 per cent of the land surface of the planet. It is one of the largest sources of greenhouse gases, responsible for 18 per cent of the world's greenhouse gas emissions as measured in CO_2 equivalents. By comparison, all transportation emits 13.5 per cent of the CO_2. It produces 65 per cent of human-related nitrous oxide (which has 296 times the global warming potential of CO_2) and 37 per cent of all human-induced methane (which is 23 times as warming as CO_2. It also generates 64 per cent of the ammonia, which contributes to acid rain and acidification of ecosystems. Livestock expansion is cited as a key factor driving deforestation, in the Amazon basin 70 per cent of previously forested area is now occupied by pastures and the remainder used for feedcrops. Through deforestation and land degradation, livestock is also driving reductions in biodiversity.

Land Transformation and Degradation

Land transformation, the use of land to yield goods and services, is the most substantial way humans alter the Earth's ecosystems, and is considered the driving force in the loss of biodiversity. Estimates of the amount of land transformed by humans vary from 39-50 per cent. Land degradation, the long-term decline in ecosystem function and productivity, is estimated to be occurring on 24 per cent of land worldwide, with cropland overrepresented. The UN-FAO report cites land management as the driving factor behind degradation and reports that 1.5 billion people rely upon the degrading land. Degradation can be deforestation, desertification, soil erosion, mineral depletion, or chemical degradation (acidification and salinization).

Eutrophication

Eutrophication, excessive nutrients in aquatic ecosystems resulting in algal blooms and anoxia, leads to fish kills, loss of biodiversity, and renders water unfit for drinking and other industrial uses. Excessive fertilization and manure application to cropland, as well as high livestock stocking densities cause nutrient (mainly nitrogen and phosphorus) runoff and leaching from agricultural land. These nutrients are major nonpoint pollutants contributing to eutrophication of aquatic ecosystems.

Pesticides

Pesticide use has increased since 1950 to 2.5 million tons annually worldwide, yet crop loss from pests has remained relatively constant. The World Health Organisation estimated in 1992 that 3 million pesticide poisonings occur annually, causing 220,000 deaths. Pesticides select for pesticide resistance in the pest population, leading to a condition termed the 'pesticide treadmill' in which pest resistance warrants the development of a new pesticide.

An alternative argument is that the way to 'save the environment' and prevent famine is by using pesticides and intensive high yield farming, a view exemplified by a quote heading the Center for Global Food Issues website: 'Growing more per acre leaves more land for nature'. However, critics argue that a trade-off between the environment and a need for food is not inevitable, and that pesticides simply replace good agronomic practices such as crop rotation.

Climate Change

Climate change has the potential to affect agriculture through changes in temperature, rainfall (timing and quantity), CO_2, solar radiation and the interaction of these elements. Agriculture can both mitigate or worsen global warming. Some of the increase in CO_2 in the atmosphere comes from the decomposition of organic matter in the soil, and much of the methane emitted into the atmosphere is caused by the decomposition of organic matter in wet soils such as rice paddies. Further, wet or anaerobic soils also lose nitrogen through denitrification, releasing the greenhouse gases nitric oxide and nitrous oxide. Changes in management can reduce the release of these greenhouse gases, and soil can further be used to sequester some of the CO_2 in the atmosphere.

Differences in economic development, population density and culture mean that the farmers of the world operate under very different conditions.

A US cotton farmer may receive US$230 in government subsidies per acre planted (in 2003), while farmers in Mali and other third-world countries do without. When prices decline, the heavily subsidized US farmer is not forced to reduce his output, making it difficult for cotton prices to rebound, but his Mali counterpart may go broke in the meantime.

A livestock farmer in South Korea can calculate with a (highly subsidized) sales price of US$1300 for a calf produced. A South American Mercosur country rancher calculates with a calf's sales price of US$120-200. With the former, scarcity and high cost of land is compensated with public subsidies, the latter compensates absence of subsidies with economics of scale and low cost of land.

In the Peoples Republic of China, a rural household's productive asset may be one hectare of farmland. In Brazil, Paraguay and other countries where local legislature allows such purchases, international investors buy thousands of hectares of farmland or raw land at prices of a few hundred US$ per hectare. Since the 1940s, agricultural productivity has increased dramatically, due largely to the increased use of energy-intensive mechanization, fertilizers and pesticides. The vast majority of this energy input comes from fossil fuel sources. Between 1950 and 1984, the Green Revolution transformed agriculture around the globe, with world grain production increasing by 250 per cent as world population doubled. Modern agriculture's heavy reliance on petrochemicals and mechanization has raised concerns that oil shortages could increase costs and reduce agricultural output, causing food shortages.

Modern or industrialized agriculture is dependent on fossil fuels in two fundamental ways:

1. direct consumption on the farm; and
2. indirect consumption to manufacture inputs used on the farm.

Direct consumption includes the use of lubricants and fuels to operate farm vehicles and machinery; and use of gas, liquid propane, and electricity to power dryers, pumps, lights, heaters, and coolers. American farms directly consumed about 1.2 exajoules (1.1 quadrillion BTU) in 2002, or just over 1 per cent of the nation's total energy.

Indirect consumption is mainly oil and natural gas used to manufacture fertilizers and pesticides, which accounted for 0.6 exajoules (0.6 quadrillion BTU) in 2002. The energy used to manufacture farm machinery is also a form of indirect agricultural energy consumption, but it is not included in USDA estimates of U.S. agricultural energy use. Together, direct and indirect consumption by U.S. farms accounts for about 2 per cent of the nation's energy use. Direct and indirect energy consumption by U.S. farms peaked in 1979, and has gradually declined over the past 30 years.

Food systems encompass not just agricultural production, but also off-farm processing, packaging, transporting, marketing, consumption, and disposal of food and food-related items. Agriculture accounts for less than one-fifth of food system energy use in the United States.

In 2007, higher incentives for farmers to grow non-food biofuel crops combined with other factors (such as over-development of former farm lands, rising transportation costs, climate change, growing consumer demand in China and India, and population growth) to cause food shortages in Asia, the Middle East, Africa, and Mexico, as well as rising food prices around the globe. As of December 2007, 37 countries faced food crises, and 20 had imposed some sort of food-price controls. Some of these shortages resulted in food riots and even deadly stampedes.

The biggest fossil fuel input to agriculture is the use of natural gas as a hydrogen source for the Haber-Bosch fertilizer-creation process. Natural gas is used because it is the cheapest currently available source of hydrogen. When oil production becomes so scarce that natural gas is used as a partial stopgap replacement, and hydrogen use in transportation increases, natural gas will become much more expensive. If the Haber Process is unable to be commercialized using renewable energy (such as by electrolysis) or if other sources of hydrogen are not available to replace the Haber Process, in amounts sufficient to supply transportation and agricultural needs, this major source of fertilizer would either become extremely expensive or unavailable. This would either cause food shortages or dramatic rises in food prices.

Mitigation of Effects of Petroleum Shortages

In the event of a petroleum shortage, organic agriculture can be more attractive than conventional practices that use petroleum-based pesticides, herbicides, or fertilizers. Some farmers using modern organic-farming methods have reported yields as high as those available from conventional farming. Organic farming may however be more labour-intensive and would require a shift of the workforce from urban to rural areas. The reconditioning of soil to restore nutrients lost during the use of monoculture agriculture techniques also takes time.

It has been suggested that rural communities might obtain fuel from the biochar and synfuel process, which uses agricultural waste to provide charcoal fertilizer, some fuel and food, instead of the normal food vs fuel debate. As the synfuel would be used on-site, the process would be more efficient and might just provide enough fuel for a new organic-agriculture fusion.

It has been suggested that some transgenic plants may some day be developed which would allow for maintaining or increasing yields while requiring fewer fossil-fuel-derived inputs than conventional crops. The possibility of success of these programmes is questioned by ecologists and economists concerned with unsustainable GMO practices such as terminator seeds.

While there has been some research on sustainability using GMO crops, at least prominent multi-year attempt by Monsanto Company has been unsuccessful, though during the same period traditional breeding techniques yielded a more sustainable variety of the same crop.

13

Agriculture and Food Safety

Traditionally, food was obtained through agriculture. With increasing concern in agribusiness over multinational corporations owning the world food supply through patents on genetically modified food, there has been a growing trend toward sustainable agricultural practices. This approach, partly fueled by consumer demand, encourages biodiversity, local self-reliance and organic farming methods. Major influences on food production include international organisations (e.g. the World Trade Organisation and Common Agricultural Policy), national government policy (or law), and war.

In popular culture, the mass production of food, specifically meats such as chicken and beef, has come under fire from various documentaries, most recently Food, Inc, documenting the mass slaughter and poor treatment of animals, often for easier revenues from large corporations. Along with a current trend towards environmentalism, people in Western culture have had an increasing trend towards the use of herbal supplements, foods for a specific group of person (such as dieters, women, or athletes), functional foods (fortified foods, such as omega-3 eggs), and a more ethnically diverse diet.

Many cultures have a recognizable cuisine, a specific set of cooking traditions using various spices or a combination of flavours unique to that culture, which evolves over time. Other differences include preferences (hot or cold, spicy, etc.) and practices, the study of which is known as gastronomy. Many cultures have diversified their foods by means of preparation, cooking methods, and manufacturing. This also includes a complex food trade which helps the cultures to economically survive by way of food, not just by consumption. Some popular types of ethnic foods include Italian, French, Japanese, Chinese, American, Cajun, Thai, and Indian cuisine. Various cultures throughout the world study the dietary analysis of food habits. While evolutionarily speaking, as opposed to culturally, humans are omnivores, religion and social constructs such as morality, activism, or environmentalism will often affect which foods they will consume. Food is eaten and typically enjoyed through the sense of taste, the perception of flavour from eating and drinking. Certain tastes are more enjoyable than others, for evolutionary purposes.

Taste Perception

Animals, specifically humans, have five different types of tastes: sweet, sour, salty, bitter, and umami. As animals have evolved, the tastes that provide the most energy (sugar and fats) are the most pleasant to eat while others, such as bitter, are not enjoyable. Water, while important for survival, has no taste. Fats, on the other hand, especially saturated fats, are thicker and rich and are thus considered more enjoyable to eat.

Sweet

Generally regarded as the most pleasant taste, sweetness is almost always caused by a type of simple sugar such as glucose or fructose, or disaccharides such as sucrose, a molecule combining glucose and fructose. Complex carbohydrates are long chains and thus do not have the sweet taste. Artificial sweeteners such as sucralose are used to mimic the sugar molecule, creating the sensation of sweet, without the calories. Other types of sugar include raw sugar, which is known for its amber colour, as it is unprocessed. As sugar is vital for energy and survival, the taste of sugar is pleasant.

The stevia plant contains a compound known as steviol which, when extracted, has 300 times the sweetness of sugar while having minimal impact on blood sugar.

Sour

Sourness is caused by the taste of acids, such as vinegar or ethanol in alcoholic beverages. Sour foods include citrus, specifically lemons, limes, and to a lesser degree oranges. Sour is evolutionarily significant as it is a sign for a food that may have gone rancid due to bacteria. Many foods, however, are slightly acidic, and help stimulate the taste buds and enhance flavour.

Salty

Saltiness is the taste of alkali metal ions such as sodium and potassium. It is found in almost every food in low to moderate proportions to enhance flavour, although to eat pure salt is regarded as highly unpleasant. There are many different types of salt, with each having a different degree of saltiness, including sea salt, fleur de sel, kosher salt, mined salt, and grey salt. Other than enhancing flavour, its significance is that the body needs and maintains a delicate electrolyte balance, which is the kidney's function. Salt may be iodized, meaning iodine has been added to it, a necessary nutrient that promotes thyroid function. Some canned foods, notably soups or packaged broths, tend to be high in salt as a means of preserving the food longer. Historically speaking, salt has been used as a meat preservative as salt promotes water excretion, thus working as a preservative. Similarly, dried foods also promote food safety.

Bitter

The rind or pith of a lemon is exceptionally bitter, while the lemon itself is characterized as sour.

Bitterness is a highly unpleasant sensation characterized by having a sharp, pungent taste. Dark, unsweetened chocolate, caffeine, lemon rind, and some types of fruit are known to be bitter.

Umami

Umami, the Japanese word for delicious, is the least known in Western popular culture, but has a long tradition in Asian cuisine. Umami is the taste of glutamates, especially monosodium glutamate or MSG. It is characterized as savory, meaty, and rich in flavour. Salmon and mushrooms are foods high in umami. Meat and other animal byproducts are described as having this taste.

Presentation

It is known that when presented with food, the consumer 'eats' first with their eyes, a universal psychological phenomenon. Food presented in a clean and appetizing way will encourage a good flavour, even if unsatisfactory.

Contrast in Texture

Texture plays a crucial role in the enjoyment of eating foods. Contrasts in textures, such as something crunchy in an otherwise smooth dish, may increase the appeal of eating it. Common examples include adding granola to yogurt, adding croutons to a salad or soup, and toasting bread to enhance its crunchiness for a smooth topping, such as jam or butter.

Contrast in Taste

Another universal phenomenon regarding food is the appeal of contrast in taste and presentation. Opposite flavours, such as sweet and saltiness, tend to go well together, such as in kettle corn and with nuts.

Food Preparation

While many foods can be eaten raw, many also undergo some form of preparation for reasons of safety, palatability, texture, or flavour. At the simplest level this may involve washing, cutting, trimming, or adding other foods or ingredients, such as spices. It may also involve mixing, heating or cooling, pressure cooking, fermentation, or combination with other food. In a home, most food preparation takes place in a kitchen. Some preparation is done to enhance the taste or aesthetic appeal; other preparation may help to preserve the food; others may be involved in cultural identity. A meal is made up of food which is prepared to be eaten at a specific time and place.

Animal-based Preparation

The preparation of animal-based food usually involves slaughter, evisceration, hanging, portioning, and rendering. In developed countries, this is usually done outside the home in slaughterhouses, which are used to process animals en masse for meat production. Many countries regulate their slaughterhouses by law. For example, the United States has established the Humane Slaughter Act of 1958, which requires that an animal be stunned before killing. This act, like those in many countries, exempts slaughter in accordance to religious law, such as kosher, shechita, and dhabiha halal. Strict interpretations of kashrut require the animal to be fully aware when its carotid artery is cut.

On the local level, a butcher may commonly break down larger animal meat into smaller manageable cuts, and pre-wrap them for commercial sale or wrap them to order in butcher paper. In addition, fish and seafood may be fabricated into smaller cuts by a fish monger. However fish butchery may be done on board a fishing vessel and quick-frozen for preservation of quality.

Cooking

The term 'cooking' encompasses a vast range of methods, tools, and combinations of ingredients to improve the flavour or digestibility of food. Cooking technique, known as culinary art, generally requires the selection, measurement, and combining of ingredients in an ordered procedure in an effort to achieve the desired result. Constraints on success include the variability of ingredients, ambient conditions, tools, and the skill of the individual cook. The diversity of cooking worldwide is a reflection of the myriad nutritional, aesthetic, agricultural, economic, cultural, and religious considerations that affect it.

Cooking requires applying heat to a food which usually, though not always, chemically changes the molecules, thus changing its flavour, texture, appearance, and nutritional properties. Cooking certain proteins, such as egg whites, meats, and fish, denatures the protein, causing it to firm. There is archaeological evidence of roasted foodstuffs at *Homo erectus* campsites dating from 420,000 years ago. Boiling as a means of cooking requires a container, and has been practiced at least since the 10th millennium BC with the introduction of pottery.

Cooking Equipment

There are many different types of equipment used for cooking.

Ovens are mostly hollow devices that get very hot (up to 500°F) and are used for baking or roasting and offer a dry-heat cooking method. Different cuisines will use different types of ovens; for example, Indian culture uses a Tandoor oven, which is a cylindrical clay oven which operates at a single high temperature. Western kitchens use variable temperature convection ovens, conventional ovens, toaster ovens, or non-radiant heat ovens like the microwave oven. Classic Italian cuisine includes the use of a brick oven containing burning wood. Ovens may be wood-fired, coal-fired, gas, electric, or oil-fired.

Various types of cook-tops are used as well. They carry the same variations of fuel types as the ovens mentioned above. Cook-tops are used to heat vessels placed on top of the heat source, such as a sauté pan, sauce pot, frying pan, or pressure cooker. These pieces of equipment can use either a moist or dry cooking method and include methods such as steaming, simmering, boiling, and poaching for moist methods, while the dry methods include sautéing, pan frying, and deep-frying.

In addition, many cultures use grills for cooking. A grill operates with a radiant heat source from below, usually covered with a metal grid and sometimes a cover. An open pit barbecue in the American south is one example along with the American style outdoor grill fueled by wood, liquid propane, or charcoal along with soaked wood chips for smoking. A Mexican style of barbecue is called barbacoa, which involves the cooking of meats such as whole sheep over an open fire. In Argentina, an asado (Spanish for 'grilled') is prepared on a grill held over an open pit or fire made upon the ground, on which a whole animal or smaller cuts are grilled.

Raw Food Preparation

Certain cultures highlight animal and vegetable foods in their raw state. Salads consisting of raw vegetables or fruits are common in many cuisines. Sashimi in Japanese cuisine consists of raw sliced fish or other meat, and sushi often incorporates raw fish or seafood. Steak tartare and salmon tartare are dishes made from diced or ground raw beef or salmon, mixed with various ingredients and served with baguettes, brioche, or frites. In Italy, carpaccio is a dish of very thinly sliced raw beef, drizzled with a vinaigrette made with olive oil. The health food movement known as raw foodism promotes a mostly vegan diet of raw fruits, vegetables, and grains prepared in various ways, including juicing, food dehydration, sprouting, and other methods of preparation that do not heat the food above 118°F (47.8°C).

Restaurants employ trained chefs who prepare food, and trained waitstaff to serve the customers. The term restaurant is credited to the French from the 19th century, as it relates to the restorative nature of the bouillons that were once served in them. However, the concept pre-dates the naming of these establishments, as evidence suggests commercial food preparation may have existed during the age of the city of Pompeii, and urban sales of prepared foods may have existed in China during the Song Dynasty. The coffee shops or cafés of 17th century Europe may also be considered an early version of the restaurant. In 2005, the population of the United States spent $496 billion for out-of-home dining. Expenditures by type of out-of-home dining were as follows: 40 per cent in full-service restaurants, 37.2 per cent in limited service restaurants (fast food), 6.6 per cent in schools or colleges,

5.4 per cent in bars and vending machines, 4.7 per cent in hotels and motels, 4.0 per cent in recreational places, and 2.2 per cent in others, which includes military bases.

Packaged foods are manufactured outside the home for purchase. This can be as simple as a butcher preparing meat, or as complex as a modern international food industry. Early food processing techniques were limited by available food preservation, packaging, and transportation. This mainly involved salting, curing, curdling, drying, pickling, fermenting, and smoking. Food manufacturing arose during the industrial revolution in the 19th century. This development took advantage of new mass markets and emerging new technology, such as milling, preservation, packaging and labeling, and transportation. It brought the advantages of pre-prepared time-saving food to the bulk of ordinary people who did not employ domestic servants.

At the start of the 21st century, a two-tier structure has arisen, with a few international food processing giants controlling a wide range of well-known food brands. There also exists a wide array of small local or national food processing companies. Advanced technologies have also come to change food manufacture. Computer-based control systems, sophisticated processing and packaging methods, and logistics and distribution advances can enhance product quality, improve food safety, and reduce costs.

Marketing and Retailing

Food marketing brings together the producer and the consumer. It is the chain of activities that brings food from 'farm gate to plate'. The marketing of even a single food product can be a complicated process involving many producers and companies. For example, fifty-six companies are involved in making one can of chicken noodle soup. These businesses include not only chicken and vegetable processors but also the companies that transport the ingredients and those who print labels and manufacture cans. The food marketing system is the largest direct and indirect non-government employer in the United States.

In the pre-modern era, the sale of surplus food took place once a week when farmers took their wares on market day into the local village marketplace. Here food was sold to grocers for sale in their local shops for purchase by local consumers. With the onset of industrialization and the development of the food processing industry, a wider range of food could be sold and distributed in distant locations. Typically early grocery shops would be counter-based shops, in which purchasers told the shop-keeper what they wanted, so that the shop-keeper could get it for them.

In the 20th century, supermarkets were born. Supermarkets brought with them a self service approach to shopping using shopping carts, and were able to offer quality food at lower cost through economies of scale and reduced staffing costs. In the latter part of the 20th century, this has been further revolutionized by the development of vast warehouse-sized, out-of-town supermarkets, selling a wide range of food from around the world.

Unlike food processors, food retailing is a two-tier market in which a small number of very large companies control a large proportion of supermarkets. The supermarket giants wield great purchasing power over farmers and processors, and strong influence over consumers. Nevertheless, less than 10 per cent of consumer spending on food goes to farmers, with larger percentages going to advertising, transportation, and intermediate corporations.

Prices

It was reported on March 24, 2008, that consumers worldwide faced rising food prices. Reasons for this development include changes in the weather and dramatic changes in the global economy, including higher oil prices, lower food reserves, and growing consumer demand in China and India. In the long term, prices are expected to stabilize. Farmers will grow more grain for both fuel and food and eventually bring prices down. Already this is happening with wheat, with more crops to be planted in the United States,

Canada, and Europe in 2009. However, the Food and Agriculture Organisation projects that consumers still have to deal with more expensive food until at least 2018.

It is rare for the spikes to hit all major foods in most countries at once. Food prices rose 4 per cent in the United States in 2007, the highest increase since 1990, and are expected to climb as much again in 2008. As of December 2007, 37 countries faced food crises, and 20 had imposed some sort of food-price controls. In China, the price of pork jumped 58 per cent in 2007. In the 1980s and 1990s, farm subsidies and support programmes allowed major grain exporting countries to hold large surpluses, which could be tapped during food shortages to keep prices down. However, new trade policies have made agricultural production much more responsive to market demands, putting global food reserves at their lowest since 1983.

Food prices are rising, wealthier Asian consumers are westernizing their diets, and farmers and nations of the third world are struggling to keep up the pace. The past five years have seen rapid growth in the contribution of Asian nations to the global fluid and powdered milk manufacturing industry, which in 2008 accounted for more than 30 per cent of production, while China alone accounts for more than 10 per cent of both production and consumption in the global fruit and vegetable processing and preserving industry. The trend is similarly evident in industries such as soft drink and bottled water manufacturing, as well as global cocoa, chocolate, and sugar confectionery manufacturing, forecast to grow by 5.7 per cent and 10.0 per cent respectively during 2008 in response to soaring demand in Chinese and Southeast Asian markets.

Famine and Hunger

Food deprivation leads to malnutrition and ultimately starvation. This is often connected with famine, which involves the absence of food in entire communities. This can have a devastating and widespread effect on human health and mortality. Rationing is sometimes used to distribute food in times of shortage, most notably during times of war.

Starvation is a significant international problem. Approximately 815 million people are undernourished, and over 16,000 children die per day from hunger-related causes. Food deprivation is regarded as a deficit need in Maslow's hierarchy of needs and is measured using famine scales.

Food Aid

Food aid can benefit people suffering from a shortage of food. It can be used to improve peoples' lives in the short term, so that a society can increase its standard of living to the point that food aid is no longer required. Conversely, badly managed food aid can create problems by disrupting local markets, depressing crop prices, and discouraging food production. Sometimes a cycle of food aid dependence can develop. Its provision, or threatened withdrawal, is sometimes used as a political tool to influence the policies of the destination country, a strategy known as food politics. Sometimes, food aid provisions will require certain types of food be purchased from certain sellers, and food aid can be misused to enhance the markets of donor countries. International efforts to distribute food to the neediest countries are often coordinated by the World Food Programme.

Safety

Foodborne illness, commonly called 'food poisoning', is caused by bacteria, toxins, viruses, parasites, and prions. Roughly 7 million people die of food poisoning each year, with about 10 times as many suffering from a non-fatal version. The two most common factors leading to cases of bacterial foodborne illness are cross-contamination of ready-to-eat food from other uncooked foods and improper temperature control. Less commonly, acute adverse reactions can also occur if chemical contamination of food occurs, for example from improper storage, or use of non-food grade soaps and disinfectants. Food can also be adulterated by a very wide range of articles (known as 'foreign bodies') during farming, manufacture, cooking, packaging, distribution, or sale. These foreign bodies can include pests or their droppings, hairs, cigarette butts, wood chips, and all manner of other contaminants. It is possible for certain types of food to become contaminated if stored or presented in an unsafe container, such as a ceramic pot with lead-based glaze.

Food poisoning has been recognized as a disease since as early as Hippocrates. The sale of rancid, contaminated, or adulterated food was commonplace until the introduction of hygiene, refrigeration, and vermin controls in the 19th century. Discovery of techniques for killing bacteria using heat, and other microbiological studies by scientists such as Louis Pasteur, contributed to the modern sanitation standards that are ubiquitous in developed nations today. This was further underpinned by the work of Justus von Liebig, which led to the development of modern food storage and food preservation methods. In more recent years, a greater understanding of the causes of food-borne illnesses has led to the development of more systematic approaches such as the Hazard Analysis and Critical Control Points (HACCP), which can identify and eliminate many risks.

Recommended measures for ensuring food safety include maintaining a clean preparation area with foods of different types kept separate, ensuring an adequate cooking temperature, and refrigerating foods promptly after cooking.

Foods that spoil easily, such as meats, dairy, and seafood, must be prepared a certain way to avoid contaminating the people for whom they are prepared. As such, the general rule of thumb is that cold foods (such as dairy products) should be kept cold and hot foods (such as soup) should be kept hot until storage. Cold meats, such as chicken, that are to be cooked should not be placed at room temperature for thawing, at the risk of dangerous bacterial growth, such as *Salmonella* or *E. coli*.

Allergies

Some people have allergies or sensitivities to foods which are not problematic to most people. This occurs when a person's immune system mistakes a certain food protein for a harmful foreign agent and attacks it. About 2 per cent of adults and 8 per cent of children have a food allergy. The amount of the food substance required to provoke a reaction in a particularly susceptible individual can be quite small. In some instances, traces of food in the air, too minute to be perceived through smell, have been known to provoke lethal reactions in extremely sensitive individuals. Common food allergens are gluten, corn, shellfish (mollusks), peanuts, and soy. Allergens frequently produce symptoms such as diarrhea, rashes, bloating, vomiting, and regurgitation. The digestive complaints usually develop within half an hour of ingesting the allergen.

Rarely, food allergies can lead to a medical emergency, such as anaphylactic shock, hypotension (low blood pressure), and loss of consciousness. An allergen associated with this type of reaction is peanut, although latex products can induce similar reactions. Initial treatment is with epinephrine (adrenaline), often carried by known patients in the form of an Epi-pen or Twinject.

DIET

Cultural and Religious Diets

Dietary habits are the habitual decisions a person or culture makes when choosing what foods to eat. Many cultures hold some food preferences and some food taboos. Dietary choices can also define cultures and play a role in religion. For example, only kosher foods are permitted by Judaism, halal foods by Islam, and in Hinduism beef is restricted. In addition, the dietary choices of different countries or regions have different characteristics. This is highly related to a culture's cuisine.

Dietary habits play a significant role in the health and mortality of all humans. Imbalances between the consumed fuels and expended energy results in either starvation or excessive reserves of adipose tissue, known as body fat. Poor intake of various vitamins and minerals can lead to diseases that can have far-reaching effects on health. For instance, 30 per cent of the world's population either has, or is at risk for developing, iodine deficiency. It is estimated that at least 3 million children are blind due to vitamin A deficiency. Vitamin C deficiency results in scurvy. Calcium, Vitamin D, and phosphorus are inter-related; the consumption of each may affect the absorption of the others. Kwashiorkor and marasmus are childhood disorders caused by lack of dietary protein.

Moral, Ethical, and Health Conscious Diet

Many individuals limit what foods they eat for reasons of morality, or other habit. For instance, vegetarians choose to forgc food from animal sources to varying degrees. Others choose a healthier diet, avoiding sugars or animal fats and increasing consumption of dietary fiber and antioxidants. Obesity, a serious problem in the western world, leads to higher chances of developing heart disease, diabetes, and many other diseases. More recently, dietary habits have been influenced by the concerns that some people have about possible impacts on health or the environment from genetically modified food. Further concerns about the impact of industrial farming (grains) on animal welfare, human health, and the environment are also having an effect on contemporary human dietary habits. This has led to the emergence of a counterculture with a preference for organic and local food.

Nutrition and Dietary Problems

Between the extremes of optimal health and death from starvation or malnutrition, there is an array of disease states that can be caused or alleviated by changes in diet. Deficiencies, excesses, and imbalances in diet can produce negative impacts on health, which may lead to diseases such as scurvy, obesity, or osteoporosis, as well as psychological and behavioral problems. The science of nutrition attempts to understand how and why specific dietary aspects influence health.

Nutrients in food are grouped into several categories. Macronutrients are fat, protein, and carbohydrates. Micronutrients are the minerals and vitamins. Additionally, food contains water and dietary fiber.

As previously discussed, the body is designed by natural selection to enjoy sweet and fattening foods for evolutionary diets, ideal for hunters and gatherers. Thus, sweet and fattening foods in nature are typically rare and are very pleasurable to eat. In modern times, with advanced technology, enjoyable foods are easily available to consumers. Unfortunately, this promotes obesity in adults and children alike.

Legal Definition

Some countries list a legal definition of food. These countries list food as any item that is to be processed, partially processed, or unprocessed for consumption. The listing of items included as foodstuffs include any substance intended to be, or reasonably expected to be, ingested by humans. In addition to these foodstuffs, drink, chewing gum, water, or other items processed into said food items are part of the legal definition of food. Items not included in the legal definition of food include animal feed, live animals (unless being prepared for sale in a market), plants prior to harvesting, medicinal products, cosmetics, tobacco and tobacco products, narcotic or psychotropic substances, and residues and contaminants.

Many plants or plant parts are eaten as food. There are around 2000 plant species which are cultivated for food, and many have several distinct cultivars.

Seeds of plants are a good source of food for animals, including humans, because they contain the nutrients necessary for the plant's initial growth, including many healthy fats, such as Omega fats. In fact, the majority of food consumed by human beings are seed-based foods. Edible seeds include cereals (maize, wheat, rice, et cetera), legumes (beans, peas, lentils, et cetera), and nuts. Oilseeds are often pressed to produce rich oils - sunflower, flaxseed, rapeseed (including canola oil), sesame etc.

Seeds are typically high in unsaturated fats and, in moderation, are considered a health food, although not all seeds are edible. Large seeds, such as those from a lemon, pose a choking hazard, while seeds from apples and cherries contain a poison (cyanide).

Fruits are the ripened ovaries of plants, including the seeds within. Many plants have evolved fruits that are attractive as a food source to animals, so that animals will eat the fruits and excrete the seeds some distance away. Fruits, therefore, make up a significant part of the diets of most cultures. Some botanical fruits, such as tomatoes, pumpkins, and eggplants, are eaten as vegetables. (For more information, see list of fruits.)

Vegetables are a second type of plant matter that is commonly eaten as food. These include root vegetables (potatoes and carrots), leaf vegetables (spinach and lettuce), stem vegetables (bamboo shoots and asparagus), and inflorescence vegetables (globe artichokes and broccoli).

Almost all foods are of plant or animal origin. Cereal grain is a staple food that provides more food energy worldwide than any other type of crop. Maize, wheat, and rice - in all of their varieties - account for 87 per cent of all grain production worldwide.

Other foods not from animal or plant sources include various edible fungi, especially mushrooms. Fungi and ambient bacteria are used in the preparation of fermented and pickled foods like leavened bread, alcoholic drinks, cheese, pickles, kombucha, and yogurt. Another example is blue-green algae such as Spirulina. Inorganic substances such as baking soda and cream of tartar are also used to chemically alter an ingredient.

Food Safety

Food safety is a scientific discipline describing handling, preparation, and storage of food in ways that prevent foodborne illness. This includes a number of routines that should be followed to avoid potentially severe health hazards. Food can transmit disease from person to person as well as serve as a growth medium for bacteria that can cause food poisoning. Debates on genetic food safety include such issues as impact of genetically modified food on health of further generations and genetic pollution of environment, which can destroy natural biological diversity. In developed countries there are intricate standards for food preparation, whereas in lesser developed countries the main issue is simply the availability of adequate safe water, which is usually a critical item. In theory food poisoning is 100 per cent preventable.

World Health Organisation (WHO) report concluded that about 40 per cent of reported food poisoning outbreaks in the WHO European Region occur in private homes. According to the WHO and CDC, in the USA alone, annually, there are 76 million cases of foodborne illness leading to 325,000 hospitalizations and 5,000 deaths.

REGULATORY AGENCIES

Australia

Australian Food Authority is working toward ensuring that all food businesses implement food safety systems to ensure food is safe to consume in a bid to halt the increasing incidence of food poisoning, this includes basic food safety training for at least one person in each business. Smart business operators know that basic food safety training improves the bottom line, staff take more pride in their work; there is less waste; and customers can have more confidence in the food they consume. Food Safety training in units of competence from a relevant training package, must be delivered by a Registered Training Organisation (RTO) to enable staff to be issued with a nationally-recognised unit of competency code on their certificate. Generally this training can be completed in less than one day. Training options are available to suit the needs of everyone. Training may be carried out in-house for a group, in a public class, via correspondence or online. Basic food safety training includes:

- Understanding the hazards associated with the main types of food and the conditions to prevent the growth of bacteria which can cause food poisoning.

- The problems associated with product packaging such as leaks in vacuum packs, damage to packaging or pest infestation, as well as problems and diseases spread by pests.
- Safe food handling. This includes safe procedures for each process such as receiving, re-packing, food storage, preparation and cooking, cooling and re-heating, displaying products, handling products when serving customers, packaging, cleaning and sanitizing, pest control, transport and delivery. Also the causes of cross contamination.
- Catering for customers who are particularly at risk of food-borne illness, including allergies and intolerance.
- Correct cleaning and sanitizing procedures, cleaning products and their correct use, and the storage of cleaning items such as brushes, mops and cloths.
- Personal hygiene, hand washing, illness, and protective clothing.

People responsible for serving unsafe food can be liable for heavy fines under this new legislation, consumers are pleased that industry will be forced to take food safety seriously.

China

Food safety is a growing concern in Chinese agriculture. The Chinese government oversees agricultural production as well as the manufacture of food packaging, containers, chemical additives, drug production, and business regulation. In recent years, the Chinese government attempted to consolidate food regulation with the creation of the State Food and Drug Administration in 2003, and officials have also been under increasing public and international pressure to solve food safety problems. However, it appears that regulations are not well known by the trade. Labels used for 'green' food, 'organic' food and 'pollution-free' food are not well recognized by traders and many are unclear about their meaning. A survey by the World Bank found that supermarket managers had difficulty in obtaining produce that met safety requirements and found that a high percentage of produce did not comply with established standards.

Traditional marketing systems, whether in China or the rest of Asia, presently provide little motivation or incentive for individual farmers to make improvements to either quality or safety as their produce tends to get grouped together with standard products as it progresses through the marketing channel. Direct linkages between farmer groups and traders or ultimate buyers, such as supermarkets, can help avoid this problem. Governments need to improve the condition of many markets through upgrading management and reinvesting market fees in physical infrastructure. Wholesale markets need to investigate the feasibility of developing separate sections to handle fruits and vegetables that meet defined safety and quality standards.

European Union

The parliament of the European Union (EU) makes legislation in the form of directives and regulations, many of which are mandatory for member states and which therefore must be incorporated into individual countries' national legislation. As a very large organisation that exists to remove barriers to trade between member states, and into which individual member states have only a proportional influence, the outcome is often seen as an excessively bureaucratic 'one size fits all' approach. However, in relation to food safety the tendency to err on the side of maximum protection for the consumer may be seen as a positive benefit. The EU parliament is informed on food safety matters by the European Food Safety Authority.

Individual member states may also have other legislation and controls in respect of food safety, provided that they do not prevent trade with other states, and can differ considerably in their internal structures and approaches to the regulatory control of food safety.

Germany

The Federal Ministry of Food, Agriculture and Consumer Protection (BMELV) is a Federal Ministry of the Federal Republic of Germany. History: Founded as Federal Ministry of Food, Agriculture and Foresting in 1949, this name did not change until 2001. Then the name changed to Federal Ministry of Consumer Protection, Food and Agriculture. At the 22nd of November 2005, the name got changed again to its current state: Federal Ministry of Food, Agriculture and Consumer Protection. The reason for this last change was that all the resorts should get equal ranking which was achieved by sorting the resorts alphabetically. Vision: A balanced and healthy diet with safe food, distinct consumer rights and consumer information for various areas of life, and a strong and sustainable agriculture as well as perspectives for our rural areas are important goals of the Federal Ministry of Food, Agriculture and Consumer Protection (BMELV). The Federal Office of Consumer Protection and Food Safety is under the control of the Federal Ministry of Food, Agriculture and Consumer Protection. It exercises several duties, with which it contributes to safer food and thereby intensifies health-based consumer protection in Germany. Food can be manufactured and sold within Germany without a special permission, as long as it does not cause any damage on consumers' health and meets the general standards set by the legislation. However, manufacturers, carriers, importers and retailers are responsible for the food they pass into circulation. They are obliged to ensure and document the safety and quality of their food with the use of in-house control mechanisms.

Hong Kong

In Hong Kong SAR, the Centre for Food Safety is in charge of ensuring food sold is safe and fit for consumption.

India

Food Safety and Standards Authority of India, established under the Food Safety and Standards Act, 2006, is the regulating body related to food safety and laying down of standards of food in India.

New Zealand

The New Zealand Food Safety Authority (NZFSA), or Te Pou Oranga Kai O Aotearoa is the New Zealand government body responsible for food safety. NZFSA is also the controlling authority for imports and exports of food and food-related products.

Food Bill 160-2 was introduced on 26 May 2010 to make some fundamental changes to New Zealand's domestic food regulatory regime. Primarily designed to drive an export led economic recovery for New Zealand, because the domestic food regulatory regime is the platform for exports. The New Zealand domestic standard is used as the basis for negotiating equivalence arrangements with trading partners. This minimizes the excessive importing country requirements that may be imposed but which do not go to food safety.

Pakistan

Pakistan does not have an integrated legal framework but has a set of laws, which deals with various aspects of food safety. These laws, despite the fact that they were enacted long time ago, have tremendous capacity to achieve at least minimum level of food safety. However, like many other laws, these laws remain very poorly enforced. There are four laws that specifically deal with food safety. Three of these laws directly focus issues related to food safety, while the fourth, the Pakistan Standards and Quality Control Authority Act, is indirectly relevant to food safety.

The Pure Food Ordinance 1960 consolidates and amends the law in relation to the preparation and the sale of foods. All provinces and some northern areas have adopted this law with certain amendments. Its aim is to ensure purity of food being supplied to people in the market and, therefore, provides for preventing adulteration. The Pure Food Ordinance 1960 does not apply to cantonment areas. There is a separate law for cantonments called 'The Cantonment Pure Food Act, 1966'. There is no substantial difference between the Pure Food Ordinance 1960 and The Cantonment Pure Food Act. Even the rules of operation are very much similar.

Pakistan Hotels and Restaurant Act, 1976 applies to all hotels and restaurants in Pakistan and seeks to control and regulate the rates and standard of service(s) by hotels and restaurants. In addition to other provisions, under section 22(2), the sale of food or beverages that are contaminated, not prepared hygienically or served in utensils that are not hygienic or clean is an offense. There are no express provisions for consumer complaints in the Pakistan Restaurants Act, 1976, Pakistan Penal Code, 1860 and Pakistan Standards and Quality Control Authority Act, 1996. The laws do not prevent citizens from lodging complaints with the concerned government officials; however, the consideration and handling of complaints is a matter of discretion of the officials.

South Korea

Korea Food and Drug Administration

Korea Food & Drug Administration (KFDA) is working for food safety since 1945. It is part of the Government of South Korea.

IOAS -Organic Certification Bodies Registered in KFDA: 'Organic' or related claims can be labelled on food products when organic certificates are considered as valid by KFDA. KFDA admits organic certificates which can be issued by:

1. IFOAM (International Federation of Organic Agriculture Movement) accredited certification bodies.
2. Government accredited certification bodies - 328 bodies in 29 countries have been registered in KFDA.

National Institute of Food and Drug Safety Evaluation

National Institute of Food and Drug Safety Evaluation (NIFDS) is functioning as well. The National Institute of Food and Drug Safety Evaluation is a national organisation for toxicological tests and research. Under the Korea Food & Drug Administration, the Institute performs research on toxicology, pharmacology, and risk analysis of foods, drugs, and their additives. The Institute strives primarily to understand important biological triggering mechanisms and improve assessment methods of human exposure, sensitivities, and risk by:

1. conducting basic, applied, and policy research that closely examines biologically triggering harmful effects on the regulated products such as foods, food additives, and drugs; and
2. operating the national toxicology programme for the toxicological test development and inspection of hazardous chemical ubstances assessments.

The Institute ensures safety by:

1. investigation and research on safety by its own researchers; and
2. contract research by external academicians and research centres.

United Kingdom

In the UK the Food Standards Agency is an independent government department responsible for food safety and hygiene across the UK. They work with businesses to help them produce safe food, and with local authorities to enforce food safety regulations. In 2006 food hygiene legislation changed and new requirements came into force. The main requirement resulting from this change is that if you own or run a food business in the UK, you must have a documented Food Safety Management System, which is based on the principles of Hazard Analysis Critical Control Point HACCP.

United States

The US food system is regulated by numerous federal, state and local officials. Although the US food safety system is one of the best in the world, it is lacking in "organisation, regulatory tools, and resources to address food borne illness".

Federal Level Regulation

The Food and Drug Administration publishes the Food Code, a model set of guidelines and procedures that assists food control jurisdictions by providing a scientifically sound technical and legal basis for regulating the retail and food service industries, including restaurants, grocery stores and institutional foodservice providers such as nursing homes. Regulatory agencies at all levels of government in the United

States use the FDA Food Code to develop or update food safety rules in their jurisdictions that are consistent with national food regulatory policy. According to the FDA, 48 of 56 states and territories, representing 79 per cent of the U.S. population, have adopted food codes patterned after one of the five versions of the Food Code, beginning with the 1993 edition.

In the United States, federal regulations governing food safety are fragmented and complicated, according to a February 2007 report from the Government Accountability Office. There are 15 agencies sharing oversight responsibilities in the food safety system, although the two primary agencies are the U.S. Department of Agriculture (USDA) Food Safety and Inspection Service (FSIS), which is responsible for the safety of meat, poultry, and processed egg products, and the Food and Drug Administration (FDA), which is responsible for virtually all other foods.

The Food Safety and Inspection Service has approximately 7,800 inspection programme personnel working in nearly 6,200 federally inspected meat, poultry and processed egg establishments. FSIS is charged with administering and enforcing the Federal Meat Inspection Act, the Poultry Products Inspection Act, the Egg Products Inspection Act, portions of the Agricultural Marketing Act, the Humane Slaughter Act, and the regulations that implement these laws. FSIS inspection programme personnel inspect every animal before slaughter, and each carcass after slaughter to ensure public health requirements are met. In fiscal year (FY) 2008, this included about 50 billion pounds of livestock carcasses, about 59 billion pounds of poultry carcasses, and about 4.3 billion pounds of processed egg products. At U.S. borders, they also inspected 3.3 billion pounds of imported meat and poultry products.

Industry Pressure

There have been concerns over the efficacy of safety practices and food industry pressure on U.S. regulators. A study reported by Reuters found that "the food industry is jeopardizing U.S. public health by withholding information from food safety investigators or pressuring regulators to withdraw or alter policy designed to protect consumers". A survey found that 25 per cent of U.S. government inspectors and scientists surveyed have experienced during the past year corporate interests forcing their food safety agency to withdraw or to modify agency policy or action that protects consumers. Scientists have observed that management undercuts field inspectors who stand up for food safety against industry pressure. According to Dr. Dean Wyatt, a USDA veterinarian who oversees federal slaughter house inspectors, "Upper level management does not adequately support field inspectors and the actions they take to protect the food supply. Not only is there lack of support, but there's outright obstruction, retaliation and abuse of power."

State and Local Regulation

A number of U.S. states have their own meat inspection programmes that substitute for USDA inspection for meats that are sold only in-state. Certain state programmes have been criticized for undue leniency to bad practices.

However, other state food safety programmes supplement, rather than replace, Federal inspections, generally with the goal of increasing consumer confidence in the state's produce. For example, state health departments have a role in investigating outbreaks of food-borne disease bacteria, as in the case of the 2006 outbreak of *Escherichia coli* O157:H7 (bad *E. coli* bacteria) from processed spinach. Health departments also promote better food processing practices to eliminate these threats.

In addition to the US Food and Drug Administration, several states that are major producers of fresh fruits and vegetables (including California, Arizona and Florida) have their own state programmes to test produce for pesticide residues.

Restaurants and other retail food establishments fall under state law and are regulated by state or local health departments. Typically these regulations require official inspections of specific design features, best food-handling practices, and certification of food handlers. In some places a letter grade or numerical score must be prominently posted following each inspection. In some localities, inspection deficiencies and remedial action are posted on the Internet.

MANUFACTURING CONTROL

HACCP Guidelines

The UK Food Standards Agency publishes recommendations as part of its Hazard Analysis and Critical Control Points (HACCP) programme. The relevant guidelines state that:

> Cooking food until the Core temperature is 75°C or above will ensure that harmful bacteria are destroyed.

However, lower cooking temperatures are acceptable provided that the core temperature is maintained for a specified period of time as follows:

- 60°C for a minimum of 45 minutes
- 65°C for a minimum of 10 minutes
- 70°C for a minimum of 2 minutes

Previous guidance from a leaflet produced by the UK Department Of Health 'Handling Cooked Meats Safely A Ten Point Plan' also allowed for:

- 75°C for a minimum of 30 seconds
- 80°C for a minimum of 6 seconds

Note that recommended cooking conditions are only appropriate if initial bacterial numbers in the uncooked food are small. Cooking does not overcome poor hygiene.

CONSUMER LABELLING

United Kingdom

Foodstuffs in the UK have one of two labels to indicate the nature of the deterioration of the product and any subsequent health issues. EHO Food Hygiene certification is required to prepare and distribute food. While there is no specified expiry date of such a qualification the changes in legislation it is suggested to update every five years.

Best before indicates a future date beyond which the food product may lose quality in terms of taste or texture amongst others, but does not imply any serious health problems if food is consumed beyond this date (within reasonable limits).

Use by indicates a legal date beyond which it is not permissible to sell a food product (usually one that deteriorates fairly rapidly after production) due to the potential serious nature of consumption of pathogens. Leeway is sometimes provided by producers in stating display until dates so that products are not at their limit of safe consumption on the actual date stated (this latter is voluntary and not subject to regulatory control). This allows for the variability in production, storage and display methods.

United States

With the exception of infant formula and baby foods which must be withdrawn by their expiration date, Federal law does not require expiration dates. For all other foods, except dairy products in some states, freshness dating is strictly voluntary on the part of manufacturers. In response to consumer demand, perishable foods are typically labeled with a Sell by date. It is up to the consumer to decide how long after the Sell by date a package is usable. Other common dating statements are Best if used by, Use-by date, Expiration date, Guaranteed fresh <date>, and Pack date.

Australia and New Zealand

Guide to food labelling and other information requirements: This guide provides background information on the general labelling requirements in the Code. The information in this guide applies both to food for retail sale and to food for catering purposes. Foods for catering purposes means those foods for use in restaurants, canteens, schools, caterers or self-catering institutions, where food is offered for immediate consumption. Labelling and information requirements in the new Code apply both to food sold or prepared for sale in Australia and New Zealand and food imported into Australia and New Zealand. Warning and Advisory Declarations, Ingredient Labelling, Date Marking, Nutrition Information Requirements, Legibility Requirements for Food Labels, Percentage Labelling, Information Requirements for Foods Exempt from Bearing a Label.

Issues Associated with Sell by/use by Dates

According to the UK's Waste and Resources Action Programme, 33 per cent per cent of all food produced is wasted along the chill chain or at the consumer. At the same time, a large number of people get sick every year due to spoiled food.

UK Government to Replace Sell by/use by Dates?

According to the UK minister Hilary Benn the use by date and sell by dates are old technologies that are outdated and should be replaced by other solutions or disposed of altogether.

How to Enhance Food Safety

There is a number of ways to enhance sell by and use by dates. These include better education of consumers on how to use, transport, and store fresh food products, but also by enhancing the use by and sell by dates by adding to the package smart indicators such as TTIs (Time Temperature Indicators). These show through a visible colour change whether the product is still fresh. TTIs are already in use by retailers and food producers in France (Monoprix and Carrefour), Switzerland (Kneuss), and other countries in western Europe.

Consumer tips: How to Keep Food Safe

1. One of the simplest measures that any person can take to prevent the spread of foodborne illness is to properly wash his or her hands before preparing or eating any meal. Many people who believe they are adequately washing their hands are sorely mistaken. According to a study conducted by the American Society of Microbiology, 97 per cent of females and 92 per cent of males said they washed their hands, but those numbers turned out to be 75 per cent of females and 58 per cent of males upon observation. A proper hand-washing technique suggested by the Missouri Department of Health and Senior Services includes using soap and warm

water; washing vigorously for 10–20 seconds, making sure to reach all surfaces of the hands including the wrists, between the fingers, and under the finger nails; rinsing well; drying hands with a paper towel; and using a paper towel to turn off the water. It is certainly important to wash your hands before preparing a meal and eating, but hands should also be washed after using the restroom, coughing/sneezing, touching cuts or skin infections, handling raw meat, and touching pets or other animals. Almost half the cases of foodborne illnesses could be prevented by better hand-washing by food handlers. In addition, hand sanitizer is a helpful follow-up to hand-washing, but it should never be used to replace this valuable technique.

2. Some foods should simply never be ingested in the first place because they have such a high risk of containing harmful bacteria that can make people ill. These foods include raw milk, unpasteurized dairy products, unpasteurized juices (such as fresh apple cider), raw meat, and raw cookie dough.
3. In cases of suspected food spoilage, food should never simply be tasted, smelled, or eye-balled in order to determine its safety. It is true that in some cases, the presence of mold or other growths may indicate that a food has reached its expiration date and should not be consumed. However, some foods may look and smell fine, but if they have been stored at room temperature for over 2 hours, microscopic bacteria may have been allowed to grow. The safe temperature for foods in refrigerators is between 2°C (35°F) and 7°C (45°F), and freezers should be kept at -18°C (0°F) or below.
4. It is not safe to let meats thaw on the counter all day, because this allows any germs present on the food to thrive. Safer alternatives to this practice include thawing the food under running water (21°C (70°F) or below) for less than 2 hours, placing the food in the refrigerator to thaw, or thawing the food in the microwave as part of the cooking process.

5. It is also important to make sure that raw meats are cooked to the appropriate internal temperature before they are consumed. Safe internal temperatures for various meats include 74°C (165°F) for poultry, 68°C (155°F) for ground meat, and 63°C (145°F) for fish and pork. It is not sufficient to judge the doneness of meat by its internal colour. According to a study performed by the USDA, "25 per cent of hamburgers with a brown internal colour were not cooked to the proper temperature." Instead of simply eyeballing the meat, it is essential to use a meat thermometer to judge the safety of consuming the food.
6. The cooking process is often the time that foodborne pathogens are allowed to enter the food we eat because of the prevalence of cross contamination. Cross contamination occurs when a person handling raw meats, eggs, fish, or other foods containing harmful pathogens touches cooking utensils, cutting boards, or cooking surfaces and spreads the pathogens to ready-to-eat foods in the process. This mode of transmission can be interrupted by washing hands after handling raw foods, washing utensils and cutting boards that have come in contact with raw foods, and disinfecting counter surfaces frequently.
7. Leftovers are ideally stored in the refrigerator in shallow containers (2 inches tall or less) so that the cooling process can be accelerated and the buildup of harmful bacteria can be prevented. Storing foods in larger containers may keep foods warm and allow harmful bacteria to grow.

14

Plant Breeding

Plant breeding is the art and science of changing the genetics of plants in order to produce desired characteristics. Plant breeding can be accomplished through many different techniques ranging from simply selecting plants with desirable characteristics for propagation, to more complex molecular techniques.

Plant breeding has been practiced for thousands of years, since near the beginning of human civilization. It is now practiced worldwide by individuals such as gardeners and farmers, or by professional plant breeders employed by organisations such as government institutions, universities, crop-specific industry associations or research centers.

International development agencies believe that breeding new crops is important for ensuring food security by developing new varieties that are higher-yielding, resistant to pests and diseases, drought-resistant or regionally adapted to different environments and growing conditions.

Plant breeding in certain situations may lead to the domestication of wild plants. Domestication of plants is an artificial selection process conducted by humans to produce plants that have more desirable traits than wild plants, and which renders them dependent on artificial (usually enhanced) environments for their continued existence. The practice is estimated to date back 9,000-11,000 years. Many crops in present day cultivation are the result of domestication in ancient times, about 5,000 years ago in the Old World and 3,000 years ago in the New World. In the Neolithic period, domestication took a minimum of 1,000 years and a maximum of 7,000 years. Today, all of our principal food crops come from domesticated varieties. Almost all the domesticated plants used today for food and agriculture were domesticated in the centers of origin. In these centers there is still a great diversity of closely related wild plants, so-called crop wild relatives, that can also be used for improving modern cultivars by plant breeding.

A plant whose origin or selection is due primarily to intentional human activity is called a cultigen, and a cultivated crop species that has evolved from wild populations due to selective pressures from traditional farmers is called a landrace. Landraces, which can be the result of natural forces or domestication, are plants (or animals) that are ideally suited to a particular region or environment. An example are the landraces of rice, *Oryza sativa* subspecies *indica,* which was developed in South Asia, and *Oryza sativa* subspecies *japonica,* which was developed in China.

Classical plant breeding uses deliberate interbreeding (crossing) of closely or distantly related individuals to produce new crop varieties or lines with desirable properties. Plants are crossbred to introduce traits/genes from one variety or line into a new genetic background. For example, a mildew-resistant pea may be crossed with a high-yielding but susceptible pea, the goal of the cross being to introduce mildew resistance without losing the high-yield characteristics. Progeny from the cross would then be crossed with the high-yielding parent to ensure that the progeny were most like the high-yielding parent, (backcrossing). The progeny from that cross would then be tested for yield and mildew resistance and high-yielding resistant plants would be further developed. Plants may also be crossed with themselves to produce inbred varieties for breeding.

Classical breeding relies largely on homologous recombination between chromosomes to generate genetic diversity. The classical plant breeder may also makes use of a number of *in vitro* techniques such as protoplast fusion, embryo rescue or mutagenesis to generate diversity and produce hybrid plants that would not exist in nature.

Traits that breeders have tried to incorporate into crop plants in the last 100 years include:

- Increased quality and yield of the crop.
- Increased tolerance of environmental pressures (salinity, extreme temperature, drought).
- Resistance to viruses, fungi and bacteria.
- Increased tolerance to insect pests.
- Increased tolerance of herbicides.

Intraspecific hybridization within a plant species was demonstrated by Charles Darwin and Gregor Mendel, and was further developed by geneticists and plant breeders. In the United Kingdom in the 1880s, it was the pioneering work of Gartons Agricultural Plant Breeders. In the early 20th century, plant breeders realized that Mendel's findings on the non-random nature of inheritance could be applied to seedling populations produced through deliberate pollinations to predict the frequencies of different types.

From 1904 to World War II in Italy Nazareno Strampelli created a number of wheat hybrids. His work allowed Italy to increase hugely crop production during the so called 'Battle for Grain' (1925-1940) and some varieties was exported in foreign countries, as Argentina, Mexico, China and others. After the war, the work of Strampelli was quickly forgotten, but thanks to the hybrids he created, Norman Borlaug was able to move the very first steps of the Green Revolution.

In 1908, George Harrison Shull described heterosis, also known as hybrid vigour. Heterosis describes the tendency of the progeny of a specific cross to outperform both parents. The detection of the usefulness of heterosis for plant breeding has led to the development of inbred lines that reveal a heterotic yield advantage when they are crossed. Maize was the first species where heterosis was widely used to produce hybrids.

By the 1920s, statistical methods were developed to analyze gene action and distinguish heritable variation from variation caused by environment. In 1933, another important breeding technique, cytoplasmic male sterility (CMS), developed in maize, was described by Marcus Morton Rhoades. CMS is a maternally inherited trait that makes the plant produce sterile pollen. This enables the production of hybrids without the need for labour intensive detasseling.

These early breeding techniques resulted in large yield increase in the United States in the early 20th century. Similar yield increases were not produced elsewhere until after World War II, the Green Revolution increased crop production in the developing world in the 1960s.

After World War II

Following World War II a number of techniques were developed that allowed plant breeders to hybridize distantly related species, and artificially induce genetic diversity.

When distantly related species are crossed, plant breeders make use of a number of plant tissue culture techniques to produce progeny from otherwise fruitless mating. Interspecific and intergeneric hybrids are produced from a cross of related species or genera that do not normally sexually reproduce with each other. These crosses are referred to as *Wide crosses*. For example, the cereal triticale is a wheat and rye hybrid. The cells in the plants derived from the first generation created from the cross contained an uneven number of chromosomes and as result was sterile. The cell division inhibitor colchicine was used to double the number of chromosomes in the cell and thus allow the production of a fertile line.

Failure to produce a hybrid may be due to pre- or post-fertilization incompatibility. If fertilization is possible between two species or genera, the hybrid embryo may abort before maturation. If this does occur the embryo resulting from an interspecific or intergeneric cross can sometimes be rescued and cultured to produce a whole plant. Such a method is referred to as Embryo Rescue. This technique has been used to produce new rice for Africa, an interspecific cross of Asian rice *(Oryza sativa)* and African rice *(Oryza glaberrima)*.

Hybrids may also be produced by a technique called protoplast fusion. In this case protoplasts are fused, usually in an electric field. Viable recombinants can be regenerated in culture.

Chemical mutagens like EMS and DMS, radiation and transposons are used to generate mutants with desirable traits to be bred with other cultivars - a process known as *Mutation Breeding*. Classical plant breeders also generate genetic diversity within a species by exploiting a process called somaclonal variation, which occurs in plants produced from tissue culture, particularly plants derived from callus. Induced polyploidy, and the addition or removal of chromosomes using a technique called chromosome engineering may also be used.

When a desirable trait has been bred into a species, a number of crosses to the favored parent are made to make the new plant as similar to the favored parent as possible. Returning to the example of the mildew resistant pea being crossed with a high-yielding but susceptible pea, to make the mildew resistant progeny of the cross most like the high-yielding parent, the progeny will be crossed back to that parent for several generations (See backcrossing). This process removes most of the genetic contribution of the mildew resistant parent. Classical breeding is therefore a cyclical process.

With classical breeding techniques, the breeder does not know exactly what genes have been introduced to the new cultivars. Some scientists therefore argue that plants produced by classical breeding methods should undergo the same safety testing regime as genetically modified plants. There have been instances where plants bred using classical techniques have been unsuitable for human consumption, for example the poison solanine was unintentionally increased to unacceptable levels in certain varieties of potato through plant breeding. New potato varieties are often screened for solanine levels before reaching the marketplace.

Modern plant breeding may use techniques of molecular biology to select, or in the case of genetic modification, to insert, desirable traits into plants.

Modern facilities in molecular biology has converted classical plant breeding to molecular plant breeding.

Steps of Plant Breeding

The following are the major activities of plant breeding:

- Creation of variation
- Selection
- Evaluation
- Release
- Multiplication
- Distribution of the new variety.

Marker Assisted Selection

Sometimes many different genes can influence a desirable trait in plant breeding. The use of tools such as molecular markers or DNA fingerprinting can map thousands of genes. This allows plant breeders to screen large populations of plants for those that possess the trait of interest. The screening is based on the presence or absence of a certain gene as determined by laboratory procedures, rather than on the visual identification of the expressed trait in the plant.

Reverse Breeding and Doubled Haploids (DH)

A method for efficiently producing homozygous plants from a heterozygous starting plant, which has all desirable traits. This starting plant is induced to produce doubled haploid from haploid cells, and later on creating homozygous/doubled haploid plants from those cells. While in natural offspring genetic recombination occurs and traits can be unlinked from each other, in doubled haploid cells and in the resulting DH plants recombination is no longer an issue. There, a recombination between two corresponding chromosomes does not lead to un-linkage of alleles or traits, since it just leads to recombination with its identical copy. Thus, traits on one chromosome stay linked. Selecting those offspring having the desired set of chromosomes and crossing them will result in a final F1 hybrid plant, having exactly the same set of chromosomes, genes and traits as the starting hybrid plant. The homozygous parental lines can reconstitute the original heterozygous plant by crossing, if desired even in a large quantity. An individual heterozygous plant can be converted into a heterozygous variety (F1 hybrid) without the necessity of vegetative propagation but as the result of the cross of two homozygous/doubled haploid lines derived from the originally selected plant.

Genetic Modification

Genetic modification of plants is achieved by adding a specific gene or genes to a plant, or by knocking down a gene with RNAi, to produce a desirable phenotype. The plants resulting from adding a gene are often referred to as transgenic plants. If for genetic modification genes of the species or of a crossable plant are used under control of their native promoter, then they are called cisgenic plants. Genetic modification can produce a plant with the desired trait or traits faster than classical breeding because the majority of the plant's genome is not altered.

To genetically modify a plant, a genetic construct must be designed so that the gene to be added or removed will be expressed by the plant. To do this, a promoter to drive transcription and a termination sequence to stop transcription of the new gene, and the gene or genes of interest must be introduced to the plant. A marker for the selection of transformed plants is also included. In the laboratory, antibiotic resistance is a commonly used marker: Plants that have been successfully transformed will grow on media containing antibiotics; plants that have not been transformed will die. In some instances markers for selection are removed by backcrossing with the parent plant prior to commercial release.

The construct can be inserted in the plant genome by genetic recombination using the bacteria *Agrobacterium tumefaciens* or *A. rhizogenes*, or by direct methods like the gene gun or microinjection. Using plant viruses to insert genetic constructs into plants is also a possibility, but the technique is limited by the host range of the virus. For example, Cauliflower mosaic virus (CaMV) only infects cauliflower and related species. Another limitation of viral vectors is that the virus is not usually passed on the progeny, so every plant has to be inoculated.

The majority of commercially released transgenic plants are currently limited to plants that have introduced resistance to insect pests and herbicides. Insect resistance is achieved through incorporation of a gene from *Bacillus thuringiensis* (Bt) that encodes a protein that is toxic to some insects. For example, the cotton bollworm, a common cotton pest, feeds on Bt cotton it will ingest the toxin and die. Herbicides usually work by binding to certain plant enzymes and inhibiting their action. The enzymes that the herbicide inhibits are known as the herbicides *target site*. Herbicide resistance can be engineered into crops by expressing a version of *target site* protein that is not inhibited by the herbicide. This is the method used to produce glyphosate resistant crop plants.

Genetic modification of plants that can produce pharmaceuticals (and industrial chemicals), sometimes called *pharmacrops*, is a rather radical new area of plant breeding.

Issues and Concerns

Modern plant breeding, whether classical or through genetic engineering, comes with issues of concern, particularly with regard to food crops. The question of whether breeding can have a negative effect on nutritional value is central in this respect. Although relatively little direct research in this area has been done, there are scientific indications that, by favoring certain aspects of a plant's development, other aspects may be retarded. A study published in the *Journal of the American College of Nutrition* in 2004, entitled *Changes in USDA Food Composition Data for 43 Garden Crops, 1950 to 1999,* compared nutritional analysis of vegetables done in 1950 and in 1999, and found substantial decreases in six of 13 nutrients measured, including 6 per cent of protein and 38 per cent of riboflavin. Reductions in calcium, phosphorus, iron and ascorbic acid were also found. The study, conducted at the Biochemical Institute, University of Texas at Austin, concluded in summary:

> "We suggest that any real declines are generally most easily explained by changes in cultivated varieties between 1950 and 1999, in which there may be trade-offs between yield and nutrient content".

The debate surrounding genetically modified food during the 1990s peaked in 1999 in terms of media coverage and risk perception, and continues today - for example, "*Germany has thrown its weight behind a growing European mutiny over genetically modified crops by banning the planting of a widely grown pest-resistant corn variety*". The debate encompasses the ecological impact of genetically modified plants, the safety of genetically modified food and concepts used for safety evaluation like substantial equivalence. Such concerns are not new to plant breeding. Most countries have regulatory processes in place to help ensure that new crop varieties entering the marketplace are both safe and meet farmers' needs. Examples include variety registration, seed schemes, regulatory authorizations for GM plants, etc.

Plant breeders' rights is also a major and controversial issue. Today, production of new varieties is dominated by commercial plant breeders, who seek to protect their work and collect royalties through national and international agreements based in intellectual property rights. The range of related issues is complex. In the simplest terms, critics of the increasingly restrictive regulations argue that, through a combination of technical and economic pressures, commercial breeders are reducing biodiversity and significantly constraining individuals (such as farmers) from developing and trading seed on a regional level . Efforts to strengthen breeders' rights, for example, by lengthening periods of variety protection are ongoing.

When new plant breeds or cultivars are bred, they must be maintained and propagated. Some plants are propagated by asexual means while others are propagated by seeds. Seed propagated cultivars require specific control over seed source and production procedures to maintain the integrity of the plant breeds results. Isolation is necessary to prevent cross contamination with related plants or the mixing of seeds after harvesting. Isolation is normally accomplished by planting distance but in certain crops, plants are enclosed in greenhouses or cages (most commonly used when producing F1 hybrids.)

The development of agricultural science, with phenomenon like the Green Revolution arising, have left millions of farmers in developing countries, most of whom operate small farms under unstable and difficult growing conditions, in a precarious situation. The adoption of new plant varieties by this group has been hampered by the constraints of poverty and the international policies promoting an industrialized model of agriculture. Their response has been the creation of a novel and promising set of research methods collectively known as participatory plant breeding. Participatory means that farmers are more involved in the breeding process and breeding goals are defined by farmers instead of international seed companies with their large-scale breeding programmes. Farmers' groups and NGOs, for example, may wish to affirm local people's rights over genetic resources, produce seeds themselves, build farmers' technical expertise, or develop new products for niche markets, like organically grown food.

Genetically Modified Plant

Genetically modified plants are plants whose DNA is modified using genetic engineering techniques. In most cases the aim is to introduce a new trait to the plant which does not occur naturally in this species. Examples include resistance to certain pests, diseases or environmental conditions, or the production of a certain nutrient or pharmaceutical agent.

Some degree of natural flow of genes, often called horizontal gene transfer or lateral gene transfer, occurs between plant species. This is facilitated by transposons, retrotransposons, proviruses and other mobile genetic elements that naturally translocate to new sites in a genome. They often move to new species over an evolutionary time scale and play a major role in dynamic changes to chromosomes during evolution.

The introduction of foreign germplasm into common foods has been achieved by traditional crop breeders by artificially overcoming fertility barriers. A hybrid cereal was created in 1875, by crossing wheat and rye. Since then important traits have been introduced into wheat, including dwarfing genes and rust resistance. Plant tissue culture and the induction of mutations have also enabled humans to artificially alter the makeup of plant genomes.

The first field trials of genetically engineered plants occurred in France and the USA in 1986, when tobacco plants were engineered to be resistant to herbicides. In 1987, Plant Genetic Systems (Ghent, Belgium), founded by Marc Van Montagu and Jeff Schell, was the first company to develop genetically engineered (tobacco) plants with insect tolerance by expressing genes encoding for insecticidal proteins from *Bacillus thuringiensis* (Bt). The People's Republic of China was the first country to allow commercialized transgenic plants, introducing a virus-resistant tobacco in 1992. The first genetically modified crop approved for sale in the U.S., in 1994, was the *FlavrSavr* tomato, which had a longer shelf life. In 1994, the European Union approved tobacco engineered to be resistant to the herbicide bromoxynil, making it the first commercially genetically engineered crop marketed in Europe. In 1995, Bt Potato was approved safe by the Environmental Protection Agency, making it the first pesticide producing crop to be approved in the USA. In 2009, 11 different transgenic crops were grown commercially on 330 million acres (134 million hectares) in 25 countries such as the USA, Brazil, Argentina, India, Canada, China, Paraguay and South Africa.

The U.S. has adopted the technology most widely whereas Europe has very little genetically engineered crops with the exception of Spain where one fifth of maize grown is genetically engineered, and smaller amounts in five other countries. The EU had a formal ban on the approval of new GM crops, until it was overturned in 2006; in a controversial move. GM crops are now *regulated* by the EU.

Genetically engineered plants are generated in a laboratory by altering the genetic makeup, usually by adding one or more genes, of a plant's genome using genetic engineering techniques. Most genetically modified plants are generated by the biolistic method (particle gun) or by *Agrobacterium tumefaciens* mediated transformation.

In the biolistic method, DNA is bound to tiny particles of gold or tungsten which are subsequently 'shot' into plant tissue or single plant cells under high pressure. The accelerated particles penetrate both the cell wall and membranes. The DNA separates from the metal and is integrated into the plant genome inside the nucleus. This method has been applied successfully for many cultivated crops, especially monocots like wheat or maize, for which transformation using *Agrobacterium tumefaciens* has been less successful. The major disadvantage of this procedure is that serious damage can be done to the cellular tissue.

Agrobacteria are natural plant parasites, and their natural ability to transfer genes is used for the development of genetically engineered plants. To create a suitable environment for themselves, these Agrobacteria insert their genes into plant hosts, resulting in a proliferation of plant cells near the soil level (crown gall). The genetic information for tumour growth is encoded on a mobile, circular DNA fragment (plasmid). When Agrobacterium infects a plant, it transfers this T-DNA to a random site in the plant genome. When used in genetic engineering the bacterial T-DNA is removed from the bacterial plasmid and replaced with the desired foreign gene. The bacterium is a vector, enabling transportation of foreign genes into plants. This method works especially well for dicotyledonous plants like potatoes, tomatoes, and tobacco. Agrobacteria infection is less successful in crops like wheat and maize.

Genetically modified plants have been developed commercially to improve shelf life, disease resistance, herbicide resistance and pest resistance. Plants engineered to tolerate non-biological stresses like drought , frost and nitrogen starvation or with increased nutritional value (*e.g.* Golden rice) were in development in 2011. Future generations of GM plants are intended to be suitable for harsh environments, produce increased amounts of nutrients or even pharmaceutical agents, or are improved for the production of bioenergy and biofuels. Due to high regulatory and research costs, the majority of genetically modified crops in agriculture consist of commodity crops, such as soybean, maize, cotton and rapeseed. However, commercial growing was reported in 2009, of smaller amounts of genetically modified sugar beet, papayas, squash (*zucchini*), sweet pepper, tomatoes, petunias, carnations, roses and poplars. Recently, some research and development has been targeted to enhancement of crops that are locally important in developing countries, such as insect-resistant cowpea for Africa and insect-resistant brinjal (eggplant) for India.

In research tobacco and *Arabidopsis thaliana* are the most genetically modified plants, due to well developed transformation methods, easy propagation and well studied genomes. They serve as model organisms for other plant species. Genetically modified plants have also been used for bioremediation of contaminated soils. Mercury, selenium and organic pollutants such as polychlorinated biphenyls (PCBs) have been removed from soils by transgenic plants containing genes for bacterial enzymes.

Transgenic plants have genes inserted into them that are derived from another species. The inserted genes can come from species within the same kingdom (plant to plant) or between kingdoms (bacteria to plant). In many cases the inserted DNA has to be modified slightly in order to correctly and efficiently express in the host organism. Transgenic plants are used to express proteins like the cry toxins from *Bacillus thuringiensis*, herbicide resistant genes and antigens for vaccinations.

Cisgenic plants are made using genes found within the same species or a closely related one, where conventional plant breeding can occur. Some breeders and scientists argue that cisgenic modification is useful for plants that are difficult to crossbreed by conventional means (such as potatoes), and that plants in the cisgenic category should not require the same level of legal regulation as other genetically modified organisms.

In research plants are engineered to help discover the functions of certain genes. One way to do this is to knock out the gene of interest and see what phenotype develops. Another strategy is to attach the gene to a strong promoter and see what happens when it is over expressed. A common technique used to find out where the gene is expressed is to attach it to GUS or a similar reporter gene that allows visualisation of the location.

The first commercialised genetically modified plants (Flavr Savr tomatoes) used RNAi technology, where the inserted DNA matched an endogenous gene already in the plant. When the inserted gene is expressed it can repress the translation of the endogenous protein. Host delivered RNAi systems are being developed, where the plant will express RNA that will interfere with insects, nematodes and other parasites protein synthesis. This may provide a novel way of protecting plants from pests.

In the USA genetically modified organisms are assessed by the US Department of Agriculture (USDA), the Food and Drug Administration (FDA) and the Environmental protection agency (EPA). The USDA evaluate the plants potential to become weeds, the FDA review plants that could enter or alter the food supply and the EPA regulate the genetically modified plants with pesticide properties. Most developed genetically modified plants are reviewed by at least two of the agencies, with many subject to all three. Final approval can still be denied by individual counties within each state. In 2004, Mendocino County, California became the first and only county to impose a ban on the "Propagation, Cultivation, Raising, and Growing of Genetically Modified Organisms", the measure passing with a 57 per cent majority.

Allergic proteins were detected during testing of a transgenic soybean inserted with a gene from the Brazil nut. The inserted gene did not translate into a known allergen, the allergenic nature of the protein was discovered when tested with serum from people allergic to Brazil nut. Three federal district court suits have been brought against Animal and Plant Health Inspection Service, the agency within USDA that regulates genetically modifies plant. Two involved field trials (herbicide-tolerant turfgrass in Oregon; pharmaceutical-producing corn and sugar in Hawaii) and one the deregulation of GM alfalfa. APHIS lost all three cases, with the judges ruling they failed to diligently follow the guidelines set out in the National Environmental Policy Act.

The European Union (EU) has possibly the most stringent regulations for genetically modified plants in the world. All genetically modified plants are considered "new food" and subject to extensive, case-by-case, science based food evaluation by the European Food Safety Authority (EFSA). The European Commission (EC) then draft a proposal that is submitted to the Section on GM Food and Feed of the Standing Committee on the Food Chain and Animal Health, where if accepted it will be adopted by the EC or passed on to the Council of Agricultural Ministers. There is also a safeguard clause that any Member State can invoke to restrict or prohibit the use or sale of a GM plant within their territory if they have a justifiable reasons to consider that the approved GM plant constitutes a risk to human health or the environment.

Currently (2010) the only genetically modified plants approved for cultivation in Europe are MON810, a Bt expressing maize conferring resistance to the European corn borerand a potato called Amflora, approved only for industrial applications. The EC has issued guidelines to allow the co-existence of GM and non-GM crops through buffer zones (where no GM crops are grown). These are regulated by individual countries and vary from 15 meters in Sweden to 800 meters in Luxembourg. All food (including processed food) or feed which contains greater than 0.9 per cent of approved GMOs must be labelled.

Regulation in Australia are provided by the Office of the Gene Technology Regulator and Food Standards Australia New Zealand. Each state in Australia individually assess the impact of release on markets and trade and can apply further legislation if they deem it necessary. Genetically modified plants are currently grown in all states except South Australia and Tasmania, who have extended their moratoriums. Health Canada and the Canadian Food Inspection Agency are responsible for evaluating the safety and nutritional value of genetically modified plants in Canada.

The Argentine government was one of the first to accept genetically modified plants, with assessment provided by the National Agricultural Biotechnology Advisory Committee (for environmental impact), the National Service of Health and Agrifood Quality (for food safety) and the National Agribusiness Direction (for theeffect on trade) The final decision is made by the Secretariat of Agriculture, Livestock, Fishery and Food. In Brazil the 27 member National Biosafety Technical Commission is responsible for assessing environmental impact, food safety and provides guidelines for transport, importation and field experiments. In 2005, the Mexican senate passed a law allowing planting and selling of genetically modified crops.

Genetically modified crops in China go through three phases of field trials (pilot field testing, environmental release testing, and preproduction testing) before they are submitted to the Office of Agricultural Genetic Engineering Biosafety Administration (OAGEBA) for assessment. The 75 member National Biosafety Committee evaluates all applications, although OAGEBA has the final decision. The cost of regulation enforcement in India is generally higher than China, while the enforcement of regulations has proved more effective in China. The National Assembly of Burkina Faso passed a biosafety law in early 2006, which established a National Biosafety Agency that would regulate GM products with the advise of various governmental and non-governmental advisory committees.

Genetically modified plants can spread the trans gene to other plants or – theoretically – even to bacteria. Depending on the transgene, this may pose a threat to the environment by changing the composition of the local ecosystem. Therefore, in most countries environmental studies are required prior to the approval of a GM plant for commercial purposes, and a monitoring plan must be presented to identify potential effects which have not been anticipated prior to the approval.

Little research has been conducted on human and animal health. However, in most countries every GM plant is tested in feeding trials to prove its safety, before it is approved for use and marketing. The project GMO-Safety collects and presents biosafety research on GMOs with more in-depth information on this topic.

The potential impact on nearby ecosystems is one of the greatest concerns associated with transgenic plants.

Transgenes have the potential for significant ecological impact if the plants can increase in frequency and persist in natural populations. These concerns are similar to those surrounding conventionally bred plant breeds. Several risk factors should be considered:

- Can the transgenic plant pass its genes to a local wild species, and are the offspring also fertile?
- Does the introduction of the transgene confer a selective advantage to the plant or to hybrids in the wild?

Many domesticated plants can mate and hybridise with wild relatives when they are grown in proximity, and whatever genes the cultivated plant had can then be passed to the hybrid. This applies equally to transgenic plants and conventionally bred plants, as in either case there are advantageous genes that may have negative consequences to an ecosystem upon release. This is normally not a significant concern, despite fears over 'mutant superweeds' overgrowing local wildlife: although hybrid plants are far from uncommon, in most cases these hybrids are not fertile due to polyploidy, and will not multiply or persist long after the original domestic plant is removed from the environment. However, this does not negate the possibility of a negative impact.

In some cases, the pollen from a domestic plant may travel many miles on the wind before fertilising another plant. This can make it difficult to assess the potential harm of crossbreeding; many of the relevant hybrids are far away from the test site. Among the solutions under study for this concern are systems designed to prevent transfer of transgenes, such as Terminator Technology, and the genetic transformation of the chloroplast only, so that only the seed of the transgenic plant would bear the transgene. With regard to the former, there is some controversy that the technologies may be inequitable and might force dependence upon producers for valid seed in the case of poor farmers, whereas the latter has no such concern but has technical constraints that still need to be overcome. Solutions are being developed by EU funded research programmes such as Co-Extra and Transcontainer.

There are at least three possible avenues of hybridization leading to escape of a transgene:

1. Hybridization with non-transgenic crop plants of the same species and variety.
2. Hybridization with wild plants of the same species.
3. Hybridization with wild plants of closely related species, usually of the same genus.

However, there are a number of factors which must be present for hybrids to be created.

The transgenic plants must be close enough to the wild species for the pollen to reach the wild plants.

- The wild and transgenic plants must flower at the same time.
- The wild and transgenic plants must be genetically compatible.

In order to persist, these hybrid offspring:

- Must be viable, and fertile.
- Must carry the transgene.

Studies suggest that a possible escape route for transgenic plants will be through hybridization with wild plants of related species.

It is known that some crop plants have been found to hybridize with wild counterparts.

It is understood, as a basic part of population genetics, that the spread of a transgene in a wild population will be directly related to the fitness effects of the gene in addition to the rate of influx of the gene to the population. Advantageous genes will spread rapidly, neutral genes will spread with genetic drift, and disadvantageous genes will only spread if there is a constant influx.

The ecological effects of transgenes are not known, but it is generally accepted that only genes which improve fitness in relation to abiotic factors would give hybrid plants sufficient advantages to become weedy or invasive. Abiotic factors are parts of the ecosystem which are not alive, such as climate, salt and mineral content, and temperature. Genes improving fitness in relation to biotic factors could disturb the (sometimes fragile) balance of an ecosystem. For instance, a wild plant receiving a pest resistance gene from a transgenic plant might become resistant to one of its natural pests, say, a beetle. This could allow the plant to increase in frequency, while at the same time animals higher up in the food chain, which are at least partly dependent on that beetle as food source, might decrease in abundance. However, the exact consequences of a transgene with a selective advantage in the natural environment are almost impossible to predict reliably.

It is also important to refer to the demanding actions that government of developing countries had been building up among the last decades.

Agricultural Impact of Transgenic Plants

Outcrossing of transgenic plants not only poses potential environmental risks, it may also trouble farmers and food producers. Many countries have different legislations for transgenic and conventional plants as well as the derived food and feed and consumers demand the freedom of choice to buy GM-derived or conventional products . Therefore, farmers and producers must separate both production chains This requires coexistence measures on the field level as well as traceability measures throughout the whole food and feed processing chain . Research projects such as Co-Extra, SIGMEA and Transcontainer investigate how farmers can avoid outcrossing and mixing of transgenic and non-transgenic crops, and how processors can ensure and verify the separation of both production chains.

Coexistence and Traceability

In many countries, and especially in the European Union, consumers demand the choice between foods derived from GM plants and conventionally or organically produced plants. This requires a labelling system as well as the reliable separation of GM and non-GM crops at field level and throughout the whole production chain.

Research has demonstrated, that coexistence can be realised by several agricultural measures, such as isolation distances or biological containment strategies.

For traceability, the OECD has introduced a 'unique identifier' which is given to any GMO when it is approved. This unique identifier must be forwarded at every stage of processing.

Many countries have established labelling regulations and guidelines on coexistence and traceability. Research projects like Co-Extra, SIGMEA and Transcontainer are aimed at investigating improved methods for ensuring coexistence and providing stakeholders the tools required for the implementation of coexistence and traceability.

15

Environmental Impact of Agriculture

The environmental impact of agriculture varies based on the wide variety of agricultural practices employed around the world.

Climate change and agriculture are interrelated processes, both of which take place on a global scale. Global warming is projected to have significant impacts on conditions affecting agriculture, including temperature, precipitation and glacial run-off. These conditions determine the carrying capacity of the biosphere to produce enough food for the human population and domesticated animals. Rising carbon dioxide levels would also have effects, both detrimental and beneficial, on crop yields. The overall effect of climate change on agriculture will depend on the balance of these effects. Assessment of the effects of global climate changes on agriculture might help to properly anticipate and adapt farming to maximize agricultural production.

At the same time, agriculture has been shown to produce significant effects on climate change, primarily through the production and release of greenhouse gases such as carbon dioxide, methane, and nitrous oxide, but also by altering the Earth's land cover, which can change its ability to absorb or reflect heat and light, thus contributing to radiative forcing. Land use change such as deforestation and desertification, together with use of fossil fuels, are the major anthropogenic sources of carbon dioxide; agriculture itself is the major contributor to increasing methane and nitrous oxide concentrations in earth's atmosphere.

Intensive Farming

Intensive farming alters the environment in many ways. Some of the disadvantages of this method of farming include:

- Limits or destroys the natural habitat of most wildlife, and leads to soil erosion
- Use of fertilizers can alter the biology of rivers and lakes.
- Pesticides generally kill useful insects as well as those that destroy crops
- Generally not sustainable - often results in desertification or, in a worst case scenario, land that is so poisonous and eroded that nothing else will grow
- Requires large amounts of energy input to produce, transport, and apply chemical fertilizers/pesticides
- Use of chemicals on fields creates run-off, excess runs off into rivers and lakes causing pollution
- Use of pesticides have numerous negative health effects in workers who apply them, people that live nearby the area of application or downstream/downwind from it, and consumers who eat the pesticides which remain on their food

Irrigation

Irrigation can lead to a number of problems:

- Depletion of underground aquifers through overdrafting.
- Ground subsidence.
- Groundwater recharge - an ecological restoration, mitigation, and remediation technique.
- Underirrigation gives poor soil salinity control which leads to increased soil salinity with consequent build up of toxic salts on soil surface in areas with high evaporation. This requires either leaching to remove these salts and a method of drainage to carry the salts away.

- Overirrigation because of poor distribution uniformity or management wastes water, chemicals, and may lead to water pollution.
- Deep drainage (from over-irrigation) may result in rising water tables which in some instances will lead to problems of irrigation salinity requiring watertable control by some form of subsurface land drainage.
- Irrigation with aline or high-sodium water may damage soil structure owing to the formation of alkaline soil.
- Runoff causing surface water and groundwater-aquifer hydrologic cycle water pollution.
- Bioretention - an ecological restoration, mitigation, and remediation technique.

A wide range of agricultural chemicals are used and some become pollutants through use, misuse, or ignorance.

- Pesticide drift
- Soil contamination
- Groundwater and water pollution
- Air pollution *spray drift*
- Pesticides, especially those based on organochloride
- Pesticide residue in foods
- Pesticide toxicity to bees

List of crop plants pollinated by bees:

- Pollination management
- Bioremediation

Soil Degradation

- Soil contamination
- Erosion
- Sedimentation

Waste

Plasticulture, the use of plastic materials in agriculture, raises problems around how to carry out the recycling of agricultural plastics.

Issues by Region

- Hedgerow removal in the United Kingdom.

- Soil salinisation, especially in Australia.
- Phosphate mining in Nauru
- Methane emissions from livestock in New Zealand
- Some environmentalists attribute the hypoxic zone in the Gulf of Mexico as being encouraged by nitrogen fertilization of the algae bloom.

Sustainable Agriculture

The exponential population increase in recent decades has increased the practice of agricultural land conversion to meet demand for food which in turn has increased the effects on the environment. The global population is still increasing and will eventually stabilise, as some critics doubt that food production, due to lower yields from global warming, can support the global population.

Organic farming is a multifaceted sustainable agriculture set of practices that can have a lower impact on the environment.

Other specific methods include: permaculture; and biodynamic agriculture which incorporating a spiritual element.

Environmental Impact of Irrigation

Environmental impacts of irrigation are the changes in quantity and quality of soil and water as a result of irrigation and the ensuing effects on natural and social conditions at the tail-end and downstream of the irrigation scheme. The impacts stem from the changed hydrological conditions owing to the installation and operation of the scheme. An irrigation scheme often draws water from the river and distributes it over the irrigated area. As a hydrological result it is found that:

- the downstream river discharge is reduced
- the evaporation in the scheme is increased
- the groundwater recharge in the scheme is increased
- the level of the water table rises
- the drainage flow is increased

These may be called direct effects. The effects thereof on soil and water quality are indirect and complex, Water logging and soil salination are part of these, whereas the subsequent impacts on natural, ecological and socio-enonomic conditions is very intricate.

Irrigation can also be done extracting groundwater by (tube)wells. As a hydrological result it is found that the level of the water descends. The effects may be water mining, land/ soil subsidence, and, along the coast, saltwater intrusion.

Irrigation projects can have large benefits, but the negative side effects are often overlooked.

The reduced downstream river discharge may cause:

- reduced downstream flooding;
- disappearance of ecologically and economically important wetlands or flood forests reduced availability of industrial, municipal, household, and drinking water; and
- reduced shipping routes.

Water withdrawal poses a serious threat to the Ganges. In India, barrages control all of the tributaries to the Ganges and divert roughly 60 per cent of river flow to irrigation reduced fishing opportunities. The Indus River in Pakistan faces scarcity due to over-extraction of water for agriculture. The Indus is inhabited by 25 amphibian species and 147 fish species of which 22 are found nowhere else in the world. It harbors the endangered Indus River dolphin, one of the world's rarest mammals. Fish populations, the main source of protein and overall life support systems for many communities, are also being threatened reduced discharge into the sea, which may have various consequences like coastal erosion (e.g. in Ghana) and salt water intrusion in delta's and estuaries . Current water withdrawal from the river Nile for irrigation is so high that, despite its size, in dry periods the river does not reach the sea. The Aral sea has suffered an 'environmental catastrophe' due to the interception of river water for irrigation purposes.

The increased groundwater recharge stems from the unavoidable deep percolation losses occurring in the irrigation scheme. The lower the irrigation efficiency, the higher the losses. Although fairly high irrigation efficiencies of 70 per cent or more (i.e. losses of 30% or less) can be obtained with sophisticated techniques like sprinkler irrigation and drip irrigation, or by precision land levelling for surface irrigation, in practice the losses are commonly in the order of 40 to 60 per cent. This may cause: rising water tables, increased storage of groundwater that may be used for irrigation, municipal, household and drinking water by pumping from wells, waterlogging and drainage problems in villages, agricultural lands, and along roads with mostly negative consequences. The increased level of the water table can lead to reduced agricultural production. Shallow water tables are a sign that the aquifer is unable to cope with the groundwater recharge stemming from the deep percolation losses, where water tables are shallow, the irrigation applications are reduced. As a result, the soil is no longer leached and soil salinity problems develop, stagnant water tables at the soil surface are known to increase the incidence of water borne diseases like malaria, filariasis, yellow fever, dengue, and schistosomiasis (Bilharzia) in many areas. Health costs, appraisals of health impacts and mitigation measures are rarely part of irrigation projects, if at all. To mitigate the adverse effects of shallow water tables and soil salinization, some form of watertable control, soil salinity control, drainage and drainage system is needed.

As drainage water moves through the soil profile it may dissolve nutrients (either fertilizer based or naturally occurring) such as nitrates, leading to a built up of those nutrients in the ground water aquifer. High nitrate levels in drinking water can be harmful to humans particularly for infants under 6 months where it is linked to 'blue-baby syndrome'.

Case Studies

In India 2,189,400 ha have been reported to suffer from waterlogging in irrigation canal commands. Also 3,469,100 ha were reported to be seriously salt affected here.

In the Indus Plains in Pakistan, more than 2 million hectares of land is waterlogged. The soil of 13.6 million hectares within the Gross Command Area was surveyed, which revealed that 3.1 million hectares (23%) was saline. 23 per cent of this was in Sindh and 13 per cent in the Punjab. More than 3 million ha of water-logged lands have been provided with tube-wells and drains at the cost of billions of rupees, but the reclamation objectives were only partially achieved. The Asian Development Bank (ADB) states that 38 per cent of the irrigated area is now waterlogged and 14 per cent of the surface is too saline for use.

In the Nile delta of Egypt, drainage is being installed in millions of hectares to combat the water-logging resulting from the introduction of massive perennial irrigation after completion of the High Dam at Assuan.

In Mexico, 15 per cent of the 3,000,000 ha if irrigable land is salinized and 10 per cent is waterlogged.

In Peru some 300,000 ha of the 1,050,000 ha of irrigable land suffers from this problem.

Estimates indicate that roughly one-third of the irrigated land in the major irrigation countries is already badly affected by salinity or is expected to become so in the near future. Present estimates for Israel are 13 per cent of the irrigated land,, Australia 20 per cent, China 15 per cent, Irak 50 per cent, Egypt 30 per cent. Irrigation-induced salinity occurs in large and small irrigation systems alike.

FAO has estimated that by 1990 about 52×10^6 ha of irrigated land will need to have improved drainage systems installed, much of it subsurface drainage to control salinity.

Reduced Downstream Drainage and Groundwater Quality

The downstream drainage water quality may deteriorate owing to leaching of salts, nutrients, herbicides and pesticides. This may negatively affect the health of the population at the tail-end and downstream of the irrigation scheme, as well as the ecological balance. The Aral sea, for example, is seriously polluted by drainage water.

The downstream quality of the groundwater may deteriorate in a similar way as the downstream drainage water and have similar consequences.

Reduced Downstream River Water Quality

Owing to drainage of surface and groundwater in the project area, which waters may be salinized and polluted by agricultural chemicals like biocides and fertilizers, the quality of the river water below the project area can deteriorate, which makes it less fit for industrial, municipal and household use. It may lead to reduced public health. Polluted river water entering the sea may adversely affect the ecology along the sea shore.

Affected Downstream Water Users

Water becomes scarce for nomadic pastoralist in Baluchistan due to new irrigation developments.

Downstream water users often have no legal water rights and may fall victim of the development of irrigation.

Pastoralists and nomadic tribes may find their land and water resources blocked by new irrigation developments without having a legal recourse.

Flood-recession cropping may be seriously affected by the upstream interception of river water for irrigation purposes.

In Baluchistan, Pakistan, the development of new small-scale irrigation projects depleted the water resources of nomadic tribes traveling annually between Baluchistan and Gujarat or Rajastan (India).

After the closure of the Kainji dam, Nigeria, 50 to 70 per cent of the downstream area of flood-recession cropping was lost.

Lake Manantali, 477 km^2, displaced 12,000 people.

Lost Land Use Opportunities

Irrigation projects may reduce the fishing opportunities of the original population and the grazing opportunities for cattle. The livestock pressure on the remaining lands may increase considerably, because the ousted traditional pastoralist tribes will have to find their subsistence and existence elsewhere, overgrazing may increase, followed by serious soil erosion and the loss of natural resources.

The Manatali reservoir formed by the Manantali dam in Mali intersects the migration routes of nomadic pastoralists and destroyed 43000 ha of savannah, probably leading to overgrazing and erosion elsewhere. Further, the reservoir destroyed 120 km^2 of forest. The depletion of groundwater aquifers, which is caused by the suppression of the seasonal flood cycle, is damaging the forests downstream of the dam.

When more groundwater is pumped from wells than replenished, storage of water in the aquifer is being mined. Irrigation from groundwater is no longer sustainable then. The result can be abandoning of irrigated agriculture.

The hundreds of tubewells installed in the state of Uttar Pradesh, India, with World Bank funding have operating periods of 1.4 to 4.7 hours/day, whereas the were designed to operate 16 hours/day .In Baluchistan, Pakistan, the development of tubewell irrigation projects was at the expense of the traditional qanat or karez users.

Groundwater-related subsidence of the land due to mining of groundwater occurred in the USA at a rate of 1m for each 13m that the watertable was lowered Homes at Greens Bayou near Houston, Texas, where 5 to 7 feet of subsidence has occurred, were flooded during a storm in June 1989 as shown in the picture.

16

List of Rice Diseases

Bacterial Diseases

Bacterial blight
[Xanthomonas oryzae pv. *oryzae* = *X. campestris* pv. *oryzae]*

Bacterial leaf streak
[Xanthomonas oryzae pv. *oryzicola]*

- Foot rot
  [Erwinia chrysanthemi]
- Grain rot
  [Burkholderia glumae]
  Pecky rice (kernel spotting)
  [Damage by bacteria underfungal and miscellaneous diseases]
- Sheath brown rot
  [Pseudomonas fuscovaginae]

Fungal Diseases

- Aggregate sheath spot
  Ceratobasidium oryzae-sativae
  Rhizoctonia oryzae-sativae [anamorph]
- Black kernel
  Curvularia lunata
  Cochliobolus lunatus [teleomorph]

- Blast (leaf, neck [rotten neck], nodal and collar)
  Pyricularia grisea = Pyricularia oryzae Magnaporthe grisea [teleomorph]
- Brown spot
  Cochliobolus miyabeanus Bipolaris oryzae [anamorph]
- Crown sheath rot
  [Gaeumannomyces graminis]
- Downy mildew
  [Sclerophthora macrospora]
- Eyespot
  [Drechslera gigantea]
- False smut
  [Ustilaginoidea virens]
- Kernel smut
  Tilletia barclayana = Neovossia horrida
- Leaf smut
  [Entyloma oryzae]
- Leaf scald
  [Microdochium oryzae = Rhynchosporium oryzae]
- Narrow brown leaf spot
  [Cercospora janseana = Cercospora oryzae Sphaerulina oryzina [teleomorph]
- Pecky rice (kernel spotting)
  Damage by many fungi including *[Cochliobolus miyabeanus Curvularia* spp. *Fusarium spp. Microdochium oryzae Sarocladium oryzae* and other fungi]
- Root rots
  [Fusarium spp. *Pythium* spp. *Pythium dissotocum Pythium spinosum]*
- Seedling blight
  Cochliobolus miyabeanus Curvularia spp. *Fusarium* spp. *Rhizoctonia solani Sclerotium rolfsii Athelia rolfsii* [teleomorph] and other pathogenic fungi.]
- Sheath blight
  [Thanatephorus cucumeris Rhizoctonia solani [anamorph]

- Sheath rot
  [Sarocladium oryzae = Acrocylindrium oryzae]
- Sheath spot
  [Rhizoctonia oryzae Stackburn (Alternaria leaf spot) *Alternaria padwickii]*
- Stem rot
  [Magnaporthe salvinii Sclerotium oryzae (synanamorph)]
  Water-mold (seed-rot and seedling disease)
  [Achlya conspicua Achlya klebsiana Fusarium spp. *Pythium* spp. *Pythium dissotocum Pythium spinosum]*

Miscellaneous Diseases and Disorders

- Alkalinity or salt damage
  [Excessive salt concentration in soil or water]
- Bronzing
  [Zinc deficiency]
- Cold injury
  [Low temperatures]
- Panicle blight
  [Cause undetermined]
- Pecky rice (kernel spotting)
  [Feeding injury by rice stink bug]
- Straighthead
  [Arsenic induced, unknown physiological disorder]
- White tip
  [Aphelenchoides besseyi]

17

Rice Varieties

Weedy Rice

Weedy rice, also known as red rice, is a species of rice (*Oryza*) that produces far fewer grains per plant than cultivated rice and is therefore considered a pest. The name 'weedy rice' is used for all types and variations of rice which show some characteristic features of cultivated rice and grow as weeds in commercial rice fields. Populations of weedy rice are found in many rice-growing regions. Weedy rice is various species and subspecies of rice which can distribute their seeds before harvest. Variations of weedy rice adapt to a wide range of natural conditions.

Weedy rice grains often have a red pericarp, so for this reason in the international literature the term 'red rice' is often used. This term, however, is not very relevant, because the rice with a red pericarp are also found in some cultivated varieties, but not in many forms of weedy rice.

In most regions of the rice production, weedy rice is introduced after the transition from transplanting rice to sowing commercial seeds directly in the rice field. It has become very significant since the mid 1980's, especially in Europe, with the weak semi-dwarf varieties of *indica* subspecies. Distribution generally promotes use of commercially purchased seeds containing weed seeds. Weedy rice can be found in 40 per cent - 75 per cent of rice fields in Europe , 40 per cent of fields in Brazil, 55 per cent in Senegal, 80 per cent in Cuba and 60 per cent in Costa Rica.

Because weedy rice and cultivated rice are so closely related, herbicides that would kill red rice would also kill cultivated rice. A genetically modified form of cultivated rice has been developed that will resist a herbicide, but this form of rice has not been approved for human consumption. This genetically modified form of cultivated rice has, however, appeared on the rice market.

Wild Rice

Wild rice (also called Canada rice, Indian rice, and water oats) is four species of grasses forming the genus *Zizania*, and the grain which can be harvested from them. The grain was historically gathered and eaten in both North America and China. While it is now something of a delicacy in North America, the grain is no longer eaten in China, where the plant's stem is used as a vegetable.

Wild rice is not directly related to Asian rice (*Oryza sativa*), whose wild progenitors are *O. rufipogon* and *O. nivara*, although they are close cousins, sharing the tribe Oryzeae. It is also not the plant described as a (zizania) in the Parable of the Tares in the Bible, which is thought to be *Lolium temulentum*.

The plants grow in shallow water in small lakes and slow-flowing streams; often, only the flowering head of wild rice rises above the water. The grain is eaten by dabbling ducks and other aquatic wildlife, as well as humans.

Three species of wild rice are native to North America:

1. Northern wild rice (*Zizania palustris*) is an annual plant native to the Great Lakes region of North America, the aquatic areas of the Boreal Forest regions of Alberta, Saskatchewan and Manitoba and Minnesota, Wisconsin and Michigan in the US.
2. Wild rice (Z. *aquatica*), also an annual, grows in the Saint Lawrence River and on the Atlantic and Gulf coasts of the United States.

3. Texas wild rice (*Z. texana*) is a perennial plant only found in a small area along the San Marcos River in central Texas.
One species is native to Asia:
- Manchurian wild rice (*Z. latifolia*; incorrect synonym: *Z. caduciflora*), is a perennial native to China.

Texas wild rice is in danger of extinction due to loss of suitable habitat in its limited range and to pollution. The pollen of Texas wild rice can only travel about 30 inches away from a parent plant. If pollen does not land on a receptive female flower within that distance, no seeds are produced. Manchurian wild rice has almost disappeared from the wild in its native range, but has been accidentally introduced into the wild in New Zealand and is considered an invasive species there.

The species most commonly harvested as grain is the annual species *Zizania palustris*. Native Americans and non-Indians harvest wild rice by canoeing into a stand of plants, and bending the ripe grain heads with wooden sticks called knockers, so as to thresh the seeds into the canoe.

The size of the knockers, as well as other details, are prescribed in state and tribal law. By Minnesota statute, knockers must be at most 1 inch in diameter, 30 inches long, and one pound in weight. The plants are not beaten with the knockers but require only a gentle brushing to dislodge the mature grain. The Ojibwa people call this plant *manoomin* meaning 'good berry'. Some seeds fall to the muddy bottom and germinate later in the year.

Several Native American cultures, such as the Ojibwa, consider wild rice to be a sacred component in their culture. The rice is harvested with a canoe: one person vans (or 'knocks') rice into the canoe with two small poles (called 'knockers' or 'flails') while the other paddles slowly or uses a push pole. For these groups, this harvest is an important cultural (and often economic) event. Named by the Ojibwe, the neighboring *Omanoominii* (the Menominee tribe, whose endonym is *Mamaceqtaw*, 'the people') is named after this plant. Many places in Illinois, Indiana, Manitoba, Michigan,

Minnesota, Ontario, Saskatchewan and Wisconsin are named after this plant, including Mahnomen, Minnesota, Menomonie, Wisconsin and many lakes and streams bearing the name 'Rice', 'Wildrice', or 'Wild Rice'.

Because of its nutritional value and taste, wild rice increased in popularity in the late 20th century, and commercial cultivation began in the US and Canada to supply the increased demand. In the US the main producers are California and Minnesota (where it is the official state grain) and it is mainly cultivated in paddy fields. In Canada, it is usually harvested from natural bodies of water; the largest producer is the province of Saskatchewan. Wild rice is also produced in Hungary and Australia. In Hungary, cultivation started in 1974 on the rice field of Szarvas. The Indian Rice Ltd. was founded in 1990. Now, the Hungarian wild rice growing and processing is managed only by this company. In Australia production is controlled by Ricewild Pty. Ltd. at Deniliquin in Southern New South Wales.

Manchurian wild rice (Chinese: pinyin: *gu*), gathered from the wild, was once an important grain in ancient China. Because of the difficulty of its domestication, it gradually lost importance with increasing population density, as its habitat was converted for use in raising rice. It is now very rare in the wild, and its use as a grain has completely disappeared in China, though it continues to be cultivated for its stems.

Almost always sold as a dried whole grain, wild rice is high in protein, the amino acid lysine and dietary fiber, and low in fat. Like true rice, it does not contain gluten. It is also a good source of the minerals potassium and phosphorus, and the vitamins thiamine, riboflavin and niacin.

Wild rice seeds can be infected by the highly toxic fungus ergot, which is dangerous if eaten. Infected grains will have pink or purplish blotches or growths of the fungus, from the size of a seed to several times larger.

Stems

The swollen crisp white stems of Manchurian wild rice are grown as a vegetable, popular in East and Southeast Asia.

The swelling occurs because of infection with the smut fungus *Ustilago esculenta.* The fungus prevents the plant from flowering, so the crop is propagated asexually, the infection being passed from mother plant to daughter plant. Harvest must be made between about 120 days and 170 days after planting, after the stem begins to swell but before the infection reaches its reproductive stage, when the stem will begin to turn black and eventually disintegrate.

The vegetable is especially common in China, where it is known as *gaosun* or *jiaobai.* Other names which may be used in English include *coba* and water bamboo.

Importation of the vegetable to the United States is prohibited in order to protect North American species from the fungus.

Wild rice is also grown as an ornamental plant in garden ponds.

Puffed Rice

Puffed rice ([Telugu - *Maramaralu*] [Tamil language Tamil]: [Pori], Malayalam: *Marathi*) is a type of puffed grain made from rice; usually made by heating rice kernels under high pressure in the presence of steam, though the method of manufacture varies widely.

Pori (Puffed Rice) has been mentioned in various Tamil literatures as an offering to Hindu deities.

Pori offered to Vinayagar (Lord Ganesh) with jaggery, mentioned in Tiruppugazh,a 15th century anthology of Tamil religious songs, written by Arunagirinathar, Tamil poet.

Puffed rice is used in snack foods and breakfast cereals, and is also a popular street food in some parts of the world. It is an ingredient of bhel puri, a popular Indian chaat item. It is also used in temples and gurdwaras as prasad.

Pori is offered to Hindu God and Goddess in all poojas in the South Indian state of Kerala and Tamil Nadu. Pilgrims of Sabarimala often pack puffed rice in their Irumudikettu along with jagery meant to be offered to Lord Ayyappan. To Lord Ganesh puffed rice (*Pori*) is offered without fail since its meant to be most liked by him, says Tamil saints. Also as snacks all over the state. Making Pori is the main family business for centuries among many villages around Namakkal, Avinashi in Tamil Nadu.

A traditional puffed rice called *muri* (*sometimes spelled mouri*) is made by heating rice in a sand-filled oven. Muri is to rice as popcorn is to corn. The processing involved makes rice less perishable. Muri is a staple food in many parts of Rayalaseema, North Karnataka, Bengal and Bangladesh. Jhalmuri or Masalamuri or Bhelpuri is a very popular preparation made from muri.

Puffed rice is referred to as *mur-mure* in some parts of India. In many parts of Rayalaseema, North Karnataka uggani along with *Mirapakai* Bajji (*Chilli Bajjis*) are popular.

Matta Rice

Kerala *Matta* rice (also known as Rosematta rice, Palakkadan Matta rice, Kerala Red rice, or Red parboiled rice) (Malayalam) is an indigenous variety of rice grown in Palakkad District of Kerala. It is different from brown rice. It is popular in Kerala and Sri Lanka where it is used on a regular basis for idlies, appams and plain rice. The robust, earthy flavour of Red Matta makes it an enticing companion to lamb, beef or game meats.

The 'Kerala Matta' rice has been very popular from early days because of the richness of rice, its unique taste and use in preparations of rice-snacks like 'Kondattam', 'Murukku' etc. The 'Palakkadan Matta ari Kanji' ('ari' in Malayalam means Rice) is also famous for its rich nutrient qualities. The Kerala Matta rice is referred to in the work 'Rice in Kerala' authored by Sri. P.C. Sahadevan and published by the Government of Kerala in the year 1966. The unique rice is mentioned in Tamil Classics like Thirukkural. During the ancient times Palghat District was part of Tamil Nadu. Rice in the days of Chera/ Chola Kingdoms was considered as a royal food. The commoners were happy with 'Chama' (an inferior variety of cereal). One adventurous farmer chanced upon this unique rice variety in the king's farm and carried it away in a 'Matta' meaning 'Areca Leaf'. The rice variety fell into the public domain and was sown by the farmer and soon became a regular rice crop in Palakkad. This rice was popularly referred to as 'Matta' and exclusively cultivated in Palakkad and later came to be known as the Kerala Matta Rice. Some of the old and popular varieties of Kerala Matta are 'Chenkazhama', 'Chettadi', 'Aruvakkari', 'Aryan', 'Vatton', 'Ilupappoocha-mpan', 'Chitteni', 'Thavalakkannan' and the newer varieties like 'Kunjukunju' and 'jyothi'.

Cultivation and Trade

Kerala Matta Rice is grown in Tamil Nadu and Kerala in South India. Matta rice gives Kerala farmers a premium of Rs. 300 for 500 kg of paddy. A three year ban on the export of matta rice was partially lifted in February 2011, allowing 25,000 tonnes to be exported in 2011.

Characteristics

Kerala Matta rice is a unique cereal having high content of nutrients and is indispensable for those who do hard physical work. It is also rich in fibre. Kerala Matta Rice is the rice having the outer bran being removed. The grains are yellowish pink from being parboiled with the reddish out layers. Rose Matta Rice maintains a pink hue as well as its flavour on cooking. Like all brown or par boiled rice, Red Matta has a lengthy cook time and requires extra water.

Uniqueness

Palakkadan matta rice is registered under the Geographical Indications of Goods (Registration & Protection) Act, 1999 by the Palakkad Matta Farmers Producer Company Ltd. It is a coarse variety of rice with bold grains and red pericarp. The rice has got a unique taste. The coarse rice with red pericarp by itself ensures high content of nutrients. 'Par-boiling' of the rice further ensures retention of nutritional value. The grains is grown on unique black cotton or regar soil, derived from rocks rich in lime peculiar to Palakkad also in 'Poonthalpadam' where the soil is heavy, containing 60-80 per cent of clay and silt and possess low permeability and high water holding capacity. These soils, the humid weather of

Palakkad, easterly winds that blow through the Palakkad gap and the rivers that flow from the Western Ghats, and the bright sunshine determine the unique taste and quality of the Kerala Matta Rice.

Preparation

The Rosematta rice is washed in a large pan and drained. In a pot with a tight cover and 1 part rice to 4 parts water the rice is boiled then simmered for ½ hour, drained and left covered for another 15 minutes.

Nutritional Facts

(As on Durbar rice pack) Serving Size 50g Calories 180 Total fat 0g; cholesterol 0g; Total Carbohydrate 42g; Sugars 0g; Protein 3g; Vitamin A 0 per cent; Vitamin C 0 per cent; Calcium 0 per cent; Iron 0 per cent.

Flattened Rice

Flattened rice (also called beaten rice) is a dehusked rice which is flattened into flat light dry flakes. These flakes of rice swell when added to liquid, whether hot or cold, as they absorb water, milk or any other liquids. The thicknesses of these flakes vary between almost translucently thin (the more expensive varieties) to nearly four times thicker than a normal rice grain.

This easily digestible form of raw rice is very popular across Nepal, North East India and Bangladesh, and is normally used to prepare snacks or light and easy fast food in a variety of Indian cuisine styles, some even for long-term consumption of a week or more. It is known by a variety of names: *Poha* or *Pauwa* in Hindi, *Baji* in Newari, *Pohe* in Marathi, *Chindé* in Bengali, *Chira* in Assamese, *Phovu* in Konkani, *Chudaa* in Oriya and parts of Bihar and Jharkhand, *Atukulu* in Telugu, *Bajeel* or *Bajil* in Tulu, *Chudwey* in Urdu (Dakkani), *Aval* in Malayalam and Tamil, *Avalakki* in Kannada, *Pauaa/Paunva* in Gujarati, and *Chiura* in Nepali, Bhojpuri and Chhattisgarhi.

Flattened rice can be eaten raw by immersing it in plain water or milk, with salt and sugar to taste, or lightly fried in oil with nuts, raisins, cardamoms, and other spices. The lightly fried variety is a standard breakfast in Malvaa region (surrounding Indore) of Madhya Pradesh. It can be reconstituted with hot water to make a porridge or paste, depending on the proportion of water added. In villages, particularly in Chhattisgarh, Poha or Chiura is also eaten raw by mixing with jaggery.

In Bhopal, poha is cooked with lightly frying mustard seeds, tumeric, chili powder, finely chopped onions and then moistened poha is added to the spicy mix and steamed for a few minutes. Jalebi is often eaten with poha.

Flattened rice is also a convenience food and very similar to instant mashed potatoes in uses and spirit.

Dishes made from Beaten Rice

Pohe

- *Dhau Baji* (Newari): A dish where beaten rice is dry roasted in a pan, then mixed with yogurt and sugar.
- *Chindé'r pulao*: A snack prepared by immersing the rice flakes in cold water, drying them, and then preparing *pilaf*-style with nuts, raisins, black pepper, green chillies, and salt and sugar to taste. This is very popular as a breakfast or evening dish in families, and may not be available in any stores or restaurants.
- *Chindé bheja*: Some flakes are immersed in a bowl of usually cold water, flavoured with lime juice, salt, sugar, and a little black pepper.
- *Bajeel Ogarne*: Here beaten rice is seasoned with mustard seeds, coconut oil, and red chillies.
- Beaten rice with curds: Here beaten rice is soaked in water and then sieved. Curd is added with table salt, preferably eaten with mango or lemon pickle.
- *Kanda Pohe* (*Avalakki OggaraNe* in Kannada): In this dish, beaten rice is soaked and sieved. Small pieces of boiled potato, onion, mustard seeds, turmeric and red chilli are seasoned and mixed with beaten rice and served hot.
- *Dadpe Pohe*: Thin or medium beaten rice is mixed with fresh coconut, grated green mangos, chili powder, and

coriander. It is then seasoned with salt and a tadka (fried mixture) of peanut oil, mustard seeds, turmeric and finely chopped onions.

- *Sweet Bajil* (*Tipe Bajil* in Tulu): Beaten rice is mixed with jaggery and grated coconut.
- *Khara Bajeel*: The beaten rice is mixed with red chilli powder, salt and coconut. Sometimes seasoned.
- *Sajjige Bajeel*: Combination of upma and Khara bajeel.
- *Chudaa Dahi (Orissa)*: Combination of yogurt, sugar and flattened rice, often with banana.
- *Aval Nanachathu (Kerala)*: Combination of grated coconut, sugar, a little water, and beaten rice. Keep for 2-3 hours so rice puffs up.

18

Rice Culture

Since its origin, the spread of rice cultivation is extensive and rice is now being grown wherever water supply is adequate and ambient temperature are suitable. The rice grain is covered with a woody husk or hull, which is indigestible and is to be removed in the first step during processing for making the rice edible. The origin of rice (Oryza sativa L.) has interested some eminent botanists and provisional inferences were made in the first half of this century. A symposium was held in Delhi during 1950 on the origin of cultivated plants of South Asia and since then research on the origin and cytogenetics of rice has been intensified in India and in Japan.

The first detailed study of an archaeological rice sample from India was from carbonized grains excavated from Hastinapur north of Delhi and was dated as being between 1100 and 700 B.C. Subsequent archaeological evidence on rice in India has been reviewed by Buth and Saraswath. They consider the specimens collected from Atranjikera in Uttar Pradesh to be the oldest found so far and estimate their period of occurrence to range from 1500 1000 B.C. Vishnu Mittre has given a detailed discussion about the origin antiquity and spread of rice cultivation in India. As regards China another ancient region of rice cultivation pottery excavated from Yang Shao has been found to carry imprints as well as rice husks. The period of that culture is estimated at 2000 B.C. but a greater antiquity has also been claimed. The region covering Burma Thailand and Cambodia is well suited to rice cultivation and has also a large population of wild rices. Therefore the discovery by a team of American archaeologists of the most ancient finds of rice from excavations in Thailand is of interest. The work reviewed by Solheim suggests that these finds reveal the first agricultural beginning in southern Asia important enough to be termed a revolution. The specimens include horticultural plants as well as rice husks. The dating suggests that these specimens belong to the period ranging from 5000 4000 B.C. This antiquity may be accepted provisionally and it may be inferred that rice cultivation spread to Vietnam Taiwan China as well as to India from this centre. However an independent and parallel origin in Assam Bengal and Kerala cannot at present be dismissed.

It has long been recognized that the wild species of *Oryza* closely related to O. sativa are widely distributed in India Burma Thailand and Cambodia. These wild populations can be grouped into at least two taxa but the distinctions are not clear cut as intermediates have been arising as a result of natural crossings. If the division into taxa is to be made it is necessary to apply the rules of nomenclature and decide on the valid names of the two species. This is a controversial issue as may be understood from the following account. One taxon of restricted distribution is found on the margins of ponds is partly floating and is potentially perennial. This species is distinguished from its close relative which is seasonal having slender grains and longer anthers in addition to some differences in plant and panicle characters. This species was used to be called *Oryza perennis* (Moench). This specific name is rejected as invalid by Tateoka in his comprehensive revision of the genus Oryza. A discussion about this and allied taxonomic difficulties is included in the book Rice Genetics and Cytogenetics. In a subsequent chapter of this monograph details of taxonomy and species relationship are elaborated. Since the specific name perennis is widely used and is also convenient to conserve as a valid name Sampath published an emended description from a specimen collected in Orissa. It is therefore permissible to consider the Orissa type to be a subspecies of a widespread varying and long anthered wild rice. The other taxon has bolder grains shorter anthers and generally stouter awns. This species has large populations and shows greater variation. Large populations of this species can be seen beside the railway track on Borrow Pits along the east coast of India north of Vijayawada and including Bengal. These plants flower during October when their conspicuous pink awns make the specific name O. rufipogon Griffith. It is possible that this species evolved from hybrids between *O. sativa* and *O. perennis*. Moench emend. Sampath because it has been repeatedly observed in many countries that where *O. perennis* grows adjacent to rice plots cross pollination from wild rice takes place. The extent of crossing is low but in the course of time a weed population builds up in the rice fields since the hybrid plants shed their seeds which remain dormant till the next season. In the course of generations a diversified population can evolve from the hybrids and can invade new habitats. It is also possible that the very large populations may be grouped together as a single species to include genotypes which had evolved from *O. perennis* before human intervention as an adaptation to habitats liable to drought.

A theory has been advanced that climatic changes during the Pleistocene Period induced physiological stresses in the herbaceous flora and the evolution of seasonal forms the existing perennial ones was accelerated. An exposition of this theory as pertaining to the Gramineae of Asia is made by R.O. Whyte (in press). To apply this concept to rice is to infer the changes as perennial climatic stress seasonal human selection cultivated rice. The term genome which is explained later in this book has to be used for supporting this hypothesis. The symbol A is used for the genome present in a species at the diploid level in *O. perennis O. rufipogon* and also in *O. sativa*. The theory of evolution precludes the separate creation of a species. Therefore the species having the A genome are interrelated and their evolution may be traceable.

A simplified statement of the ancestry of the cultivated rice is as follows. The perennial long anthered species is the ultimate ancestor but possibly another taxon with bolder grains and seasonal habit was the immediate ancestor. For details the review of Nayar may be seen. Under this topic there is a need for further research to arrive at a firm conclusion.

For the human selection to operate there must be genetic variability present in populations which must be responsive to the procedures of primitive agriculturists. The details of cultivation practices in ancient times cannot be traced but it can be inferred that in some areas the scrub or the jungle was cut burnt crudely leveled and the seeds of crops were sown. In river valleys and deltas the procedures would be slightly different suggesting a more advanced agriculture. The method used by primitive agriculturists for harvesting and seed selection is not known. Initially the seeds of wild rice must have been used. The perennial wild rice is partly out crossing hence heterozygous and different populations show differences in genetic composition. Hybridization between different genotypes followed by inbreeding would lead to rapid changes in plant characteristics. Mutations for nonshedding awnless grains would be intensively selected by the primitive agriculturists. Sampath has suggested that hybridity in the molecular structure of some key enzymes could have played a part in the evolution of *O. sativa*. Studies on population genetics of the wild rices of the world have been carried out by Dr H.I. Oka and his collaborators at the National Institute of Genetics Misima. These studies contribute substantially to an understanding of the origin of *O. sativa*. Two of his collaborators gave experimental findings and summarized his interpretation. In a joint contribution the dynamics of plant domestication as applicable to rice is discussed. In view of such significant studies any further advance under this topic can come only as the result of combined cytogenetic and biochemical studies on hybrids and hybrid progenies of wild rices.

Rice Breeding

Rice breeding in India started in 1911 in undivided Bengal with the appointment of Dr G.P. Hector as Economic Botanist with his headquarters at Dacca which is now in Bangladesh. In 1912 Madras province had the first crop specialist fully devoted to rice. The period from 1911 1979 may be considered under three distinct periods as far as rice breeding in India is concerned viz. of mainly pure line selections and very few hybridizations of inter racial hybridization between japonicas and indices and of inter racial hybridization with semi dwarfs especially Taiwanese indices.

Prior to 1930 Bengal and Madras were the only provinces which had full time specialists for the crop. When the Indian Council of Agricultural Research was established in 1929 it initiated rice research projects in many states which did not have a rice programme and this gave an impetus to the development of rice research in the country and by 1950 there were 82 research stations devoted to rice in 14 States of India. These research stations released 445 improved varieties mainly by the pure line method of selection. Of course a few (e.g. Co. 15 Co. 16 Co. 25 Co. 26 Co. 29 Co. 30) were hybrid derivatives from indica crosses but numerically they were insignificant when compared to those evolved through pure line selections.

Researchers have delineated the development of Rice Research Stations in India. The establishment of these different stations was prompted by the need to cater for different ecological conditions. Researchers had listed the broad breeding objectives which made possible the development of 445 improved varieties in the country. They were:

1. Earliness;
2. Deep water and flood resistance;
3. Lodging resistance;
4. Drought resistance;
5. Non shedding of grains;
6. Dormancy of seed;

7. Control of wild rice;
8. Disease resistance; and
9. Higher response to heavy manuring.

Thus the earlier breeding efforts were directed towards the development of varieties adapted to specific stress situations or for resistance to diseases prevalent in the region or what the Japanese called ecological breeding . When synthetic fertilizers began to be popular after World War II efforts were made to identify varieties which respond to heavy manuring. There were no major pest problems and the progress though not spectacular did not pose possibilities of serious disaster. Through pure line selection the advantages of natural selections over centuries had been fully made use of and there were no problems of antagonism involved in the introduction of new genes to an incompatible environment. The surviving genotypes seemed to be more suited to their environment underscoring the significance of survival and adaptation in evolution.

After the establishment of the Central Rice Research Institute in 1946 at Cuttuck there had been a systematic screening of exotic types from the genetic stocks and many Chinese Japanese Taiwanese and Russian types were tested for the purpose of direct introduction in the country. The result showed that the early duration local varieties like Benibhog were superior to the exotic introductions. Notable among the Chinese introductions were Ch. 4 Ch. 45 Ch. 55 Ch. 62 and Ch. 63 of these Ch. 45 proved to be a good yielder combined with earliness and Helminthosporium resistance and had been used as a donor in some of the modern varieties.

Prior to 1947 Chinese varieties were first introduced in Kashmir Valley possibly due to reasons of geographical proximity or contiguity and have been found suitable and so extensively cultivated. The most notable of these introductions is Ch. 1039 which is the leading variety of Kashmir Valley even today.

The end of the Second World War and the subsequent population explosion stimulated the Food and Agricultural

Organisation of the United Nations to take up the problem of improving production of this major Asian and world cereal on an international basis and the result was a collaborative project of japonica × indica hybridization in South East Asian countries. Japan had started using chemical fertilizers from the beginning of this century and so japonicas the cultivated rices of Japan showed response to fertilizer under Japanese conditions up to 60 100 kg N/ha whereas the indicas cultivated types in Asia responded to N fertilizer only up to 20-30 kg N/ha.

The rationale of the F.A.O. project was to transfer the high yielding ability and response to heavy fertilizer inputs that characterize the japonicas into the local indica varieties which were adapted to their respective conditions of culture and had tolerance to the prevalent diseases and pests of the region.

A parallel scheme of japonica × indica hybridization was also drawn up by the Indian Council of Agricultural Research (ICAR) with the same objectives of identifying varieties with response to fertilizer and having the major features of the local varieties of the different states.

These two projects used 192 improved indica varieties selected by the participating Asian countries and Indian states and produced a total of 710 different japonica × indica hybrids. F1 seeds of these hybrids were distributed to the different participating countries or states for growing the F2 and subsequent generations in their respective regions to breed varieties suited to those agro climatic conditions.

These projects could claim only very limited success as only four varieties were released from the seven hundred and odd hybrid combinations. Malinja and Mahsuri in Malaysia Adt. 27 in Tamil Nadu state of India and Circna in Australia were the varieties named.

Another scheme was lunched by Central Rice Research Institute (CRRI) in 1960 to evolve high yielding fertilizer responsive hybrid varieties with japonica in 11 states. The development of the semi dwarf varieties in Taiwan and

Philippines and their introduction into India put an abrupt end to this scheme in 1966 even before the results could be properly assessed.

But in another later attempt at Central Rice Research Institute Rao and Nagaraju achieved remarkable success in the development of japonica × indica hybrids fully achieving the objectives envisaged in the original international and national hybridization projects. Their success might be attributed to the choice of short statured japonicas (as against the tall ones previously used) grown in South Japan which climatically is fairly similar to Taiwan (and not from Hokkaido the coldest region where rice is grown). So varieties adapted to mild temperate region were seen to be more productive under tropical conditions than those from extremely cold temperate zone. This emphasises the importance of selecting suitable parents with adaptability in rice improvement/ hybridization programmes.

During the period of japonica×indica hybridization time and again it was stressed that the japonicas had high yielding ability and response to fertilizer. But in India the introduced japonicas had been a total failure except in the hills and some cool areas. Japonicas were both photoperiod and temperature sensitive and so flowered in 35 40 days and did not get enough time for proper vegetative growth and tillering and so were not half as productive as the indicas under Indian conditions nor did they exhibit any of the virtues for which they were famous in Japan. Therefore the limited success of the first two japonica × indica hybridization projects was natural as the very premise of the project of transferring the high yield potential and response to fertilizer of japonicas was not apparent in them under Indian conditions. Besides the character of response to high fertility is an interaction of environment and genotype and when the environment was changed the interaction also gave different or negative results. The chances of getting hybrid recombinants with the desirable attributes of both the parents from such a wide genetic scrambling were a slender as getting highly productive hybrids as transgressive segregants from any other inter or intra racial crosses involving ordinary or poor yielding parents.

It was obvious that the short photoperiod and tropical conditions of the Indian plains transformed the entire physiology of growth development and productivity of japonicas which therefore could not provide productive recombinants in a Mendelian proportion. The ecological specialization to divergent situations had caused genetic incompatibility between the races and the *japonica* × *indica* hybrids were seen to have a very high degree (even to 99%) of spikelet sterility in the segregating populations. This is an interesting instance of interaction between genotype and environment ruining the genetic potential for productivity in crop plants themselves or in their hybrid derivatives.

In Japan during the rice season the days are longer and there is a higher level of solar radiation that in tropical countries. In tropical region of India the day length is fairly constant during the crop season but with low solar radiation due to the overcast sky of the monsoon period. Where the long duration crops are raised though the days are bright there is a shortening in day length after the autumn equinox contributing to a reduction in the availability of per day solar radiation. This is one of the significant differences between the rice growing environments of tropical and temperate regions.

As indicated earlier CRRI has been exploring the possibility of direct introductions of exotic types from leading rice producing countries like Japan Taiwan etc. Some of the Japanese varieties when tried under 90 kg N and 35kg P_2O_5 per ha were found promising (though on par or inferior to local varieties in yield) especially Norin 17 Norin 18 and Zuiho. The Taiwanese introduction Hsunchu was found not as productive as the local or Japanese types. The subsequent introduction of intermediate types from Taiwan proved successful in many parts of the country like Taichung 65 in Karnataka Taichung (Native) 1 in Bihar Tainan 3 and

Kaohsiung 18 in Kerala and Hsunchu in U.P. almost setting the stage for the next phase in Indian rice breeding.

The development of Taichung (Native) 1 from the semidwarf mutant Dee geo woo gen was major event in rice research in Asia and particularly for India T(N) 1 recorded a productivity which was considered impossible in the tropics before. It was felt then that through extensive cultivation of non lodging semidwarf hybrids rice production could be substantially increased in a short time as in wheat. Enunciation of the plant type concept from an elaboration of the morphology in terms of the physiological efficiency of the semidwarfs stimulated breeding activity throughout most of South Asia and especially India which operated its most intensive rice breeding programmes since 1965 under the All India Co ordinated Rice Improvement Project (AICRIP). Initially the aim was to identify semidwarf varieties that would yield well from Kanyakumari to Kashmir so as to make the seed multiplication and distribution system effective. Padma and Jaya were the first varieties that emerged from this programme. Subsequently varieties were released by Central Variety Release Committee and by the different state agencies. The numerical superiority of state releases stresses the importance of regional adaptation in rice varieties. Most of these varieties have a yield potential of 3 5 tonnes/ha.

The most significant aspect of this period is the prolific release of hybrid varieties. During this phase 123 varieties were released in twelve years compared to the 51 hybrid varieties released during the four decades prior to 1965. This surge in hybrid releases was facilitated when semidwarf plant habit became one of the easily identifiable selection criteria for breeders.

The plant type or semidwarf varieties with the genetic architecture for physiological efficiency of grain production have been found to be superior to the tall traditional varieties in both kharif and rabi seasons but more so in the rabi season. The following table illustrates the superior response of semidwarf varieties to nitrogen inputs for grain production in comparison to the traditional varieties during rabi season when the cultivation is under controlled irrigation and ample solar radiation.

As with japonica × indica hybridization the inter racial hybridization programme with Taiwanese varieties or derivatives also ran into difficulties. It was unfortunately reported in the early phase of the semidwarf period that through adoption of semidwarf varieties with improved management practices the production problem could be solved as was done in wheat. But rice being cultivated during the monsoon when no other cereal could be grown in heavy rainfall areas normally faced problems of adaptation to specific ecology and the newly introduced semidwarf types were found unsuitable in a variety of stress situations such as water logging salinity drought low solar radiation due to clouded atmospheric condition etc. when these semidwarf varieties were cultivated under high fertility conditions they were found susceptible to most of the pests and diseases of rice. Continuous and intensive cultivation of these semidwarfs caused disease and pest epidemics which gave premonitions of famine or ruin as in Bihar Andhra Pradesh Kerala Indonesia and elsewhere. These facts again stress the importance of adaptability in monsoon rice varieties to the tracts in which they are to be grown. It is well known that monsoon fosters most of the pests and diseases of rice and high levels of fertilizer inputs aggravate their intensity. In such a situation it is unwise to advocate varieties of identical genetical constitution over wide tracts. Genetic diversity is still the best insurance against disease and pest epidemics as is illustrated by the Indonesian and Kerala catastrophes.

The concern with disease and pest epidemics has intensified efforts for incorporation of multiple resistance by which is meant resistance to more than one disease or pest in the varieties to be developed. Many of the traditional indicas have been found to be the major donors for disease and pest resistance.

Thus having implicitly accepted the production superiority of the semidwarfs and widely popularized them we have to embark on breeding plant type varieties with tolerance to physiological stresses like drought water logging saline tolerance cold tolerance resistance to diseases and pests and good cooking and eating qualities rather to transfer the desirable traits of the local varieties to the plant type background.

In monsoon dependent rice cultivation uplands with rainfall of 700 1100 mm get exposed to moisture stress periodically due to breaks in monsoon lasting for different periods of a week to ten days of erratic distribution of rainfall. Such areas constitute about a sixth of the world s rice acreage and third of the kharif rice area in India and it is necessary to stabilize yields from such lands to keep up the upward trend in rice production.

Uplands are defined as those lands which are not bunded and wherein water is not therefore impounded during cultivation. Upland rice cultivation entirely depends on rainfall and it is a way of harvesting rain by adopting varieties of suitable duration according to the rainfall pattern.

Four kinds of situations are possible for such a kind of rice cultivation:

1. Rains adequate or assured during vegetative and reproductive phases.
2. Rains inadequate or unreliable during vegetative phase but adequate during reproductive phase.
3. Rains adequate during vegetative phase but inadequate during reproductive phase.
4. Rains inadequate during both vegetative and reproductive phase.

The crux of the problem in upland breeding (exposed to moisture stress) as in items and is to find out suitable donors with drought tolerance during the vegetative and reproductive phases as under situation in item rice cultivation is not possible and in item there is no problem of moisture stress.

As there are uplands in all the rice growing states many local varieties suited to such conditions have been identified.

Through screening a number of varieties with varying degree of drought tolerance have been identified (e.g. Mtu. 17 Mettasannavari from Andhra Pradesh Ch. 45 from Bihar Sathi 34 36 from Gujarat Ptb. 28 Ptb. 29 Ptb. 30 from Kerala B 76 from Orissa Lalnakanda 41 from Punjab Tkm.1 from Tamil Nadu and N. 22 and Sudha from Uttar Pradesh.

Among these it was found that Lalnakanda 41 Ch. 45 and N. 22 have drought tolerance at the vegetative phase while Mtu. 17 showed drought tolerance even at the reproductive phase.

The first attempt recorded to breed varieties with drought tolerance was in Tamil Nadu during the mid fifties and a drought tolerant variety Co. 31 was released. Kerala also reported some drought tolerant breeding lines from the cross Krasnodar × Kattamodan Culture No. 356 especially.

With the introduction of Taichung (Native) 1 during 1965 efforts were made to transfer drought tolerance to semidwarf hybrids and Bala from the cross N. 22 × T (N) 1 was the first high yielding variety with drought tolerance that was released in the country. As Bala was hard threshing efforts were made to identify lines with easy threshing and good grain qualities. CR. 113 CR. 115 CR. 141 and CR. 143 had many lines with better threshability and grain qualities than Bala . One line viz. CR. 141 192 from the cross (N. 22/T(N) 1 × T. 90 IR. 8) had been named Kiran in Bihar. Hybrids more productive and tolerant to drought than any of the parents had been identified in the cross CR. 125 (Lalnakanda 41 × Mtu. 17) × T(N) 1.

International Rice Research Institute (IRRI) geneticists have standardized the testing procedure for drought tolerance of upland rices and have made considerable progress by evolving a large number of promising cultures suited for uplands. Many of these are tested in most rice growing countries including India through the International Rice Testing Programme (IRTP). As the upland rice problems are faced by every rice growing state in India a good number of cultures have been generated by states using local donors and at present many are under trial in the AICRIP testing programme.

Efforts were also made at Central Rice Research Institute (CRRI) to evolve varieties with drought tolerance through induced mutation in traditional varieties. Considerable success was achieved through this approach and many mutants with higher yield potential and drought tolerance than the parents had been identified in Ch. 45 and Mtu. 17 . Mutant Number 2 and 12 of Mtu. 17 had been in district trials in Meghalaya and Manipur. Of special significance is Mtu. 17 Mutant No. 4 which showed very high tolerance to drought even during the flowering phase.

Another mutant from CR. 113 designated CRM. 13 3241 is possibly the earliest induced productive major cereal in the world maturing in seventy days when direct seeded under a temperature regime of over 25°C. This mutant yields about 1½ 2 tonnes/ha normally but with good management has shown potential up to 5 tonnes/ha. In many State Farms under the Department of Agriculture of Orissa Government it had recorded yields 2½ 3½ tonnes/ha. By relying on the earliness of this variety known or predictable drought spells can be avoided or there is a possibility to raise another rice crop after the drought or flood ravages and the resumption of normal monsoon. This variety is to be named shortly by the Orissa Department of Agriculture. In Assam it is found to be promising as pre flood kharif variety (March June) suited for direct seeded condition where it could be grown with the rains received during March June. In Tripura it has been found to be useful in Tillo lands (low mounds). This mutant is under extensive trial in West Bengal. Arunachal Pradesh and Madhya Pradesh.

Kharif is the main rice crop or season for India extending from June to December practically coinciding with the onset of the south west monsoon and complete recession of north east monsoon. Of the total 38.9 million hectares under rice in India about 20 million ha or 50 per cent of the area are under lowland where there is standing water of varying depths depending on the topography of the land for varying periods. The lowlying areas can be classified into:

- Water logged area (ill-drained conditions);
- Flooded areas; and
- Deep water areas.

The classification is mainly based on the toposequence of rice fields. With the onset of monsoon medium lands have shallow rainfed conditions but water gets accumulated later at the peak of monsoon. So in the high rainfall zones medium duration photosensitive varieties are grown in such lands. Where the rainfall is low photosensitive varieties which flower in 100 110 days are preferred. The intermediate lowlands constitute about half of the water logged areas and photosensitive varieties are grown in such lands. In the semi deep and deep water areas there is stagnation of water with the onset of heavy rains (normally from mid July onwards) and there is no way to drain off inundated water. Under such situations only broadcasting with the onset of monsoon is the usual practice.

The soils on which rice is grown in India and their classification.

The major soil groups producing rice are Riverine alluvium red yellow red loamy hill and submontane tarai laterite coastal alluvium red sandy or gravelly patches of mixed red and black medium and shallow black soils.

The soils can generally be classified for purposes of rice cultivation in India into:

- Alluvial soils (Haplaquents Ustifluvents Udifluvents Haplustalfs Ustochrepts);
- Calcareous alluvial soils (Calciorthids);
- Coastal and deltaic alluvium (Propsualfs);
- Red soils (Paleustalfs Rhodustalfs Haplustalfs);
- Red and yellow soils (Haplustults Ochraqults Rhodustalfs);

- Lateritic soils (Plinthaqults Plinthustults Plinthudults Oxisols);
- Black soils (Ustochrepts Uatropepts Pellusterts Chromusterts Pelluderts);
- Mixed red and black soils (association of Alfisols and Vertisols);
- Grey brown soils (Calciorthids);
- Brown hill soils (Palchumults);
- Submontane soils (Hapludalfs);
- Terai soils (Haplaquolls);
- Desert soils (Lithic Entisols Psamments Calciorthids);
- Saline alkali soils (Salorthids Salargids and Natrargids); and
- Peaty and saline peaty soils (Histosols).

For a comprehensive and meaningful development of research programmes on a regional basis the Indian Council of Agricultural Research has identified eight agro climatic regions in the country and these regions also represent the typical rice growing regions of the country. The agro climatic regions encompassing the different states with soils rainfall temperature etc. which are significant from the point of view of rice cultivation are given in Table 1. This broad division into general agro climatic regions is suited for general agricultural purposes. The soils are also subdivided into agro climatic regions based on the degree of wetness as measured by moisture index which is the excess of precipitation over the potential evapotranspiration expressed as a percentage of the potential evapotranspiration divided into 8 classes designated one to eight with increasing wetness and with each one of them again divided into subclasses A B C D and E which are in an ascending order of coolness based on the mean average temperature.

The area occupied by rice in West Bengal and Bihar is nearly the same followed by Orissa, Madhya Pradesh, Uttar Pradesh, Andhra Pradesh, Tamil Nadu, Assam, Maharashtra and Karnataka. These states put together account for more than 90 per cent of the total rice producing area. They also constitute the traditionally rice growing areas in the country. The rest of the states have however limited areas under the rice crop.

The humid western Himalayan region. This region comprises submontane soils hill soils and terai soils in the states of Jammu and Kashmir Himachal Pradesh and the Kumaon and Garhwal divisions of Uttrakhand.

The soils that are found in the rice growing tract of Jammu and Kashmir are formed from the alluvium brought by the major rivers Chenab Ravi Tawi and their tributaries. They occur mostly in the Jammu and Kathua districts. They vary in depth are light in texture and their pH ranges from 6.5 to 8.7 they are high in organic matter nitrogen and K_2O but are deficient in phosphorus.

The submontane soils include the valley floor and the karewa soils which occur in the Anantnagh Baramulla and Srinagar districts. The valley floor has been constituted by the alluvium deposited by the Jhelum and the Indus. They are silty loam to clay loam and are neutral to alkaline (pH 5.4 8.5).

The karewa soils are somewhat eroded and formed from the deposits which are of lacustrine nature. Their texture is heavy their contents of nitrogen and organic matter are moderate to high and their total P and K ranges from 0.09-0.3 and 0.1 to 0.2 per cent respectively.

The hill soils occur in Uttrakhand in the districts of Almora, Chamoli, Pithorgarh, Uttar Kashi and Dehra Dun. They are shallow with fragments of rock occurring within a few centimeters at higher elevations but about three meters in valleys and lower depressions. They are derived from biotite schists and phyllitic materials under moist conditions. The soils groups fall under the categories of red loam brown forest soil meadow soil and podzolic soil.

The *terai* soil occurs as a narrow strip from the north west to the extreme north east. The soil remains saturated throughout the year because of sufficient precipitation and high ground water-table. They have been formed from the transported materials laid down by different rivers originating from the Himalayas. They are productive and respond to fertilizers. They are classified as Molisols in soil taxonomy.

In Himachal Pradesh the hill soils are formed over a variety of parent rocks comprising sandstones gray micaceous sandstones and shales in the sub-Himalayan region where they are located. The soils are loam to silty loam and medium to high in organic matter total nitrogen phosphorus and potash. They are poor in available nutrients. The cation exchange capacity is low to medium.

The humid Bengal, Assam basin and the humid eastern Himalayan region and the Bay islands. For convenience these two regions are dealt with together. The altitude of the rice growing areas ranges from a few metres in Sundarbans in West Bengal to about 1660 metres in the north eastern part of the Himalayas in the Mizoram State and up to more than 2000 metres in Arunachal Pradesh.

The crop is often grown on flat lands to facilitate the supply of water needs. It is grown successfully over a wide range of slopes ranging from nearly level to very steep (podu or thum) cultivation in hilly areas. One of the main limiting factors is the availability of water.

Owing to the adaptability of the rice crop to soils having a wide range of characteristics it is not possible to categorize a particular soil group as rice soil or assess its best use as rice land.

The major groups of soils listed in the table for the two regions included riverine alluvium the terai soils red loamy sandy or gravelly red yellow and laterite soils. Some of the important soil series cultivated for rice in West Bengal extracted from the Soil Survey Reports are Canning, Kharbona, Jagdishpur, Sasanga, Hanrgra, Totpara and Banpara. They are placed in Entisol Inceptisol and Alfisol in soil taxonomy.

The alluvial soils deposited by the rivers mostly occupy the major part of the wetland rice soils thus contributing the largest share to rice production in the country. They are derived from the deposition mainly as silt deposited by the numerous tributaries of the Ganges and the Brahmaputra systems. The different weathering products of the Himalayas are deposited during the course of their flow through the plains.

In the wetlands the water table is high the drainage is poor and the entire profile remains in a reduced state. Mottled horizons are common and the accumulation of calcium carbonate in the lower horizons is also observed in soils. The flooded condition of paddy soils brings about the movement of iron and manganese compounds from the upper layers and their precipitation in the reduced zone of the lower horizon.

In West Bengal the Rarh region which comprises portion of Murshidabad Bankura the whole of Burdwan and the western half of Midnapore are classified under old alluvium. According to Mukerjee et al. and Digar the textures vary from sandy loams to heavy clays with a hard pan.

The laterite and lateritic soils are found between the Damodar River and the Bhagirathi River interspersed with basaltic and granitic hills. They may be classified into two groups. The first group consists of soils of Midnapore Bankura Burdwan and Birbhum. In these soils the ratio of SiO_2 Al_2O_3 is quite high and because of chemical weathering followed by considerable leaching the soils are deficient in N P_2O_5 and K_2O. They respond to N and P fertilization. At some places buried laterites are also observed at considerable depths underlain by alluvium. These soils give better response to P_2O_5 and the yield of rice is significantly increased by the application of P_2O_5 rather than by that of N.

The red soils of Birbhum Bankura Burdwan and West Dinajpur sometimes misclassified as laterites are transported from the hills of Chhotanagpur Plateau. They are acidic poor in Ca N and available P. They are highly leached and respond to N and P.

The coastal soils in the districts of 24 Parganas and Midnapore after reclamation are producing good crop of rice. They are also rich in plant nutrients. The terai soils in the

Jalpaiguri and Cooch Behar districts lying at the foot of the Himalayas are of raw humus type sandy and gray to black.

Soils in the Assam Valley are acidic specially the old alluvial soils whereas the new alluvium is slightly acidic to neutral and in some cases slightly alkaline. The soils are high in available P and K and moderate in organic matter and nitrogen.

The lateritic soils occur in the north eastern mountainous upland areas of Assam. Drainage in the uplands is good. The groundwater laterites are poorly drained. In some parts of West Bengal by the augmentation of irrigation sources from groundwater reserves through the sinking of tube wells rice is grown in low medium and upland situations. Though rice is adapted to a wide range of soils as mentioned earlier the type of soils suitable for it mainly depends upon the conditions under which the crop is grown rather than upon the nature of the soil.

By the increase in demands for more areas to be brought under the rice crop the conservation of moisture during certain periods becomes necessary owing to insufficient irrigation water. Therefore effective soil depth and suitable texture are very important.

In wetland cultivation soil structure is of little significance but good soil structure ensures better water transmission and moisture preservation for the dryland crop.

The rice crop is better grown mostly in acidic soils whose pH ranges from 5.5 to 6.5. It is successfully grown in saline soils of Sudarabans in the Gangetic delta.

The major groups of soil growing rice in the region are calcareous alluvial riverine alluvial saline alkaline red yellow loam red sandy or gravelly and mixed red and black. The alluvial soils owe their origin from the materials brought and deposited by the great rivers from the mountains. They are rich in potash and calcium but are deficient in organic matter nitrogen and phosphorus. The older alluvium is generally deficient in phosphorus lime and organic matter whereas the recent alluvium is well supplied with nutrients because of fresh accumulation of river silt. The soils are placed in Entisol Inceptizon and Alfisol categories.

In the irrigated tracts of the Punjab state the soils are light textured and alkaline. Organic matter and nitrogen are low.

In Uttar Pradesh the alluvial soils occupy nearly 60 per cent of the area in the east west south and central parts of the state. They have developed from the alluvium deposited by the Ganga and the Yamuna and their tributaries. The soils can be broadly classified under:

1. light textured alluvium of the west and north west;
2. alluvium in the centre possessing intermediate textures; and
3. alluvium in the north east derived from the calcareous parent material.

Saline and karail soils occur all along the Ganga river on the left side in the districts of Meerut, Aligarh, Bulandshar, Manipuri, Etah Kanpur, Fatehpur, Allahabad, Lucknow, Pratapgarh and Sultanpur. The parent materials are alluvial deposits in the riverine areas and finely washed materials in the lower depressions. The soils are highly alkaline indurated and have hard pan which obstructs the downward movement of water.

The *karail* soils are black finer in texture and occur in the lower basin of Ganga. They occur in the districts of Allahabad, Varanasi, Ghazipur and Balia. They are formed from the black alluvial deposits transported by the Yamuna from Central India.

The Ganga divides Bihar into two halves north and south. The alluvium north of the Ganga has texture varying from sandy loam to clay loam and the pH is neutral to alkaline. Alkaline soils are generally found where the lime content is high. The alluvium south of the Ganga comprising the districts of Patna, Ganga and parts of Shahabad is gray to black and light loam to heavy clay. Lime is less and soil pH is slightly alkaline changing to the acidic range in the southern extremity.

The middle part which lies in a depression gets flooded during the monsoon. The available K_2O and P_2O_5 are high.

The red soils occur in the districts of Ranchi, Hazaribagh, Santal Parganas, Singhbhum and Manbhum. They are acidic (pH 5.0 6.8) and contain higher and soluble Fe_2O_3 than Al_2O_3. They are rich in available K_2O but are low in P_2O_5.

The wide use of newly released varieties and proper seed production from breeder and foundation seed to the growers seed stock on the farm are essential for high level rice production with minimum input. New and superior varieties however can make their contribution to practical agriculture only if the seed reaches the farmer in varietally pure state in adequate quantities in an undamaged condition free of weed seed and at a reasonable price.

The general purpose of seed production is to increase those old and new varieties which are superior to standard varieties for commercial distribution. The production of seed rice consists of growing the primary seed called foundation seed and then increasing this seed in sufficient quantities to meet the request of the practical farmer for his seed stock supplies. To produce high quality seed a grower must have a superior seed source of a well adapted variety. Formerly each farm would obtain a certain amount of such seed and multiply it to establish its own seed stock on the farm. But today modern harvesting and processing methods bulk drying and storage have increased the possibility of seed mixing. This led to the need for sources of pure seed. As a result the seed certification programme now in effect in this county is an important part of rice production.

Production of primary seed is carried out by institution for rice research and their experimental stations and farms. They produce foundation seed (super elite and elite) and multiply promising varieties for release to the growers. Production of farm seed stock is done largely by the commercial grower who breeds foundation seed through three generations the third of which is sown for commercial grain output.

The classes of seed termed breeder foundation and certified seed can be described as follows:

Breeder seed is seed directly controlled by the plant breeding institution and is the source of select seed handled at selected nurseries for the production of seed of the certified classes.

Foundation seed is the progeny of breeder or select seed handled at seed increase nurseries to maintain specific genetic purity and identity. Foundation seed is usually the first year increase from breeder seed. It is produced on fields that have not grown another variety or a lower class of the same variety during the 2 previous years. The distribution of foundation seed to growers usually is handled through specialized seed production farms and/or stations under a breeding center that increase this seed to the commercial growers as a certified class seed. For new varieties or for old varieties in short supply specified amounts of seed may be increased or reduced depending on demand.

Certified seed is the progeny of breeder and more so that foundation seed is handled so as to maintain a satisfactory level of genetic purity and identity. It is produced in riceland areas specifically allotted for seed increase purposes. The production and certification of seed is not a part of the breeding programme.

The *super elite* and *elite seed* is distributed to growers to be increased to quantities sufficient to maintain a seed stock necessary to satisfy the grower s needs. Usually the third year increase from certified or foundation seed is used for commercial grain production. Thus seed of a commercially established variety is renewed once in three years. For the production of the various classes of certified seed it is necessary to have clean land and to prevent mixtures in seeding harvesting and processing. The careful tending of all fields to remove undesirable weeds other crop and off type plants may increase the production costs but is very essential.

Varietally pure high quality seed in a viable condition can be obtained only through the proper use of the whole spectrum of agronomic practices. This includes adequate seedbed preparation crops grown preparatory to seeding rice the use of high quality seed optimum dates and methods of seeding adequate fertilization and finally proper mechanical treatments (threshing cleaning and grading). Practical experience has indicated that seed rice grown in good soil that receives the best fertilization and cultivation treatments is usually larger in size than seed of the same variety grown in poor soil and inadequately cultivated. The higher the level of cultivation the slower the process of varietal deterioration under commercial farming. Strict observance of the seed production cultivation requirements usually results in seed with high varietal and field qualities which will be preserved well in the 5th or even 6th generation. Any retreat from the established seed rice cultural requirements may bring about a rapid deterioration in the quality of even the first year seed. This will undoubtedly reduce the grain output of table rice in the area.

Usually the fields where rice will be grown for seed are treated much better than the commercial rice paddies to benefit the rice grower with seed rice of high standard. To avoid mixing each variety is sown with a separate clean seeder. The results of rice research and advanced practice indicate that perennial grasses cultivated fallows and new lands developed for rice are good for seed rice production. The land should be thoroughly worked to a fine tilth and adequately fertilized. Saline lands are considered inadequate for seed production and should be avoided. The irrigation and drainage facilities should be operable and in good shape and the land levelled to allow rapid flooding and draining if necessary.

The best time to sow rice for seed is when the soil temperature at a depth of 3.5 cm is 14 to 16°C which for most rice growing areas occurs in late April and early May.

To obtain a high germination rate the seed usually kept cooled during storage in the winter period is aerated and warmed up either in grain bins or grain driers and treated with granosan M.2.3 weeks before seeding.

The rate of seeding depends on the variety and may vary from 4.5 million to 6 million viable seeds per hectare. Where the elite seed is being increased for commercial release the rate of seeding is reduced to 4.5 million viable seeds per hectare. Good results can be obtained by drilling 3 million viable seeds per hectare in rows spaced at 30 cm. This method has proved effective for rapid multiplication of new and promising varieties since under such a wide row method of seeding the multiplication coefficient increases enabling the grower to achieve higher yields at a much lower rate of seeding. Under this method a rate of 100 kg viable seeds per hectare gave 7.16 t/ha of seed rice according to the USSR RRI data.

The wide row method of sowing rice for seed provides for a uniform ripening of seeds on the main and lateral panicles improves plant resistance to lodging and increases the productivity of the plant stand. All this in turn reduces the risk of blast disease and produces seed of a higher class. In addition this method allows for easy weeding to maintain varietal purity and identity of seed by removing off type and other crop plants from the field.

The time to sow rice for seed is equally important. Early seeding results in a thinned stand establishment during emergence while with delayed seeding the seed usually fails to fully mature and as a result exhibits poorer germination.

Seed rice plantings require optimum levels of nutrients particularly phosphorus. Excessive applications of nitrogen fertilizers should be avoided because high nitrogen contents delays maturity especially when the weather during the growing period is cool and rainy. In addition high nitrogen weakens the strength of the stem of the rice plant which leads to severe lodging which results in poorly filled grain high spikelet sterility problems at harvest time and germination in the panicle.

Insofar as possible seed fields should be managed so as to minimize lodging and produce satisfactory yields without excessive vegetation growth. This is impossible with high single rates of nitrogen which must be applied in divided or split dressings. In seed fields ammonium sulfate and urea are preferred over all other sources of nitrogen.

Phosphorus fertilizers appear to improve seed quality. Depending on the forecrop and degree of soil salinity phosphorus is applied as basal at rates from 90 to 150 kg P_2O_5 per hectare before seeding. Potash is also essential for seed fields to facilitate maturity obtain well filled grain and reduce the percentage of empty spikelets. Potassium is usually applied as topdressing during leaf tube formation at 30 to 60 kg K_2O per hectare.

The uses of specific varieties that differ in maturity grain type processing and cooking qualities of rice grain have increased the possibility of seed mixing. In this respect the production of seed that is varietally pure and free of persistent weed seeds become extremely important. Preventing intermixing throughout the various phases of seed production requires very close attention by the grower. Commercial varieties could become badly mixed with other varieties and infested with weedy strains of rice. These strains are the red rices that reduced grain and milled yield during harvesting and processing.

All the strains of red rice are characterized by severe shattering rapid growth high yield and a tolerance to adverse environments. Red rice produces many tillers (up to 60) and the progeny from one seed may amount to 1500-1600 viable seeds. Usually the grower inadvertently spreads red rice by planting contaminated seed. Because herbicides do not selectively control red rice in the rice crop infestations should be removed from seed rice fields by other methods if one is to avoid deteriorated quality in seed rice and prevent further spreading of the weed. Red rice contaminates not only the seeding material but also the soil. Tests have indicated that without proper weeding the quantity of red rice in the seeding material the following season increases 5 to 10 fold.

To control red rice it is necessary to know the biology of its strains. Control is difficult yet possible through crop rotations weeding operations renewal of seed sources adequate tillage etc. Red rice infestations of soil can be prevented through using land cropped with perennial grasses seeded fallows and new riceland for elite propagation and seed rice fields. Red rice plants that appear in the first year alfalfa crops following rice do not produce seed because they are cut out with each cut of alfalfa for hay.

Red rice seeds shed into the soil remain viable for several years and are able to sprout from a soil depth of 10 cm. Thus the emergence of a red rice seed plowed under in the fall to depths of 2 and 10 cm would be 20 to 10 per cent respectively. All plants that emerged would develop well and produce seed.

Flooding or flushing the soil to provoke red rice emergence is an effective means of red rice control. The method is particularly useful in cultivated fallows where a flood is established after the fallow grown crop has been harvested to soak the soil to refusal. The weeds and volunteer rice plants are then killed by disking or working the field over once with a chisel or plow. Besides mechanical eradication of the soil borne red rice use of high quality seed rice that is free of red rice and other weed seeds is an effective way of controlling repeated infestations.

Red rice infestation increases without regular rogueing of seed fields or when rice follows rice continuously. Infestation will also increase if the grower relies on his own seed stock for several seasons or if the seeding material is badly mixed.

Seed rice fields should be rogued several times during the last part of the growing season to eliminate not only the red rice plants but also the mixed varieties or rogues. The first rogueing is done at tasseling when the panicles of the early rices are visible. The second rogueing is initiated when the seed rice variety has fully developed and the rogues can be checked for the absence or presence of awns and colouration of the panicles. All awned plants are then removed from the seed fields growing awnless varieties of rice and conversely all the awnless plants are removed from the fields growing awned varieties.

Length and diameter grading of seed rice has been extremely useful in removing the larger diameter red rice grains from the seed of long grain varieties. The use of such graders is important in controlling red rice. In the medium and short grain varieties the only means of red rice control is the use of seed and land which is free of red rice because no method of separation has as yet been devised. The propagation of seed containing red rice soon results in a wild infestation of the soil with red rice strains and further complicates the maintenance of pure seed.

Field inspection of seed rice fields by the Seed Certifying Agency is carried out 5 to 6 days before harvest time to establish the varietal purity and identity of seed rice and to note the degree of infestation with red rice diseases and pests. Where required one additional rogueing may be recommended. Field inspection together with laboratory analyses of seed samples are used for further seed certification. In order for the rice to be eligible for certification the seed rice has to satisfy specific requirements and standards which are available from an official certifying agency. In general these requirements deal with application procedures field and harvest inspections post harvest seed movement seed processing and sampling. All rice growing areas use these standards as the minimum requirements for seed rice.

The time and method of harvesting seed rice are both important as they influence seed quality. The practice of water management in seed crops is equally important. Drying the fields for harvesting requires the close attention of the grower. Care should be taken when drying a field that the water recedes gradually e.g. at a rate of 1 cm per day. Day to day observation has to be carried out over soil which is drying in areas where rice seed is not dormant and able to swell and germinate in the panicle. If this is the case the depth of water in the rice paddy should be lowered immediately to a minimum and in low lying areas withdrawn completely. To be of high quality seed rice must be harvested at the proper stage of maturity. If the seed crop is cut when immature field yields are reduced and the breakage in threshing is excessive because of the light and chalky kernels. If the seed crop is left in the field until overripe the kernels may check.

The difference in moisture between the inside and the outside of the kernel is said to be the cause of checking or shattering of the grain. When too much moisture is removed due to high temperatures stresses and strains occur in the kernel which result in the microcracking of kernels. The checking of rice depends also on the shape of the grain the degree of maturity the variety and growing conditions but the moisture content still remains the decisive factor. Insofar as the checking of rice is not only the result of the outside (weather) factors but also of the mechanical impact it receives during threshing cleaning artificial drying and grading it is best to employ a method of harvesting that will result in seed with minimum damage percentage. Two staged threshing from the windrow is the preferred method during harvesting seed rice to reduce mechanical damage. The combine threshes about 80 to 85 per cent of the grain for seed during the first pass. What is left is threshed during the second round. The USSR RRI tests confirmed by practical observations of growers have indicated that the least losses occur with double stage threshing in which the speed of the thresher cylinder during the first pass (peg tooth cylinder 550 rpm and raspbar cylinder 750 780 rpm) is slower than during the second pass (700 and 1000 rpm respectively).

Harvesting should not be started until 90 to 95 per cent of the grain in the panicle are fully mature. This is established by taking an average sample. Seed rice should be harvested within the shortest time possible and with a minimum interruption between cutting and threshing. The normal procedure is to cut rice let it stay in the windrow for 3 to 5 days to dry and then thresh it from the windrow. Leaving the windrows in the field is unadvisable because of adverse weather factors that may cause the grain to check and lower its quality. Where the two staged harvest method is used for different varieties threshing should by all means be done with thoroughly cleaned combines. To keep varieties segregated use is also made of direct combining where the rice plants are not very badly lodged and the grain yields do not exceed 5 t/ha. In such cases the drying of the grain can be promoted by applying such chemical desiccants as magnesium sulfate which has proved useful in seed fields in testes conducted in various rice areas about the country. Spraying magnesium chlorate at 25 kg/ha hastens the drying of the grain and straw by 10 to 12 days. This practice prevents lodging reduces by 10 to 15 per cent the checking of kernels and permits direct combining. No grower however should use a desiccating material on the maturing seed crop until he has checked its legal status with reference to chemical residue tolerances.

In most rice growing farms crops are rotated because under continuous cropping with rice the soil becomes depleted in fertility and organic matter. The resulting deterioration of the physical condition of the rice soil makes cultivation difficult and the soil becomes infested with weeds and diseases that reduce the yield and quality of the rice grain.

Proper choice and establishment of a rotation programme is very important for maintaining high and stable production controlling weeds and red rice increasing the irrigation water and land use efficiency as well as the use of farming machinery and labour. Rice rotations help maintain and improve soil tilth and productivity between rice crops provide nutrious forage for livestock on the rice farms and increase the total agricultural output per hectare of riceland. The preferred system of cropping for any farm depends on the soil type local climatic conditions and economic considerations. In any case both the riceland and rice grower should benefit from crops rotated with rice. Rotational crops are selected so as to help eradicate weeds reduce populations of injurious pests control diseases and lower production costs.

Although the biology of rice makes it superior to other crops in that it responds well to repeated or continuous cropping rice in this country is rotated with other crops for the reasons discussed earlier. Rice rotations are also feasible because the increase in rice yields despite a smaller proportion of cropland in rice each year due to rotation is sufficient to maintain or even increase the total rice production on rice farms. A high and stable yield of rice under continuous cropping can be however obtained only with heavy application of commercial fertilizers. The USSR Rice Research Institute has reported that the 27 year average yield of rice grown in a six year rotation was by 1.73 t/ha more than when rice was grown continuously. Rotating rice with other crops is 1.5 times more economical than maintaining a continuous rice culture. In establishing a cropping system a four year rotation of rice gave 0.45 t/ha or 10 per cent more rice than the first yield. The yields of rice declined 0.47 t/ha within the same period under continuous cropping. In rotation experiments in the USSR Far East the yield of rice in a seven year rotation system was found to be 1.5 times that of rice under continuous cropping. Similar results were reported from the Uzbek SSR Rice Research Institute.

Continuous planting of lands to rice leads to heavy infestation of riceland with the rice culture related weeds to the detriment of the soil s physical condition and depletion of its fertility.

The beneficial effect of crop rotation on the rice yields can be attributed to many factors. First rotations enrich the plow line soil layer in organic matter and eliminate aquatic and other injurious weeds. Rotations facilitate oxidation of the chemically reduced nutrients improve porosity reduce the bulk mass by improving soil texture (less amount of particles smaller than 0.25 mm). They are also helpful in controlling insects and diseases and providing better opportunities for surface levelling through timely operations. On commercial rice farms rotations ensure comparatively high and stable grain yields.

Rice rotations in this country were first used in the old Kuban delta land which were formerly overgrown with boggy reed vegetation. An 8000 ha area had been developed for rice and six and seven year rotation systems were tried on its low productive overmoist and partly salinized soils. In the years 1971-75 average yields on the rice farms.

Rice rotations have come into use also in the new Kuban delta ricelands to benefit the rice growers with 5.5 t/ha and more rice which is 1-1.5 tons more than the average yields on the neighbouring farms where rotations are not yet customary.

Cropping systems or rotations have been used by many rice farms in other rice producing areas of the Soviet Union just to demonstrate that crop rotation is essential to ensure rice yields of about 6.0 t/ha or even more.

Under a rotation programme it is sought to use a maximum of cropland in rice following crops that are proven the best predecessors or forecrops. Such crops for rice are those that improve soil productivity and help the rice grower obtain good returns from a hectare of cropland. For this purpose the irrigated ricelands should for the greater part of the year be preferably used for raising high yielding crops. Since livestock has been extensively developed in most rice growing areas such crops are grown basically for feed purposes. In this way crop rotations are a useful tool in matching up the cultivation of rice and livestock raising.

Usually the rice systems are designed and engineered for a particular rotation pattern. The choice for a cropping pattern is therefore very important the determining factors being agricultural specialization soil type water and drainage conditions in the locality and the agronomic function of the rotation system. The idea of crop rotation implies that crops be periodically changed e.g. flooded rice is followed by a dryland crop. Such alternation of crops is mutually beneficial because it helps eliminate the deteriorative effect on the rice soil of extensive floods by allowing the soil to dry out when it is in a dryland crop. The cropping systems should be selected so that the proportion and the order of crops in the cropland are easily adaptable to different economic situations without readjusting the irrigation facility layout. Research and farming have proved that long time rotations such as the seven eight and nine year rotational programmes are most suitable in this respect.

Of the numerous long time cropping systems the eight year rotation with perennial grasses and seeded or cultivated fallows is preferred as the most flexible one. Under such a cropping pattern 62.5 per cent of the land is used for rice this proportion being easily increased to 75 per cent when necessary. The rice soil benefits from this system in receiving a double amount of organic matter first from turning under the perennial grasses then from the annuals. In addition the eight year rotation system provides better opportunities for the basic land forming and levelling operations in each field check. In most rice producing areas this cropping pattern has been the basis for design and construction of new riceland developments. Also other scientifically grounded cropping systems involving rice for various periods have been in use on rice farms of other locations in the Kuban delta lands.

Many rice farms use the eight year rotation with the following orders and frequency of crops first two years perennial grasses (alfalfa clover) third to fifth year rice sixth year seeded fallow followed by two annual crops of rice (with 62.5% of the land being used for rice 25 per cent for perennial grasses and 12.5 per cent for cultivated fallows under the system). About one fourth of the cropland in the Kuban delta is in a seven year rotation first and second year. Perennial grasses (alfalfa clover) third to fifth year rice sixth year cultivated fallow and seventh year rice or first year cultivated fallow second and third year rice fourth year other grain crops overseeded with perennials fifth year grasses and sixth and seventh year rice (with 57.1% of land in rice under the system). Where the long time rotation is impracticable but the agronomic practices are advanced and labour and power resources are plentiful the rice growers choose to use short term cropping systems such as the three year rotation first year seeded fallow and second and third year rice (with 66.7% of the cropland in rice) and four year rotation first year cultivated fallows and three years in rice i.e. three fourth of the time the land being used for rice under the system.

In the Monsoon climate of the Far East the cropping patterns vary. The eight year rotation may have a different order of crops depending on the depth of snow pack in the winter. Thus in localities where snow cover is permanent an eight year rotation may be first to third year rice half of the fourth year green manure crop the other half maintenance of the irrigation facilities fifth and sixth year rice seventh year barley or oats over cropped with clover eighth year clover (with 62.5% of the land in rice). Where snow is marginal the order and frequency of crops is first to third year rice half of the fourth year green manure crops the other half maintenance of the irrigation facilities fifth and sixth year rice seventh year cultivated fallow and eighth year forage crop the percentage of land in rice being the same. In other localities recommendations are for a seven year rotation as follows first year grain crop second year feed crop third and fourth year rice fifth year green manure crop sixth and seventh year rice (with 57% of cropland being used for rice). A six year rotation allows for one year in grain crop two years in rice one year in soybeans for green manure and two years in rice (with 66.7% of land in rice). The practice for newly developed ricelands has been a four year rotation consisting of three years in rice followed by half a year of green manure crops and the other half used for maintenance of the irrigation facilities (with 75% of land in rice under the cropping system).

With allowance for the local traditions and climate the cropping patterns are essentially the same but may vary in length from four to nine years also in the order of crops and in the proportion of land in rice which may range from 43 to 66.7 per cent. Whatever the order and frequency of crops in rotations rice growers have to follow the general tendency of crops in rotations rice growers have to follow the general tendency of allotting a maximum and economically feasible proportion of the land to rice as a staple culture and grow catch crops on it in between rice croppings.

Intensified Cropping Systems

Because of the high cost of land development for rice one way to ensure good returns from a hectare of irrigated land is by putting the riceland to intensive agricultural use. Considering the limited geography of rice in this country another way is to extend the acreage for rice in a rotation in addition to increasing the yield of rice through improved agronomy and superior varieties. Research on rotating rice with other crops has proved it possible to repeat rice cropping (up to four years) in the same field. Obtaining high and stable yields under such a system of cropping requires periodic incorporation into the soil of organic matter optimum applications of fertilizer good water management sufficient treatment of the field with herbicides and adequate agronomic practices. Rotational experiments conducted by the USSR Rice Research Institute indicate that the yield and gross output of rice can be increased thr ough using rotations making better use of perennial grasses increasing to more than three years the length of repeated cropping of rice after perennial grasses and through growing catch crops between rice croppings.

The eight year rotation system developed by the researchers for the Kuban delta ricelands can be considered as intensified rotation with 75 per cent of land in rice. The coefficient of land use under this system increases from 1.25 to 1.75 due to growing catch crops and better use of perennial grasses.

The Growth of Agricultural Plants

The growth of agricultural plants and cultural methods used for soil cultivation and particularly application of water and fertilizers cause various changes in the physical chemical and biological properties of the soil. This in turn affects the growth and development of crops that are grown on the same field the following years by increasing or decreasing their yield. The knowledge of how the individual species or groups of plants may influence the crop grown in alternate years is very important for appraising these plants or species as the forecrops for setting the proper order and frequency of crops in a rotation.

It has been proved by many tests and practical rice farming that perennial legumes fallow grown annual legumes and green manure crops leguminous gramineous mixtures and cruciferous plants and catch crops grown for seed and green manure are best for growing in rotations ahead of rice.

For other rice growing areas the crops preceeding rice in rotations are essentialy the same. In addition sweet or sour clover crimson clover mixed with berseem or Egyptian clover are sown in Kazakhstan, Uzbekistan and Turkmenia. The Sudan grass and spring wheat are grown in fallow fields and as catch crops in the Ukraine and Kazakhstan while corn (maize) sorghum joughara mixed with mung beans sweet clover and vetch oats mixtures are sown in Kazakhstan, Uzbekistan and Tajikistan.

The rice soil benefits much from alfalfa and clover if grown for two years. The grasses improve the physical condition of the soil increase the content of organic matter and soil productivity. Perennials facilitate the conversion of almost insoluble phosphorus compounds into readily soluble ones whose quantities tend to increase with the age of grasses. With a two year old grass cover the soil has a maximum of available phosphates. In rice rotations the total yield of alfalfa hay (four cuts) may reach 8-10 t/ha with the cost of one feed unit much lower than that of annual legumes. High yield of alfalfa in rice rotations is due to good agronomic practices including check flood irrigation or sprinkling and fertilizer applications.

The beneficial effect of alfalfa on the rice soils is higher when the two year old grass is left over winter to be turned under the following spring after the first cut of hay. In this case it gives additional 25-30 t/ha of green matter (5 tons on dry matter basis) before the field is sown to rice. The method of turning under alfalfa in spring has become customary with the rice farms in the Kuban rice areas ensuring stable yield of good quality hay in addition to 5 t/ha of early of mid season rice each year and increasing the organic matter in the soil in the form of roots and other plants debris. The higher the yield of perennial grasses grown ahead of rice in rotation the higher their beneficial effect on the rice soils and consequently on rice yield. Grasses therefore must be given the best agronomic care including seasonal irrigation and fertilizer treatments combined with soil slitting to produce highest yields of hay already in the first year.

Modern agronomic practices and adequate timing of optimum nitrogen and phosphorus fertilizer applications make it possible to maintain and sometimes increase the yield of rice grown three years continuously after grasses.

The yields of rice in an eight year rotation depending on the forecrop were as follows (the data of the USSR RRI).

Practical rice growing in the Kuban ricelands showed that alfalfa grown for two years ahead of rice and plowed under in the spring before seeding rice gives assured 5.0-5.5 t/ha of rice grain and with fertilizers up to 6.0-7.0 t/ha. Similar yields of rice in grassland broken at fall are attainable only with the application of 90 100 kg/ha of nitrogen fertilizers and phosphates (P_2O_5).

The chief aim of fallowing fields is controlling weeds check land leveling and reshaping and maintaining water structures. But because the land development for rice is costly it is unwise to allow the land to lie idle and hence pure fallowing is not encouraged. The fallow fields are therefore seeded or cultivated which permits the chief aim of fallowing to be achieved plus the fallow grown crops additionally gathered.

Seeded or cultivated fallows are fields used for growing various agricultural crops which when ripe leave fields free from plants soon after harvest for the land leveling operation. such crops in the Northern Caucasus are winter wheat mixed with winter peas or vetch grown for hay or green chop spring vetch mixed with oats winter and spring peas mixed with oats or barley and winter barley. The fallow grown crop in the Lower Volga rice farms is mostly winter rye mixed with vetch for green chop. In the Far East ricelands such crop is soybeans.

The use of mineral fertilizers for the fallow grown winter crops is mandatory in all the rice producing areas. The rates vary with the area and soil productivity. The soils in the Kuban delta lands require 120 kg N in addition to 90 kg P_2O_5 per hectare applied as basal fertilizer during the fall plowing for grains in pulses. Nitrogen applications are split into 90 kg/ha at seedbed preparation and 30 kg/ha as an early dressing.

For early spring crops such as barley wheat peas and oats mixed with vetch and peas the fertilizers are applied at seedbed preparation or at harrowing.

The yields of vetch and oat mixtures sown in fallows for hay are about 5 t/ha winter wheat and peas produce by early spring 3 to 4 t/ha and winter peas sown in autumn produce up to 3 t/ha of nutritious green matter.

All these crops are however susceptible to excess moisture. Crop failures may result from too much water held in checks after heavy rainfall and cloudburst unless adequate drainage is provided.

The choice and composition of fallow grown crops relies on the economic considerations availability of seeds and the possibility for annual land levelling in the checks which is a key operation for obtaining high rice yields the following season. In selecting and allotting lands to the accompanying crops of rice rotation and fallows the physical condition of the flooded soils is particularly important. Alfalfa barley corn and peas do not grow well where drainage is poor and the water table high. Their yields are low from excess water and poor thin stands. Adequate drainage is therefore the only remedy from water logging and inundation of rice fields and the adjacent areas which are in dryland crops. Of the crops which can tolerate high ground waters crimson clover berseem (Egyptian clover) and mung beans are the most tolerant.

Benefits to the staple rice culture from cultivated fallows in the rotation are high only with good weed control proper grading and levelling of land and increased organic matter in the soil due to fallow grown annual legumes and grasses. The intensive use of land through seeded fallows makes possible double cropping of riceland so that two crops are harvested the same year provided all operations are expertly timed.

Double cropping implies growing catch crops for use either at fall or early next spring as feed or green manure the same year after the main fallow grown crop is harvested field levelled and given the semi fallow tillage. Growing catch crops is also important for improving soil productivity and rice yield. The name catch crop applies to crops grown the same year following the staple crop and intended for feed or green manure. They are also known as stubble crops. The term is also applicable to crops sown in the spring into the cover crops to keep growing still for some time after the cover crop is harvested. Such crops are also called the companion or nurse crops the name applies to crops sown in summer or in the fall following the staple crop and harvested for feed purpose the following spring before a main crop is sown and known as the wintering crop and also to crops sown on fields free from the previous crop harvested early in season for green chop sillage or hay and sometimes called the postharvest crops which elsewhere can be grown as the main crop.

The agricultural plants selected to be grown as catch crops should be high yielding and early maturing recommended for this or that area and well adapted to heavy and periodically flooded soils. Among such crops are pulses (winter and spring vetch and peavine) winter rye winter wheat barley oats spring rapeseed all sown in pure or mixed stands.

In the Northern Caucasus and the Lower Volga rice areas the fallow grown catch crops are sown in the summer or fall and thus are called summer crops. The same crops to be grown in rice fields are sown as winter crops. In the rice producing areas of the USSR Far East the catch crop is soybeans (when grown in fallows it is for green manure although soybeans can be grown for grain).

Winter rye is good as a catch crop. Some of its winter varieties are winter hardy and shoot out well early in the spring at low temperatures (close to zero) producing fairly good yield of nutritious green matter so valuable early in the spring for its vitamins.

In many rice growing areas of this country and particularly in the Cis Caspian Lowland rotational crops are grown in saline soils. In such cases adequate drainage and importation are necessary to avoid water logging inundation and salinization of the land in accompanying crops and grasses that are adjacent to rice fields on the one hand and make the best use of the rotation on the other. Of the accompanying crops peas oats and corn are less tolerant to salts than are rye wheat sorghum and particularly alfalfa. Gourds and melons tolerate better high concentrations of salts. Soils moisture content is an important regulator of the degree of salt tolerance of the rotational crops. The higher the moisture content the more tolerant the plants to salinity during their early development.

To provide high and stable yield each rotational crop in a rice cropping system should be grown under optimum agronomic conditions. It has been established that the rice yield to a large extent depends on the productivity of the preceeding crops. Thus yield or rice following one year alfalfa depending on its crop of hay was as follows.

Good timing of catch crops is also important in a rice rotation. It is advisable that in the rice fields which are planned the following season for catch crops rices are early maturing and sown in the current year as early as possible. In that way the crop of rice is ready to harvest much early giving the grower time enough to prepare the land for catch crops of the following year.

Tilling soil for rice is not much the same as tilling for other cereals and dryland crops. Its principal aim in rice production is to obtain high yields of rice through improving the rice soil and taking advantage of its potential productivity.

While the dryland crops require soil nutrients in the oxidized form the rice plant benefits more when the nutrients are chemically reduced or deoxidized. The dryland crops require that the capillary noncapillary porosity ratio (determined by the water stable soil structure and soil moisture brought to capillary capacity) be optimum while this soil parameter for rice is practically for rice is practically unimportant.

Nutrition of the rice plant is in large measure assured by inundation during part of all of the growing period. Flooding is very much essential for optimum grain yields that are why the ideal soil types for rice production are those that conserve water. Most rice soils often referred to as heavy soils because of their high clay and silt content present special soil management problem that are overcome through soil cultivation practices intended also to help make the best use of the natural soil potential. These measures include tillage and seedbed preparation maintenance of organic matter and soil texture drainage for successful mechanized rice operations cultivation of other crops in rotation with rice fertilizer application use of green manures and weed control.

Soil tillage practices vary from place to place depending on soil type climatic conditions crop that preceedes rice in rotation physical condition of the soil character and degree of field infestation herbicides used and other factors. Tillage in rice production pursues many purposes.

Forming a sufficiently deep and biologically active plowline layer by working the field several times over with various types of plow.

Creating conditions in the plow line that help immobilize soil nutrients i.e. regulate oxidation and reduction through loosening drying and aerating of soil.

Wetting the rice fields that are to be sown at early dates and to a greater depth so as to establish the moisture content sufficient to bring about emergence of rice seedlings without additional flush irrigation.

Preparing the riceland with a soil structure that will ensure a uniform coverage and germination of seeds good stand establishment and further development of the plant during growing season.

Controlling weeds pests and diseases of rice and other rotational crops by plowing in the fall one time over with a chisel and a second time in the spring with a mouldboard.

Precise levelling of the field surface (to within ± 5 cm from the median plane of the rice check surface) to maintain desired depth of flood water in the field and to drain as rapidly as required.

Covering organic and mineral fertilizers at desired depths.

Preparing a suitable seedbed for rice.

The harvesting of mature rice and post harvesting operations are important aspects of rice culture. Rice crops usually mature later in the season than other grain crops. The time to harvest rice therefore varies from early September in the European USSR to mid September in the Far East. For the best results harvesting should continue for no more than 20 25 days. Delaying or extending the time of harvesting increases losses reduces both yield and grain quality and does not provide enough time to adequately prepare the land for next season s crops.

Factors that determine the duration of the harvest are the time and date of seeding the maturity period of the rice variety the level of infestation soil and drainage conditions in the rice fields and the weather before and during harvesting.

Draining at the proper time before harvesting is required to sufficiently dry the soil to use the heavy rice harvesting machinery. It is however equally important to maintain the water in the rice field long enough to permit the rice crop to reach proper maturity.

When to drain depends on the soil type drainage facilities and weather conditions in any given season. Some soils dry quickly others slowly. Rice growers soon familiarize themselves with the time to dry their soil and soon learn to judge when the best time is to drain the fields for harvesting without letting the rice crop suffer from a lack of soil moisture. In a year with a typical amount of heat and rainfall the date when rice will be ready to cut can be estimated by observing the date of flowering and initiation of heading. Rice normally requires 40 to 50 days from flowering to maturity.

The flow of water into the checks is usually reduced by the time rice reaches the soft dough (milky) stage and is discontinued altogether when the rice matures to the hard dough (waxy) stage so that the water will recede slowly at a rate of 1-1.5 cm per day. Where the soils are saline the fields are drained. The level of groundwater should preferably be maintained low through proper drainage to avoid waterlogging the checks. Less time is required to dry the soil where drainage furrows have been opened in the spring. In fields without drainage furrows pools of water are likely to appear. In such cases the water is either pumped out or removed through hand made furrows.

Usually riceland may be drained when the rice crop has fully headed and the panicles have turned down and ripened in the upper parts. This stage normally occurs about 2-3 weeks before the rice crop is ready to harvest.

Water intake should be discontinued progressively beginning with the low lying checks that are usually downstream from the headwork then successively with the checks at higher elevations. This results in a simultaneous and uniform drying of the paddies in each large check. By the time the rice crop is ready to cut the soil should be dry enough to support the harvesting machines and equipment.

Premature drying of the field checks will delay the filling of grain so the rice crop harvested too early will have a greater quantity of immature empty and poor quality grains and will produce a smaller yield of head rice at milling. On the other hand it is equally important not to miss the time of maturity. When rice stands too long in the field losses are increased due to lodging premature germination in the panicle and shattering.

The pre harvest application of chemical desiccants is a frequently used practice to speed the drying of rice in the field before harvest. Of all the known materials applied as sprays a 60 per cent magnesium chlorate water solution has proved the most effective when it is used at 25 kg to 150 liters water per hectare. After treatment with this desiccant about 2-3 per cent grain moisture and 4 6 per cent leaf moisture is removed daily. Within 4 to 6 days as soon the grain moisture content is brought down from within 20-27 to 15-16 per cent the rice can be harvested.

The aerial application of desiccants gives best results when carried out on clear bright days early in the morning or afternoon. Average diurnal temperatures should be about 9 10°C with a maximum wind velocity of 4 m/s. Very good results are obtained if there is no rain for about 6 to 8 h after spraying. The application of chemical desiccants at optimum dates (when 85 90% of kernels are fully mature) increases the grain yield improves the seed quality and reduces both labour and harvest time by 10 to 15 days. Rice treated with desiccants is usually harvested by direct combining.

Chemical materials used as desiccants should be considered poisonous so no grower should use a desiccating chemical on the maturing rice crop until he has checked its legal status with reference to chemical residue tolerances. When used with caution however desiccants can give good results without the traditional after effect such as a drop in milling quality kernel dislocation and an off flavour that may occasionally be imparted to the rice.

A new method of speeding up the drying of rice has recently been proposed by Professor E.P. Aleshin and has proven effective in improving harvesting conditions and grain quality and in reducing harvest losses. It relies entirely on a solution of water soluble phosphorus fertilizers plus small amounts of 2-4 D amine salt which is applied as a top dressing on rice in the milky stage of ripening.

Pre Harvest Operations

After the irrigation water has been withheld and the soil is sufficiently dry the rice around the check s border is cut with either a self propelled crawler mounted reaper a combined harvester thresher or a crawler mounted swather. This is done 2-3 days before the all out harvesting of the rice begins in the fields enabling more time for the soil to dry out and the rice to mature as well as eliminating the risk that the harvesting machines will run onto hydraulic structure invisible to the operator.

Square shaped rice paddies and large checks are divided into strips 50 to 70 m wide by cutting swaths from one end of the field to the other. Two cross swaths are cut from both sides of the field to provide a 6 to 10 m wide headland for the harvesting equipment. This increases the efficiency of the harvesting machines by about 15 to 20 per cent reducing hand labour and field losses.

The time to harvest food and seed rice can be determined by observing the date when 85 and 95 per cent of the grains in the respective panicles are fully mature. If the crop is left in the field until it is overripe the kernels may check. This will cause breakage during combining and milling and a reduction in the yield of whole kernels (head rice). Biological yield losses from harvesting delayed by three days amount to about 0.2 t./ha. The losses rice to 0.5-1.0 t/ha when harvesting is delayed by 10 to 15 days. It follows that the prime time for cutting the rice crop should not be missed by the grower. Any delay will result in reduced yield due to shattering during hot dry days and slow threshing if the weather is humid and cool.

The time to harvest depends largely on the weather. The mid season varieties of rice (Kuban-3) which are sown about the same date should be harvested within 8 to 10 days and the late rices (Krasnodarsky-424) within 10-12 days. It has been established that standing rice does not hold its maximum yield for long. In the Kuban river riceland for instance rice keeps its optimal grain yield (to within ± 5% of the maximum) only 8 to 10 days.

Harvesting Rice

Most rice in the Soviet Union is harvested mechanically either with self propelled combine harvesters or with a tractor drawn header or swather which threshes from the windrow. Harvesting by hand may be resorted to only on very small acreages when the weather is rainy and the use of harvesting machines is impractical.

Direct combining or single phase harvesting and separate or two phase harvesting are the two major methods to harvest rice in this country.

Over 80 per cent of the total rice acreage in the USSR is harvested by the two phase method. Essentially this is cutting the rice with a swather or windrower and threshing it from the windrow with a pickup combine when the grain is adequately dry. The rice is then dried artificially before it is stored or milled. Careful adjustment of the reaping machine and the thresher leads to grain of a high milling quality and market value.

The two phase method permits rice to be cut at earlier dates followed by threshing from the windrow 3-5 days after. This results in grain with much less moisture content thus reducing the cost of artificial drying. If the rice crop is left in the windrow too long the grain may check (crack) increasing breakage during threshing and milling and markedly reducing the yield of head rice and quality of seed rice. It is therefore better to thresh from the windrow at the proper time and avoid large intervals between cutting and threshing.

Direct combining or combine harvesting is more efficient and economic in that it provides grain of the highest milling quality and considerably reduces fields losses. It is more effective over the two phase method particularly when the weather at harvest time is unstable because it permits rice to be removed from the field in one operation with no danger of weather damage. Hopefully with improved combines along with a wider use of desiccants grain driers cleaning facilities and less lodging rice varieties that produce less vegetative growth direct combining will find a wider application in the near future.

Already in some rice growing areas self propelled rice combines provide the major means of harvesting rice.

With either method obtaining a control yield of threshed grain by cutting and threshing 2 swaths in 2-3 representative (typical) field checks or rice paddies has become an important practice in all rice producing areas. Practical observation confirmed by growers results indicate that the operator is the most important factor in preventing high combine losses. Therefore control threshing is usually done first by highly skilled combine operators who determine for the other operators where to adjust the thresher device in the combines and the cutter head in the swathers and reapers.

With the common two phase harvest method rice is cut with a tractor mounted side delivery windrower or reaper. Front mounted swathers having two active cutter bars are good for cutting badly lodged rice. A header or windrower is also suitable in such cases as it delivers uniform windrows from 4.5 to 5 m wide swaths. Such windrows dry quickly. Self propelled headers or swathers with the knife divider removed and the reel adjusted to the rear shield of the frame can also be successfully used to cut rice crops that are badly lodged. These adjustments reduce the number of cut out panicles lower losses by reel shattering and improve the operating condition of the reel and the delivery chain. The cam action reel should be adjusted 200 250 mm frontwise relative to the cutter so that the rake just touches the plant stem at 2/3 of its height from the base. The reel is adjusted in level with the cutter bar to cut lodged rice below the point of bending i.e. 50-70 mm from the top so that the reel rake then only cleans the knife and pushes the cut plants onto the delivery chain. The reel speed should always exceed the ground speed of the swather. This effects proper reaping at 15-20 cm from the ground surface and minimizes field losses. The height at which the rice is cut is very important because the proper amount of straw serves as a cushion to the grain during threshing resulting in a lower cylinder loss and less breakage.

Rice in a paddy or large check may be cut either by the strip or by the continuous method. With the first method each swather or combine works a strip of rice crop 50-70 m wide. It starts on one of its longer sides makes a 90° turn at the corner and an idle run along the shorter side of the strip to turn again and cut rice along the other longer side in the opposite direction working clockwise from the check s field margin towards the center line of the strip.

Strip harvesting is good for harvesting field checks where the swather can pass over the levees from one rice paddy to another. The efficiency of the harvesting equipment is 15-20 per cent higher as the idle run distance on the head land is considerably reduced. The method is usually used for cutting badly lodged rice or under extremely muddy conditions when turns are difficult to make due to large clods on the headland.

The continuous method is effective where soil is more dry and rice is not lodging. The method requires no headland as the harvester cuts the rice going counterclockwise along the check and makes a turn to the right (270° loop) each time it reaches a field corner.

Usually several harvesters form a group that completes harvesting a field check within 3-4 days (15-20 hectares per each swather). The group method permits the rice crop to be quickly cut and threshed with a pickup combine as soon as the windrows are sufficiently dry. Where the harvest time is late August and early September and the days are warm and dry threshing from the windrow is normally begun 3-5 days after cutting. Where the harvest time is late September and early October the interval between cutting and threshing may be longer. Threshing from the windrow may not begin until the grain (not the stem) moisture content reaches 16 to 20 per cent. Field observations confirmed by grower s reports indicate that if rice is left in windrows until over dried this results in grain of poor quality creating heavy losses during threshing and milling.

The threshing operation in a field check 15 to 20 ha in size is also done by a group of 4 to 5 pickup combines. They are assisted by tractor drawn or self propelled grain carts which haul the threshed grain from the combine to the field side trucks who in turn haul the grain further to the driers or the elevator. With an average efficiency of 3-4 ha per combine such a harvesting team may complete a field check in 2-3 days. In both methods total field losses can be minimized and grain quality improved by threshing the rice straw with unthreshed grain a second time. Double threshing requires that 85 to 95 per cent of the grain the threshed during the first threshing round while the remaining grain is threshed during the second round with a pickup combine harvester. The combine thresher should be adjusted so that no threshed grain will go into the new windrow as the straw leaves the combine. The windrows should be uniform in shape and not too large so that they do not crowd the feed. The more straw is fed the higher the cylinder losses particularly if the grain s moisture content is excessively high. Because the rice kernel is susceptible to cracking the cylinders should be run at a slower speed than usual for small grain crops.

To obtain maximum grain yields it is necessary for the cylinder and the concave to be in good condition and for the concaves and other parts of the combine to be properly adjusted. The major combine losses are attributed to the cutter bar cylinder rack and cleaning shoe. Other losses may be due to overloading or improper machine adjustment or a combination of the two. Overloading as a result of excessive ground speed is usually a major cause for heavy loss in all types and sizes of combines. Modern combines can be adjusted to do a good job of threshing with a minimum of shelling and cracking of the grain.

With a lath reel pickup grain losses are about two times less than with the pegged reel version of the pickup attachment. For this reason the lath reel pickup is preferable to the pegged reel pickup. High losses of unthreshed grain usually result from either improper cylinder (drum) or concave adjustments or both. Losses of threshed grain may also come from poor separation in the straw wakers and cleaning shoe. Several tests should be made with each machine to determine the effect of adjusting or changing the ground speed. Cylinder speed should be varied with the rice varieties and the grain straw moisture content.

Reducing the cylinder speed helps minimize shelling and cracking of the grain but may increase the loss of unthreshed grain. For the second round of threshing the speed of the fan and cylinders should be greater than the rated one by 20 per cent.

Rice harvesting machines include various tractor driven swathers and reapers self propelled headers and windrowers and self propelled combined thresher harvesters equipped with crawler tracks half tracks or tyres. In rainy season wide mud cleats may be bolted onto the tracks to increase support to the harvester. Other tractors and combines are equipped with tyres with mud lugs or cages so that they can be operated on the sloping levees and under extremely muddy conditions.

The rice farming machines usually operate by either the traction or floating principle. By the first the tracks or tyres penetrate the muddy tilth to reach the hard pan on which they find a firm support for traction. By the second principle machines have to move by flotation acquiring support on the top muddy soil with the help of cage wheel or track extensions (extendable lugs). Ricegrowers would very much appreciate special self propelled rice combines equipped with the rice special tyre . Some self propelled harvesters are equipped with large bins or hoppers for collecting the threshed grain. The hoppers are emptied by mechanically augering the rice into self propelled bankouts or tractor driven carts that take the rice to trucks which wait alongside the field. The rice is then hauled to driers or to aeration bins where it is unloaded by use of grain augers or other bulk handling means.

Grain Moisture Content

Because the grain moisture content varies with the time of day the combine threshing parts should be re adjusted several times during the day at 9 10 a.m. and 6 7 p.m. for the wet straw and between 12 and 4 p.m. for the dry straw.

Rice must be of high milling quality to command a premium price and to obtain this high quality and maximum yields rice must be cut at the proper stage of maturity (moisture content).

When the rice crop has reached the proper stage and grain moisture harvesting should proceed quickly because the loss of moisture in standing rice can be very rapid. If rice is harvested at the proper stage the grains are fully mature in the upper portions of the panicle and are in the hard dough stage at the base of the panicle. Observations indicate that maximum yields of head rice were obtained when rice was harvested at moisture content of about 18 to 24 per cent and then immediately dried to 13 and 14 per cent. Varieties differ as to the range of moisture content at which they yield the best quality milled rice. This range is rather wide varying from 16 to 25 per cent for some varieties. Many rice growers determine the moisture content of hand harvested samples of their rice with various types of moisture meters before they begin all out harvesting.

Thus when harvesting for maximum quality a lot of factors must be considered but moisture content of the grain at harvest time is among the most important. Good results may be obtained with the use of chemical desiccants which hasten pre harvest of the crop if applied timely and properly.

Post harvest tillage and preparation for the next crop require that the rice fields be cleaned of rice straw and other plant residues. The straw can be removed from the field after it is bailed picked up and stacked off field to be processed for animal feed. Some other suggested uses are as bedding construction material for manurial purposes or as a mulching material for purpose of soil protection. The straw can be removed from the fields either as the harvest proceeds or immediately after the harvest. For soil mulching the straw is simply cut in the rice field with special straw spreaders or choppers and the straw particles are then spread uniformly over the stubble to facilitate plowing under with a disk plow. Some combines are now equipped with straw spreaders that cut up the straw as it leaves the combine. Various other machines such as straw rakes pickup choppers stackers and loaders assisted with special tractor driven straw carts are used to facilitate the operation and haul straw stacks from the fields.

Processing Rice for Storage and Milling

The cleaning and drying of rough rice is very important for safe grain storage. Timely and proper processing of the field run rice usually results in attaining grain of the highest quality and commercial value with lower input per unit volume of rice dried and stored. The post harvest procedures include pre cleaning or scalping drying and grading of the rough rice. Usually the rough rice coming from the field unless the fields are clean contains considerable foreign material such as stems weed seeds and trash. It is therefore advisable to clean it partially with a scalper aspirator machine before putting it into the bin for aeration. In some areas facilities and conditions may require that the rice first be dried. Such drying may require that the rice be passed though the drier several times. Frequently the rice is also aerated between passes to remove foreign matter and light weight immature grains before it is put into storage.

Preliminary cleaning of rough rice can be done on the on farm facilities that should include a fanning mill with a wind aspirator to remove light grains hulls and other light weight foreign material a screen with large perforations to remove any remaining sticks stems lumps and large weed seeds and a finely perforated screen to remove fine broken rice grain small weed seeds and other small particles of foreign material. The pre cleaned rice is then put into bins for aeration.

Aeration

Is the procedure used to cool and ventilate grain during storage to improve quality and prevent spoilage. This can be accomplished by turning the grain at regular intervals by transferring it from one bin to another with a grain loader or grain thrower or by circulating air through the stored grain.

For proper drying moisture must be removed from inside the rice kernel. Drying too fast can result in internal cracking or checking of the kernels. To prevent this drying is usually done in several stage with the moisture reduced only about two per cent at each drying. After each stage the rice is tempered in a bin so that the kernel moisture will equilibrate.

Weeds and Their Control

Weeds compete with rice for light nutrients space and water they also adversely affect the microclimate around the plant and harbour diseases and pests. They reduce yields lower the market value of the crop by reducing quality and increase the cost of production harvesting drying and cleaning.

Slightly more than 250 species of plants have been registered as weeds that infest rice fields in the Soviet Union. Of these about 20 species are persistent weeds that infest old ricelands and some 10-12 species are weeds frequently found in crops that are grown in rotation with rice.

Weeds that infest rice fields differ from those that infest dryland and even irrigated crops. They are from the species that thrives best in extremely wet or flooded soil.

Plants that infest rice fields can ecologically be grouped as hydrophylous marshy aquatic and floating weeds and algae.

Hydrophylous weed plants include barnyard grass (*Echinochloa contracta Stev. E. phyllopogon Stapf.* and *E. crus galli L.*).

The weeds in this group are common to all rice growing areas and grow equally well in waterlogged soils and fields flooded with shallow water. Prolonged and deep flooding is fatal for the young weed grass.

Barnyard grass is an annual plant and is the most persistent weed in seed rice and food rice plantings. Early in season it is often hard to differentiate between the young rice seedlings and those of the weed grass because of various morphological and biological characters that are quite similar in both species. However, the rice leaf is more rigid robust and rough than that of the barnyard grass which has a wider vein in the centre and is a paler green. The stalk in rice is somewhat flat at the base and it is round in barnyard grass.

One barnyard grass plant may produce from 600 to 800 seeds in average rice stands and from 3000 to 6000 seeds in thin stands. The heat requirement of barnyard grass is about the same as that of rice. *Echinochloa* spp. germinates at temperatures not lower than 12°C in very wet or flooded soils. The optimum temperature for germination is from 20 to 25°C. Shed in the soil the weed seed remains viable for 3 years it may germinate and give seedlings in dryland from a depth of 6 cm when the soil is compact and from 12 cm when the soil is loose. It germinates and sprouts seedlings from topsoil covered with a shallow layer of water about 1-3 cm.

Echinochioa contracta Stev. tillers well in rich soils and in thin stands. It can be long awned medium awned and awnless. All three forms of the species are subject to shattering thus infesting rice fields badly. The weight of 1000 grains varies from 6-7 g to 11 g. The matured seed has no dormancy period and since it sheds in wet gound it germinates rapidly from late September to early October when the soil is sufficiently moist the weather warm and temperatures about 16-18°C. In the spring the seed of the weed sprouts from a soil depth of 1-12 cm as soon as the soil temperature reaches 12-14°C. By late May its germination percentage is about 93-98. The best soil conditions for sprouting are a soil moisture content of about 90-100 per cent of the least field capacity and a temperature of 20 to 25°C. In the spring 100 per cent of the weed seeds germinate and sprout from a 1-3 cm soil depth 80 per cent from a 5 cm depth and 56 per cent from a 10-12 cm soil depth in rice fields where a flood about 15 cm deep is maintained. After a year in rice about 20 per cent of the seeds within a soil layer from 0 to 20 cm may still be viable. The young grass can stand shallow water but a flood of about 25 cm would be fatal.

Echinochloa phyllopogon Stapf. can be either awned or awnless. The awnless forms shatter more and infest rice soils directly. The awned from are more resistant to shattering and infest rice fields through uncleaned seed rice. The weed has a well developed root system and produces many tillers. 1000 grains weigh 4-7 g. The seed is not dormant and germinates rapidly producing vigorous seedlings at excessive soil moisture and soil temperatures of 14-15°C. The young weed grass can stand deep water but floods up to 25-30 cm in hot weather will kill the weed within 5 to 7 days. Morphologically *E. phyllopogon* is closer to rice than other forms of the species and has about the same maturity period. The seed of the weed buried deep in the soil remains viable up to 5 years and is able to sprout in compact soil up to 10 cm deep. The seed however fails to produce seedlings from a soil layer of 2 cm under submergence but the established seedlings can stand deep water for the rest of the growing period.

Echinochloa crus galli L. can be long awned medium awned or awnless. The long awned forms usually infest fields where rice is cultivated under continuous submergence. The weed can sprout from a soil depth of 3-5 cm in a field with a 10 cm deep water cover but it fails to produce seedlings through a layer of water as high as 15-20 cm.

Because they are ecologically closer to dryland weeds the medium awned and awnless forms normally infest rice fields under rotational irrigation. These forms of barnyard grass mature even earlier than do the early rices and shatter more than other weed grasses. The small sized seed has a period of dormancy. The 1000 grain weight varies between 1.5 and 2.0 g. Once shed the seed volunteers in early April from a soil depth of 1 cm but not until mid April from a depth of 3-5 cm. In the spring up to the time for seeding rice about 80 per cent of barnyard grass seeds present in a soil depth of 1-5 cm will emerge and about 50 per cent will sprout in a soil layer between 0 and 20 cm provided that air temperatures are 12 to 23°C and soil moisture accounts for 70 to 85 per cent of the least field capacity. When irrigation water is provided from April 16 to May 20 about 28 per cent more seeds that survived the winter within the 0-20 cm soil layer will emerge.

However about 17 per cent of such seeds will still remain within the rice field. Under rotational irrigation water applications for crops other than rice (usually grasses) can during one summer in a dryland crop yield up to 95 per cent of barnyard grass plants from the 1-25 cm soil layer. *E. crus galli* is a viable plant that grows back every time the main crop of grass is cut.

Rice cutgrass (*Leersia oryzoides* L.) a perennial grass has recently become a problem in Uzbekistan, Kazakhstan and in the Northern Caucasus. The weed grass infests primarily rice fields under rotational irrigation and also irrigation ditches. It propagates by seed and other propagules called rhizomes. During its growing period one rice cutgrass plant produces rhizomes up to 1 m long with 12-15 internodes. The winter buds start to grow in the spring when temperatures are from 8 to 12°C. The culm of the plant varies in height from 50 to 150 cm and its leaf is sharply indented on the edges. The inflorescence is an expanded panicle up to 18 cm long that bears many spikelets (from 500 to 700).

Marshy weed plants are largely perennials that infest fields which are continuously in rice as well as low lying fields checks which are waterlogged most of the time. The weeds in this group thrive exclusively or waterlogged and submerged lands and can withstand deep water and prolonged submergence. The weeds propagate by seed and by vegetations. Their propagules are rhizomes tubers or root tubers. These start to grow in the spring at soil temperatures about 10-11°C. Because it seedling usually emerge earlier than those of rice they compete vigorously with each other for the growth essentials.

Common reed (*Phragmites communis* Trin.) thrives in waterlogged areas and ricelands where table water is high. It propagates vegetatively through its well developed rootstock that penetrates soil to 1.5 m as well as through above ground propagules that creep over the soil surface. The common reed has no special soil requirements and grow well in both saline and good soils.

Bulrush (*Boldoschoenus compactus* Hoffm.) and clubrush (*B. maritimus* Palla) are sedge weeds. The stalk is 85 cm tall and triangular at the base. The leaf is long (70 cm) narrow and rough. The mature seed is small and dormant and is shed long before the early rice is harvested. Most of the seeds (up to 50-80%) over winter on check surfaces then germinate and produce shoots in the spring when temperatures stabilize about 20°C and soil moisture approaches field capacity. Seedlings may even grow through a thin sheet of water about 1-2 cm. In the soil the seed remains viable for about 5-8 years. Both forms propagate by seed and by tuber. During one season each tuber lying at a depth of 11-15 cm produces from 10 to 47 new tubers and in a year old grassland up to 11 tubers. Tuberization occurs primarily within the 2-10 cm layer of soil. In old riceland the number of tubers within the depth of the plow line may sometimes be as high as 1000-2000 tubers per sq m. Tubers that are buried at a depth of 20-23 cm for more than 9 years lose about 70-75 per cent of their viability. Drying and freezing of the soil in old riceland markedly reduces the viability of propagules within the top soil. Drying of the soil (i.e. soil moisture under 14%) is fatal to tubers.

Spikerush (*Junceilus serotinus* Rottd.) is another persistent weed of the sedge family. The triangular culm is about 1 m tall. It propagates by seed and by rootstock. The seed s dormancy and germination rates are about the same as in bulrush seed. Propagation is however usually vegetative through the roötstock. One fruit bearing organ produces up to 47 new cord like rhizomes in one season. The rhizomes are spaced at 3 to 20 cm apart and sit at the end of the old rootstock. Freezing and drying of soil is lethal only to the surface confined rhizomes.

Common cattail also mace reed and narrow leaf cattail are perennial weeds with a thick creeping rootstocks buried at a depth of 5-10 cm. These weeds have a 2 cm and a 0.5-1.0 cm broad leaf respectively. Both weeds propagate by seed and by rootstock. The small sized seeds have a pappus and are grouped into cylindrical inflorescences each containing up to 4,50,000 seeds. The seed germination rate is about 100 per cent in the year when the plant flowers. The seed produces shoots at temperatures no lower than 20°C in overwet soils or fields with a thin water layer. Draining of fields and drying of the soil kills the young plants. The weed infests mostly irrigation and drainage ditches and newly developed rice lands it also thrives where cultural practices are poor.

Common water plantain (*Alisma plantago aquatica* var. maritima L.) is a perennial weed that infests rice fields in the Ukraine, Northern Caucasus, Kazakhstan and Uzbekistan. Oriental water plantain (*A. plantago asiatica*) is a weed that causes problems in the Far East rice lands. It is a prolific plant that propagates by seed and by tubers. Its maturity period is shorter than that of rice. The matured seed shatters and thus infests rice soils. One plants is able to produce anywhere from 15,000-20,000 and more achenes with a high seedling vigour. The seed germinates rapidly both in soils with moisture that is close to field capacity and in submerged soils with a floodwater temperature of 15-18°C. From the 1 cm layer of submerged soil water plantain emerges shortly after rice and completes with the rice seedlings for strength and becomes robust until the rice row stand close. The competition is particularly vigorous where the stands of crop are thin. Weed shoots develop from the buds that sit on the propagative tubers and soon appear to form leaves (in June and early July) that float on the floodwater surface shading and suppressing the young rice.

When buried in wet soil water plantain propagules with auxiliary buds can remain viable indefinitely and are able to withstand heavy frosts. Even a mild frost however can kill tubers when they are brought to the surface during soil cultivation. Smoothing underwater check surfaces following land preparation operations during the summer is considered an effective means of controlling water plantain.

Pickerel weed (*Monochoria korsakovi* Regal et Meack.) is an annual broadleaf weed that can survive in deep water. Pickerel weed usually infests rice fields and irrigation and drainage ditches. It is common in the far eastern rice producing areas and is a major weed where rice is shallowly seeded. Outbreaks of Monochoria have been recently reported in the Northern Caucasus – particularly in the Kuban delta ricelands.

The mature plant is 50-60 cm tall and has a succulent stem with thick broad leaves. It propagates by seed which is enclosed in a ball with a large pericarp. One Monochoria plant produces up to 20000 seeds. The mature seed germinates well in a soil with moisture close to field capacity or in flooded soil. The young weed plant usually emerges in rice fields from mid June to early July. The weed is susceptible to shade. A good rice stand will suppress Monochoria in that a large number of the plants will die for lack of daylight. Most of the remaining plants (up to 95%) fail to produce inflorescence and therefore do not flower. The weed however thrives in thin stands and then competes vigorously with rice thus reducing grain yields. An efficient means of controlling Monochoria is to sow rice early and deep thus permitting seedlings to be obtained using naturally stored moisture. An additional means of combatting the weed is to level the fallow fields when they are under water.

Arrowhead or duck potato (*Sagittaria trifolia* L.) is a perennial plant with arrow shaped leaves. It propagates by seed and tuber forming stolons at depths ranging from 6-9 to 15 cm. These are underground shoots bearing about 8 tubers at each end. The tuber has a crown bud from which a seedling can develop earlier than from the seed itself. At soil depths of 20-25 cm the tubers remain viable for about a year or so. Drying of the soils kills tubers while a layer of water stimulates the tuber developing seedling which can survive in deep water and can break surface through depths of up to 50 cm. The small sized seed remains viable for about 5 years.

Acquatic Weeds

Acquatic weeds include both the annuals and perennials which can grow and bear fruit while immersed or floating on the water surface. Some of these weeds propagate by seed (chara and naiad) others both vegetatively and by seed (pondweeds). Drying of the soil is harmful to all the weeds under this group.

Chara and naiad are annual weed plants 15-20 cm tall that propagate by seed. They infest mostly the irrigation canals and rice field areas around turnouts. Drying of the fields for 2-3 days kills the weeds.

Clasping leaf pondweed floating pondweed and common pondweed are perennials that propagate both by seed and vegetatively. The shallow rooted rhizomes are able to easily break from the soil and are dispersed by flowing water. The weeds are unable to tolerate dry conditions and therefore infest primarily irrigation and drainage facilities as well as fields where rice is grown continuously. The economic losses attributable to these weeds are large. They infest waterways thus greatly reducing the water carrying capacity of the delivery canals by raising the water level in the drainage ditches. This in turn causes the water table in the non irrigated downstream lands to rise thus injuring or sometimes killing the dryland crops grown there. Proper choice of rotational crops can effectively control these weeds.

Floating Weeds

Thrive in rice fields and drainage and irrigation ditches. This group includes ninebark duckweed or duck s meat horned pondweed and many others. These weeds are mostly annual and propagate by seed.

Algae

Are lower plants several unicellular and multicellular forms of which commonly infest rice fields. When temperatures are high algae of various sizes and shapes rapidly develop colonies in the water (usually in mid May and June). One such algae is diatom which is the first to appear. Others are green algae blue green algae and brown algae. All these algae frequently form scum that deposits a dirty film on the emerging rice seedlings which retards and frequently prevents further growth of the young rice plants. Algae scum is most harmful during emergence of the rice plants.

Weed Control Practices

Effective systems of weed control combine preventive mechanical cultural and chemical methods. Nonchemical methods include several or all of the following practices using weed free seed rice crop rotations seedbed preparation and land levelling selecting the proper methods of seeding and water and fertilizer management. Chemical methods are based on the use of herbicides that effectively control weeds in rice if applied properly and timely.

Weed control practices differ depending on the species and amount of weeds the structure of cropped acreage in the rotation the availability of irrigation water drainage conditions in the rice field and rice varieties.

The non-chemical practices can be preventive mechanical and cultural. Proper combination of some or all of such practices will provide an effective weed control system.

Practices that prevent weed infestations or their spread in clean fields include the use of high quality seed rice that is free of weed seed irrigation with water that is free of weed seeds and other weed propagules and cultivation with clean equipment.

Plowing disking harrowing rotary tilling or combinations of these mechanical methods are used to prepare rice fields seedbed and eliminate young weeds. In new ricelands presowing tillage of fall plowed fields or spring plowing is done several days before seeding to level the check surfaces and make a fine tilth in the top layer (8-10 cm). One of the main goals of all methods of seedbed preparation is to eliminate all weed growth up to the time of seeding. Deep plowing in the fall (up to 20-25 cm) with inversion of the soil layer to turn down the topsoil infested with weed seeds and subsequent tilling in the spring without inversion (subsoiling or chiseling) so as not to bring the seeds to the surface is a good practice to control barnyard grass and other gramineous weeds. The method chosen depends on type of soil soil condition (mellowness) other crops in rotation the method of seeding climate and the kinds of weed present. Primary cultivation usually provides good conditions for weed seed germination and emergence and subsequent cultivation eliminates young weeds and conserves soil moisture. Old weeds that may survive on incomplete seedbeds are not so easy to control therefore thorough preparation is important.

In the major rice growing areas the old riceland is harrowed late in March or in April to bring up barnyard grass. The rice fields are then disked and harrowed again to eliminate young weeds. If the spring is dry the old rice fields are flushed one or two times to provoke weed emergence 6 to10 days before weed control cultivations. The number of presowing soil cultivations needed to control barnyard grass depends on how compact the topsoil is.

The seeding method influences weed problems. The depth of tillage regardless of implements used should not exceed 5 6 cm in the field where rice is to be drilled and is unlimited in these areas where the rice is broadcast onto the dry ground or in water. Time intervals between weed control cultivations and between seeding the rice and flooding the soil should be minimized. If this condition is satisfied the layer of water will prevent the emergence of the barnyard grass whose seeds are only 2 cm deep in the soil. Firming the soil with a roller packer is a good way to bring up weed grasses due to the capillary rise of water to the topsoil usually infested with weed seeds. On the average the rate of weed emergence per square meter on ground that has been firmed is twice that on unpacked ground. The young weeds that emerge after soil firming are easily eliminated by proper cultivations. However the barnyard grass that emerges along with the drilled or dry seeded rice is difficult to control by cultural or mechanical methods. Water seeding reduces the growth of barnyard grass and other weed grasses during rice emergence. Herbicides are essential for controlling annual grasses that infest dry seeded rice and other weeds that infest water seeded rice such as the aquatic weeds and sedge.

Pest Management in Aromatic Rices

Diseases and pests attacking normal rice cultivars also attack aromatic rices only their relative importance may vary.

Diseases and pests which are favoured by late maturity (lower temperature) dense crop canopy and/or low nitrogen are more prevalent in aromatic rices because of their long duration and tall stature. Many aromatic rice varieties are in cultivation in their native areas since ages. Their nitrogen requirement is very low. They have become adapted and show less susceptibility to different diseases and pests in their native areas of cultivation. However some of the improved high yielding aromatic rice varieties an highly susceptible to diseases and pests like neck blast sheath rot sheath bight yellow stem borer white backed plant hopper (WBPH) brown plant hopper (BPH) leaf folders etc. Even traditional varieties may suffer severaly once they are cultivated beyond their native areas. There is hardly any disease or pest attack on Tapovan basmati in village Tapovan areas (Tehri Uttaranchal). However same variety was severaly attacked by neck blast and sheath rot when grown in plains. This paper reviews the disease and pest profile and discusses the importance of integrated pests management (IPM) in aromatic rices.

Diseases

Since aromatic rices are grown under both irrigated and rainfed ecosystems which include lowland upland and high altitude ecologies most of the diseases are reported from one or other areas. The most destructive diseases on aromatic rices are neck blast sheath rot sheath blight bacterial blight and brown spot.

Brown Spot

Helminthosporiosis or brown spot disease of rice caused by Cochliobolus miyabeanus (Ito & Kuribayashi) Drechseler (anamorph Bipolaris oryzae (Breda de Haan) Shoemaker) is one of the most important diseases of the traditional aromatic rice more so under rainfed conditions. Disease appears as small oval or circular dark brown spots on leaves and glumes . Spots are relatively evenly distributed on the leaf surface. The disease is primarily seedborne however secondary spread is rapid under favourable environment. Disease is aggravated by poor fertility conditions like low nitrogen phosphorus and potassium. Due to lodging problem in tall aromatic rice varieties low dosage of nitrogen is applied. This results in high incidence of brown spot. Proper application of nitrogen particularly in slow release form suppresses disease development. However one must be careful as high N may aggravate lodging problem. Disease can be managed by seed treatment followed by foliar spray of fungicides like mancozeb carboxin bitertanol etc. Application of Si also reduces disease intensity. Biocontrol agents like Bacillus subtilis applied through seed soil or foliar spray have been found to be effective. A number of aromatic rice land races/germplasms have been identified as resistant under natural condition. However among the improved aromatic rice varieties only Pusa Basmati- 1 is reported to be resistant.

Sheath Blight Complex

In rice sheath blight complex three species of Rhizoctonia R. solani (teleomorph Thanetephorus cucumeris) R. oryzae (teleomorph Waitea circinata) and R. oryzae sativae (teleomorph Ceratobasidium oryzae sativae) are involved. Rhizoctonia solani inciting sheath blight is the most widely distributed species on rice. First symptoms are greenish gray spots that develop on leaf sheath near the waterline. The elliptical or oval spots enlarge to 2 to 3 cm and coalesce with each other. Disease may spread to upper sheath and occasionally to leaves. Losses may vary depending upon the time of appearance of the disease. Rhizoctonia solani has got very wide host range. However based primarily on the astomosis behaviour it has been subdivided into 13 intra specific groups [an astomosis groups (AGs) and sub groups]. However all the isolates of R. solani obtained from rice belong to AG 1 IA and only isolates from AG 1 IA and AG 1IB are capable of producing typical symptom of rice sheath blight. Isolates from other groups were either non pathogenic or induced hypersensitive/resistant reaction on rice. However rice isolates of R. solani exhibit a wide variation in their morphological and virulence characteristics even if they are obtained from same field. Disease is favoured by high N and P high plant density and dense canopy. High yielding dwarf broad leaf N and P responsive varieties like Pusa Basmati-1 are particularly susceptible to sheath blight. Nitrogen increases sheath blight essentially via indirect effects increased tissue contacts in the canopy and higher leaf wetness. In addition to dosage time of application of nitrogen also affects sheath blight development. High K disfavours disease.

There is a lack of resistance against sheath blight. However some of the varieties/lines of aromatic rices have shown reasonably good degree of tolerance. Crop rotation if followed properly could be one of the effective methods in keeping the soil population of rice isolates in check. Balanced application of NPK spray of borax and sulphates of Zn Cu and Fe reduce sheath blight incidence. A number of fungicides like propiconazole pencyuron diclonazine flutolanil mancozeb iprodione carbendazim are effective against the disease. New generation compound acibenzolar S methyle is reported to reduce sheath blight severity when applied through soil or as spray on plants by inducing plant defense mechanism. A number of biocontrol agents like *Pseudomonas fluorescens Bacillus* sp *Trichoderma virens* or *T. harzianum* alone or in combination with organic manure (*Gliricidia maculata* leaves) have been found effective in reducing the sheath blight infection under field conditions. *Trichoderma harzianum* is an efficient mycoparasite of R. solani. Preliminary studies have shown that rice wheat rotation which is the most popular in northern India does not favour sheath blight development in spite of the fact that wheat is susceptible to rice isolates of R. solani. However summer rice maize or mentha do favour sheath blight.

Blast

Rice blast caused by Magnaporthe grisea is a serious problem in aromatic rices even under low land irrigated system because of the long duration of crop. It is most serious problem in aromatic rises in Iran, Pakistan and India. In 1964 neck blast epidemic was experienced in Basmati rices in Punjab province of Pakistan. During 1989 blast epidemic in Basmati in Haryana (India) resulted in loss of Rs. 110 million. Blast epidemic in Kalanamak for two consecutive years 1998 and 1999 resulted in sharp decline in area under this variety in its native belt i.e. districts Siddharthanagar, Basti, Gorakhpur etc.

Blast has two phases leaf blast and panicle blast. Leaf blast is characterized by elliptical or spindle shaped lesions with whitish gray or greenish centre and brown or purple margins with yellow halo. Panicle blast which is more damaging appears as a dark necrotic lesion covering partially or completely around the panicle base or secondary branches. It may lead to breaking of panicles resulting in few or no grain setting. At the time of grain filling in aromatic rices temperature is comparatively low which favours panicle blast development. Disease is favoured by high nitrogen. Soils with poor silica availability are blast conducive. In most parts of the world population of pathogen is reported to be clonal. However in Himalayan hills population structure of *M. grisea* exhibits high diversity in rice strains. Some evidence suggest recombination of rice and non rice infecting strains in Indian Himalayas as a cause for this high diversity. In view of this information there is urgent need to analyze variability in M. grisea population affecting late maturing aromatic rices grown in Himalayan foothills. It may have lot of bearing on blast management particularly on resistance breeding.

A number of effective fungicides like carbendazim, carpropamid, tricyclazole, pyroquilone, ediphenphos, etc. are available against rice blast. In aromatic rices they are being used widely by the farmers. New generation chemicals like tricyclazoles carpropamid etc. are environmentally safe and provide good protection. Rather than being directly fungitoxic these chemicals act as antipenetrants by blocking melanin biosynthesis in appressoria. Some of the biocontrol agents like Pseudomonas fluorescens *Bacillus* sp. and mixed formulation of *Pseudomonas fluorescens* + *Trichoderma harzianum* have been found effective against the disease. Application of silica fertilizers reduces blast incidence. Host resistance is the most effective method for the management of rice blast. Unfortunately most of the popular varieties of aromatic rices are susceptible to neck blast. Nevertheless a wide variation in reaction towards neck blast was noticed in different Indian germplasm/land races of aromatic rices.

Sheath Rot

Sheath rot caused by researchers which was considered only a minor disease till a few years ago has now attained the status of a major disease. It is primarily because of the introduction of some of the high yielding varieties. It might increase further with the popularization of the hybrid varieties. Typical symptoms are oblong to irregular brown to gray lesions on boot leaf sheath near panicle. Lesions may coalesce covering the entire sheath. Disease is highly damaging as it infects boot leaf sheath and under severe condition it may totally inhibit panicle emergence. Burning of the infected stables planting of the tolerant varieties spray of fungicide like carbendazim at tillering and boot leaf stage and biocontrol agents are some of the methods recommended for the disease management. A wide variation was observed in natural incidence of sheath rot in different germplasm/land races of Indian aromatic rices. Early planted rice crops could escape disease incidence.

False Smut

Like sheath rot false smut caused by *Ustilaginoidea* virens is another disease which has gained importance only during the last few years with the introduction of some of the high yielding varieties. Infected grains are transformed into yellow greenish or greenish black velvety looking spore balls. Incidence of the disease is likely to increase with the popularization of hybrid varieties. Disease is favoured by high nitrogen. Sanitation practice like manual removal of sclerotia before harvesting proper dose of nitrogen and spray of fungicides like foltaf mancozeb etc. are some of the recommended management practices.

Foot Root

Bakanae or foot rot a seed borne disease is caused by *Gibberella fugikuroi* (*Anamorph Fusarium moniliforme*). Infected seedlings/plants are elongated nearly twice the height of the normal plants with thin yellow green leaves. Elongated plants die. Infected plants that survive until maturity bear only partially filled grains or empty panicles. High nitrogen and temperature range of 30 to 35°C favour the disease. This is one of the major diseases in Basmati belts of Haryana (India) and Punjab (India and Pakistan). In 1991 most of the Basmati fields in Punjab province of Pakistan were badly affected by this disease. Outbreaks of this disease were observed in Haryana during 1989 1990 and 1992. Foot rot can be effectively controlled by seed dressing with fungicide like carbendazim.

Stem Rot

Stem rot caused by Magnaporthe salvini (sclerotial stage *Sclerotium oryzae* is endemic in eastern U.P. Infection starts near the waterline as blackish dark irregular lesions on the outer leaf sheath and gradually enlarges. Eventually fungus penetrates into culm and weakens the stem leading to lodging. The disease is favoured by high nitrogen while K and Si application reduce disease incidence. Application of balanced fertilizer burning of stubble after harvest avoidance of waterlogging for long period and planting of moderately resistant varieties are some of the recommended methods for the disease management. Some of the aromatic rice varieties are reported to be resistant to stem rot.

Narrow Brown Leaf Spot

This disease is caused by *Cercospora oryzae*. Incidence of the disease has increased in recent past particularly in Bijnore (U.P.) and Dehradun (Uttarakhand). The disease is characterized by small narrow elongated dark brown spots spread uniformly over the leaf surface. Work is in progress to develop disease resistant varieties. Some of the non aromatic resistant varieties like Mahssuri Bhawani IR 26 IR 28 IR 29 and IR 30 may serve as donors.

Bacterial Blight

This disease is caused by bacterium *Xanthomonas campestris* pv. oryzae (Ishiyama) Dye. Disease may appear both in nursery (Kresek phase) as well as in field. Kresek phase is characterized by wilting of seedlings. In mature plants lesions usually start near the leaf tip or margins or both and extend down the outer edges. Young lesions are pale green to grayish green later turning yellow to gray necrotic. Lesions may extend to entire leaf length. Disease is more serious under irrigated conditions. Bacterial blight is a widely distributed and devastating disease of rice. Some of the aromatic rice cultivars like Pusa Basmati 1 are highly susceptible to bacterial blight. It is favoured by high N. Planting of resistant cultivars is the best method of disease management. A number of resistant varieties are available among non aromatic rices. Among aromatic rices HBC 19 Pakistani Basmati Ghanal and IET 9691 showed resistance to bacterial blight. Proper use of nitrogen and avoidance of shade and water stagnation in field help keeping the diseases in check.

Grain Discolouration

It is characterized by darkening of glumes of spikelets brown to black including rotten glumes. Disease intensity ranges from sporadic discol ouration to discolouration of entire glumes. A number of fungi viz. *Sarocladium oryzae, Cochliobolus miyabeanus, Alternaria alternata, Magnaporthe salvini, M. grisea* etc. are reported to be involved in grain discolouration. High rainfall at the time of maturity favours development of grain discolouration.

Insect Pests

Insect pests pose serious threat to cultivation of rice in almost all regions of the world where rice is grown. More than 800 insects species have been recorded damaging rice in one way or another although majority of them are of little importance. In a particular area insect pests attacking aromatic rice are the same as those prevalent on non aromatic rices. Nevertheless mainly due to long duration tall stature and dense canopy the aromatic rice cultivars are more susceptible to insect infestation as compared to non aromatic rice due to which the farmers in many traditionally aromatic rice belt have given up its cultivation. In India the aromatic rice is damaged seriously by yellow stem borer *Scripophaga incertulas* Walker leaf folder, *Cnaphalocrosis medinalis* Guenee white backed plant hopper, *Sogatella furcifera* and brown plant hopper Nilaparvata lugens.

Yellow Stem Borer *Scripophaga incertulas* (Walker) (*Lepidoptera Pyralidae*)

The most serious insect pest of Basmati rice in the entire northern Indian belt is yellow stem borer. Studies conducted in Punjab over five years revealed that non protection of Basmati 385 may result in 80-97 per cent white ears in crop due to stem borers. Yellow stem borer epidemic was recorded in Basmati belt of Haryana and Punjab during 1998 where 50 per cent incidence of white head was noticed. The yellow stem borer lays eggs near the tip of leaf blade which are covered with buff coloured hairs derived from anal tuft of female moth. One female moth lays an average of 2 to 3 clusters of egg each containing about 60 to 100 eggs. About a week after hatching the larvae from the leaf sheath bore into the stem and staying in the pith feed on the inner surface of the walls. Such feeding often results in severing of the apical parts of the plants from the base. When this kind of damage occurs during vegetative stage of the plant central leaf does not unfold turns brown and dries off although the lower leaves remain green and healthy. This condition is called dead heart. The affected tillers dry out without bearing panicles. After panicle initiation severing of the growing plant parts from the base result in the drying of the panicles which may not emerge at all and those that have already emerged do not produce grains. This condition is known as white ear head . The borer remain active in the field almost from nursery stage to crop maturity. However they cause more injury to the plant from the middle to later part of the crop growth. It has been observed that among the three stages of crop growth maximum tillering stage registers highest infestation followed by flowering and early tilering stages. It has also been noted that the variety having more tillers per hill suffer more from yellow stem borer. The economic injury threshold for dead heart and white head are reported to be 5.7-12 and 9.4-14.7 per cent respectively. These values seem to be quite high value aromatic rices. It may be revised as 5 and 3 per cent respectively for dead heart and white head.

Hoppers

Hopper burn caused either by white backed plant hopper (WBPH) or brown plant hopper (BPH) is quite common to aromatic rices. They may result in serious losses. In recent years incidence of green leaf hopper is on increase in Basmati in Uttarakhand Tara.

1. Brown planthopper Nilaparvata lugens (Stal.) (Homoptera Delphacidae)

   The nymphs and adults of brown plant hopper suck the phloem sap from the basal portion of the plant which result in yellowing and wilting of plants and finally leading to hopper burn. The eggs of BPH are usually laid in groups in the tissues of the lower part of rice plant mainly in the leaf sheath but at times also in the leaf blades. One female may lay 400-500 eggs which hatch in 7-10 days. In the Basmati belts the population of this insect remains very high in September October.

2. White backed planthopper *Sogatella furcifera* (Horvath) (Homoptera Delphacidae)

   In U.P. and Uttaranchal white backed planthopper is more common than BPH. It lays eggs in masses in the leaf sheath tissues of the plant which hatch in 3-14 days. During the period of feeding variety and stages of crop also affect the symptoms. If the attack is before heading stage lower leaves followed gradually by the upper leaves turn yellow to bronze. There are stunting and reduction in the number of productive tillers. When the damage is in the panicle formation stage the number of grains and panicle length decrease considerably. There is adverse effect on the ripening when WBPH attacks during maturation period. The flag leaf and panicle are aggressively attacked by nymphs and adults the population of which remain high from early September to mid October.

Rice Leaf Folder *Cnaphalocrocis medinalis* (Guenee) (*Lepidoptera Pyralidae*)

The rice leaf folders belonging to Cnaphalocrocis and Marasmia have recently acquired the pest status in rice. However *Cnaphalocrocis medinalis* has become a major pest of rice causing moderate to severe damage in most of the rice growing regions. In Bihar the infestation of this insect reached to 78.1 per cent leading to 90 per cent yield loss in scented rice. Similarly untreated fields of Basmati rice in Haryana and adjoining areas have been reported to suffer 30-80 per cent loss in yield due to attack of leaf folder which may cause up to 28.5 per cent leaf damage after increasing its population to 20 larvae/hill. Unbalanced use of fertilizers especially excessive application of nitrogenous fertilizers seems to be one of the important factors of increasing menace of leaf folders.

The eggs are laid in batches of 10 to 12 arranged linearly along the middle on either surface of the leaves. One female lays approximately 100 eggs. The damage is caused by caterpillars which fold the leaves longitudinally by fastening margins with silken threads and feeding inside the fold. During feeding the larvae of *C. medinalis* sit along the length of the leaf blade and scrape out the soft tissues between vascular bundles longitudinally. As a result only bundle unit bundle sheath sclerenchyma the aboxial epidermis and the cuticle are left intact. In severely attacked condition the crop gives scorched whitish appearance of infested plants and consequently of leaves. They create a leaf tube during the later stages of feeding. Several natural enemies viz. *Cotesia* sp. *Trichogramms* sp. *Bracon* sp. etc. have been found parasitizing leaf folder larvae in the field and keeping the population below ET level.

Rice Hispa *Dicladispa armigera* (Olivier) (*Coleoptera chrysomelidae*)

It is widely distributed in Myanmar, China, India, Nepal, Pakistan and Sumatra. Female beetle lay eggs singly near the tip of the leaf blade and partially inserted in the mesophyll tissue of the ventral surface of the leaf. One female lays an average of 55 eggs which hatch in 3-5 days. The grub mines the leaf between epidermis producing irregular longitudinal white blotches. The adults feed on all portion of leaf producing white parallel streaks along the mid rib of the leaf leaving only the lower epidermis. The damage by this insect is restricted in early stage of the crop.

Rice ranks second in consumption of chemical pesticides particularly the insecticides. Their indiscriminate use has affected the ecology adversely. In addition to environmental pollution and health hazards this has led to resurgence of pests and pesticide resistance leading to failure of chemical protection and heavy loss to crop. Serious outbreak of hopper burn due to WBPH was observed in Pusa Basmati 1 fields heavily applied with phorate granule in schedule based operation during 2001 at Pantnagar. With the development of several alternate methods of insect control now it is being realized that to tackle the insect pest problems in aromatic rice safely more emphasis should be given on the use of resistant varieties manipulation of agronomic practices conservation and enhancement of natural enemies and need based application of safe insecticide molecules.

Water Management Practices for Rice

In modern rice culture water management is of great importance as it stimulates better crop growth and higher grain production. Water management involves the manipulation of the hydrologic cycle at various stages to make water available when necessary to remove it when there is an excess of it and to improve its quality if required. It thus involves irrigation drainage and the conservation of water. A major factor underlying stagnation in the yield of the rice crop appears to be poor water management.

In the states of Tamil Nadu, Jammu and Kashmir, Punjab and Haryana where more than 85 per cent of the area is irrigated the yield per hectare are relatively high. The states which have the poorest irrigation have the lowest yields.

Irrigation stabilizes yield. It has been stated that the rainfall during the rainy season in most of the rice growing states in India is generally sufficient for rice cultivation but it is erratic in time space and quantity. This situation either causes drought or floods both of which adversely affect the yield of this crop. With the provision of irrigation facilities the adverse effects of drought can be avoided. Irrigation dams help to control floods and regulate water supply besides stabilizing yields. Statistics show that in Asia during the past 20 years about 10 per cent of the cultivated area in each year has been affected by floods or drought.

It has been proved that not only can irrigation ad drainage help to stabilize the yield of the rice crop but well managed water can also increase its yields. Under scientific management the required quantity of water is made available to the crop when needed. Experiments have demonstrated that a 100 per cent increase in yield may be realized with no other changes in agro technical methods than controlled irrigation with proper management.

The Effect of Land Submergence on the Growth and Yield of Rice

Studies have been undertaken by many workers to determine the effect of land submergence on the growth and yield of rice.

The Depth of Submergence

The advantages of land submergence led the workers to initiate work to know the optimum depth of submergence for obtaining the maximum yield.

Ganguli working in Assam reported that the water level of 7.62 cm throughout the growth period of rice was the best whereas Pillai inferred that the maintenance of 5.08 cm of standing water with frequent changes with fresh water resulted in high rice production.

In the black soils of Siruguppa of Mysore submergence under 5 cm deep water resulted in the highest grain and straw yield obtained under the following three treatments:

1. 5 cm submergence;
2. saturation to hair cracking; and
3. flowing water.

A thin layer of water is sufficient to maximise the yield of rice no additional advantage occurs from very deep submergence which entails only wastage of water.

Bhatia and Dastane found that a depth range up to 0-4 cm seems to be the optimum for high yielding dwarf rice.

The above workers further added that for dwarf rice varieties deeper submergence may be harmful as shown above. Researchers found that the grain yield of rice was better under submergence than under mere saturation during summer and spring and also that the crop under shallow submergence (5 ± 3 cm) gave as good a yield as deep submergence (10 ± 3 cm).

Ghildyal and Jana on the basis of pot experiments observed in general that the highest yield was obtained during a cool and dry season with 0-3 cm of water.

The results of the experiments conducted recently under the All India Co-ordinated Scheme for Research on Water Management and Salinity have shown that the field submergence under water 5 to 10 cm deep does not produce any significant difference in the yield and hence shallow submergence up to 5 cm is economical.

From an experiment conducted at Bhubaneswar on a sandy loam soil with a pH of 4.9 Sahu and Rout reported that the lowland rice (T-1242) gave the maximum yield when the soil was kept submerged under 15 cm of water. The yield was reduced by 26.4 per cent under field capacity and by 29.2 at 75 per cent available moisture as compared with the yield under deep continuous submergence though the efficiency per unit of water used was higher from the first two treatments.

Researchers observed in a lateritic sandy clay loam soil with a pH of 5.1 at Kharagpur that the yield of rice was higher under shallow flooding (3 cm) than under deep flooding (15 cm). Researchers from Tamil Nadu reported that among the various depth of submergence the 5 cm depth of water proved in general to be the optimum depth of submergence for getting the best yield.

According to researcher a small quantity of water used at shorter intervals was more beneficial to the rice crop than larger quantities at longer intervals.

The results of studies made at Kharagpur on a lateritic soil (pH 5.4 hydraulic conductivity 0.51 cm/hr of low fertility 0.04 per cent N 0.0055 per cent available P and 0.1 per cent available K) under the co ordinated Project for Research on Water Management and Salinity show the monsoon season shallow submergence and deep submergence were as good as saturation for IR. 8 rice because of the effect of rains low evapourative demands. But during summer shallow submergence scored over deep submergence or saturation.

The work done at Chakuli (sandy loam soil) Orissa at Siruguppa (heavy black soil with 50% clay). Mysore and at Roorkee (alluvial soil) Uttar Pradesh under the Co ordinated Scheme showed that submergence up to 5 and 10 cm did not show any significant difference in yield and therefore submergence up to 5 cm only was economical.

The results discussed above show that for tall rice varieties a slightly higher depth of submergence may be tolerated whereas for new dwarf high yielding rice varieties a depth of 5 cm is enough to get a good yield.

Effect of Partial Submergence

Since the continuous submergence of the field involves a huge quantity of assured water many workers started experiment to find out the critical period of land submergence for economizing on water.

According to researchers tiller initiation primordium initiation and flowering are the most critical stages. A shortage of water during these stages could reduce grain yield appreciably. Therefore submergence at these stages should be practised. Further Ray and Pande emphasized the point that the flowering stage was the most critical period.

The data revealed that the highest grain yield at Chakuli was obtained when the soil moisture was maintained at saturation till tillering followed by submergence under 5 cm of water till harvesting (M1). Continuous submergence (M8) did not show any additional advantage while continuous saturation till flowering brought about a reduction in yield.

At Kharagpur the highest grain yield was obtained during kharif under the treatment in which saturation was maintained till tillering followed by submergence till harvesting (M1) whereas during rabi the treatment submergence till flowering followed by saturation till harvesting (M3) produced the highest grain yield though the treatment saturation till tillering followed by submergence till harvesting (M1) also produced more or less similar yield. Continuous submergence required the greatest quantity of water without any additional benefit in terms of grain yield. The results of another experiment conducted using IR. 8 during kharif 1971 at Kharagpur showed that submergence under 5±2 cm of water maintained only during the active vegetative and reproductive phases and saturation during other phases produced the maximum grain yield.

The result of the studies taken up at Siruguppa (Mysore) also reveal in general that tillering to flowering was the most critical stage when the rice crop should not be subjected to any moisture stress.

As already stated in most cases the shallow submergence of the fields has been reported to be beneficial. However where the water table is shallow even shallow submergence may be avoided meaning thereby that a reasonably good yield of rice can be obtained by maintaining the rice field just moist (0 3 atm.) to avoid cracking. A number of experiments at the Indian Agricultural Research Institute during kharif have also corroborated this result.

Mane working on rice variety NP. 130 reported that there was a good scope of economising on irrigation water in the rice fields by applying water at 0.2 or 0.5 atm. tension and not going in for continuous submergence.

Rao studied the influence of moisture regimes on the yield and yield components of the rice variety under the conditions of a shallow water-table.

Neither the grain yield nor any yield component was influenced significantly by moisture stress up to 0.3 atm. tensions where the water table was shallow. This observation suggests that where the water table is shallow there is no need to submerge the fields.

Recently researcher found a suitable water management practice for rice using the varieties maturing nearly in 115 to 120 days (viz. Sabarmati and Jamuna). He recommended that with a much less quantity of water (by scheduling irrigation at 0.3 atm. tension) in the rice fields as compared with the conventional practice of keeping the water standing in the rice fields a good yield of rice (even better than that from the latter practice) could be obtained by scheduling irrigation in respect of rice at 0 0.3 atm. tension but supplementing the crop with a foliar spray of nitrogen (urea) potassium silicate and ferrous sulphate (under poor Fe status) and controlling weeds with a suitable herbicide. However caution must be exercised to avoid stress during critical stages such as active tillering and flowering. He was of the opinion that the applying of silicate maintained leaf turgidity and the rest of the nutrients compensated for the loss caused by slightly oxidized condition prevailing in the field because of scheduling irrigation at 0.3 atm. tension.

Water Requirement of the Rice Crop

Earlier studies on the water requirement of the rice crop were directed towards transpiration ratios and were conducted mostly with plants grown in pots. This procedure reduced the significance of these studies. Researchers reviewed the work on the water requirement of crops including rice. According to researchers the latest definition of water requirement is regardless of source the quantity of water needed to grow a rice crop under field conditions . This definition embraces evapotranspiration application loss (percolation and seepage) and special needs (e.g. the leaching of excess salts and preparing the field). They reported that owing to the difference in the different components of water requirement the water requirements of the same variety or crop may differ widely from place to place.

It seems that water requirement of the rice crop varies widely depending upon the soil climate season varieties and management practices because the above mentioned components are the function of these entities.

The importance of insect pests is generally recognized the damage they do is widespread and very evident but the loss of crop caused by diseases should not be overlooked or considered negligible. The crop is liable to many diseases any one of which may suddenly inflict widespread damage.

In recent years the effect of plant protection has significantly increased. Although average losses in most fields have been appreciably reduced due to adequate plant protection measures losses in individual rice growing areas and fields from specific diseases and pests are at times high and markedly reduce that total grain output in the country.

Practical plant protection includes not only destructive measures but also the use of resistant rice varieties methods that result in unfavourable conditions for the development of injurious organisms and practices that conserve useful enthomofauna. Such protection also allows one to control economically important pests which rely on population thresholds by using in the first place natural limiting factors and then other plant protection methods that are consistent with economical ecological and toxicological requirements.

Rice Diseases

Most of the world s major rice diseases are known to occur in the Soviet Union.

Blast for one is a major disease caused by the fungus *Pyricularia oryzae* Cav. It occurs in almost all rice producing areas and is the most noxious disease of rice. The fungus mostly attack the leaves and to a lesser extent the nodes and panicles. The disease results in both leaf blast and head blast. The latter condition is where the panicles frequently break over due to infection weakened structural tissues in the panicle and is sometimes known as rotten neck.

Atmospheric moisture and temperature conditions are of primary importance in the infection and spread of the fungus that causes blast. Frequent rains heavy nightly dews high relative humidities and temperature (18-20°C) favour wide scale outbreaks of the disease Rice plants under high levels of nitrogen fertilization are more susceptible to blast. The outbreaks of disease may be caused by use of susceptible varieties or uncleaned seeds mixed with the seeds of varieties consistently susceptible to blast. Blast is heavier on late sown than on early sown crops. The infection is persistent in seeds on the stubble in straw and reed growths.

The average losses in yield of the fungus affected plants account for 25 per cent. The milling yield of head rice is decreased by about 23-25 per cent. Treatment of the rice crop infected with *P. oryzae* includes spraying with 0.4 per cent zineb solution (80% wettable powder) at a rate of 2.4 kg/ha or with rhizid P (50% emulsible concentrate) at a rate of 0.5 1.0 kg/ha in terms of the active ingredient. The rate of application is 200 1/ha. The treatment of the crop should be completed 20 days before harvesting.

Preventive measures include early fall plowing seeding with clean certified seed from the varieties selected best for that area s growing season the application and uniform distribution of nitrogen fertilizer and seed dressing or disinfecting with coloured granosan M dusts at 0.04 kg (active substance) per ton of seed.

Other rice diseases such as brown spot sclerotical rot root rot and bacterial disturbances are rare and of less economic significance.

Recommended control and prevention practices against fungi and bacteria attacks include the removal of rice straw burning of plant residue deep fall plowing with inversion of the soil layer and rotational planting (with cultivated fallows and leguminous grasses). Seed dressing with coloured granosan M dusts (0.04 kg/ton active substance) is mandatory.

General symptoms of rice diseases are abnormal plant growth and changing leaf colour. A disturbance in plant development manifestes itself in retarded growth and excessive or reduced tillering. The stems and leaves may develop galls or cecidia streak mozaic and necrotic areas. The leaf may change its colouration from green to yellow green or yellow orange. Diseases are transmitted basically by suctorial insects. To prevent the spread of such diseases rice fields are treated with phosphororganic substances in the early stages of plant development to kill cicads (Cicadidae) insect vectors of virus and micoplasma inhabiting clumps of grasses particularly barnyard grass.

White tip disease of rice caused by an ectoparasitic foliar nematode *Aphelenchoides besseyi* Christie is another widespread noxious disease of rice.

The most distinguishing symptom of white tip is the presence of leaves with white tips of 2.5-5 cm long. The tips of the developing leaves may be twisted and wrinkled and the flag leaf may be twisted and wrinkled and the flag leaf may be twisted near the panicle. The infected plants are generally stunted.

The nematodes are seed borne and are spread from one crop to the next in seed rice and stubble. They become active after rice is sown and migrate towards the growing point of the young rice plants where the nematode feed and reproduce. Anywhere from 8 to 13 generations can be reproduced during a growing season. Feeding injures the developing leaves and panicles before emergence. Later on the injuries are white necrotic leaf tips and small sterile panicles. Grain yields from diseased plants are markedly reduces.

Several methods can be used to control white tip. Resistant seed varieties nematode free seed should be used in planting re cleaned seed lots free from shrunk and light weight seeds can be used for seeding. Infected rice straw should be removed from the fields and burnt. Fall plowing and rotations also help control or prevent the spread of white tip in rice.

Pests of Rice

Several pests frequently damage rice severely. Among them is the larva of Dioptera and Orthoptera which may cause serve injury by feeding on young rice plants particularly in rice grown in saline soils. Economically important population thresholds constitute 40 larvae per 1 sq. m.

The tadpole shrimp Triops (Apus) cancriformis Schaft. although not an insect is also a pest of rice. The adult spherical shield shaped shrimp is about 3.0-3.5 cm long. The eggs are ball shaped reddish black and 0.4 mm in diameter and are laid by the female shrimp in water or soil. This gives the eggs shelter for many years after water is withdrawn. In the spring 3 to 4 days after flooding the field the eggs hatch and the young larvae or maggots as they are commonly called emerge to become fully grown adults in 14-15 days. The young larvae first feed on the organic matter and within 8-9 days reach 7-10 mm in length. They then migrate to the rice and cause severe injury by pruning the young roots and shoots. Germinating seeds lying on the soil surface become easy targets for the maggots. The tadpole shrimp survives for one generation and late in June it disappears.

Since the immature stages are spent underwater among the rice roots most of the shrimps larvae can be destroyed by draining the fields and allowing them to dry for a day or two. Appropriately leveled checks timely opened drainage furrows and peripheral ditches are essential for rapid drainage.

Esteria (lumnadia) *Leptestheria* spp. a shellfish is another aquatic pest of rice its body is enclosed in a bivalve translucent shell and is 9 10 mm long and 4 5 mm broad in fully developed specimens. It moves with the use of its antennae and lays its eggs in a shell. Its white ball shaped eggs are 0.13 mm in diameter and dropped into water as they accumulate within the shell. The eggs settle on the soil surface and may stay there for years. Three days after the field is flooded the eggs laid in the previous season hatch and larvae emerge.

Esteria matures within 8 to 10 days the first 5 to 7 of which are spent feeding on organic matter. Upon reaching maturity the full grown Esteria quickly migrates to the soil surface and begins to feed on the young rice plants. What ensues is the destruction of a significant number of these plants. The life cycle of Esteria is one generation and it can be found in rice fields until late June.

Draining and withholding water for 1-2 days controls larvae development by disturbing its life cycle thus eliminating the risk of injury to rice seedlings.

The caddis fly (Trichoptera) *Limnophylus stigma* is an insect pest of rice. Several species of this numerous insect order are present in the Far East and Central Asia injuring rice severely in certain years. The 10-16 mm long larva is what inflicts damage on the rice plants. The larva lives in the water enclosed in a cigar shaped tube that it builds around its body from minute plant debris and trash. The tube size varies from 12 to 20 mm. The larva holds the tube fast on its body with its last body segment and moves about with its head and three pairs of thorax legs. The larvae migrate to rice fields and feed on rice seedlings thus reducing the density of plant stands.

Draining the field for 1-2 days or treating it with chlorinated lime at a rate of 10-12 kg/ha helps control the caddis fly.

The barley leaf miner *Hydrellia griseola* Fall. is a dangerous pest of young rice in the Far East Northern Caucasus and the Ukraine. A grey fly 2.5 mm long the miner usually infests rice fields in April and in the Far East in May. Its white eggs elliptical in shape and 0.6 mm long are laid on the upper leaf surfaces and along the veins of rice leaves that are afloat. Damage is done 2-3 days after the eggs hatch and the maggots appear. The miner maggots attack the leaves and feed on their parenchyma. This reduces the photosynthetic capacity of the leaves and consequently impairs the rice yield. The pale yellow maggots are elliptical and 3.0-3.5 mm long. They pupate in the mines they have made in the leaves and develop pale brownish pupa. Within 6-9 days they emerge as flies. The barley leaf miner produces 3-4 generations and attacks all rice seedlings regardless of the date of seeding.

Lowering the water or draining the fields for 2-3 days or treating fields with a 20 per cent emulsifiable methaphos at 0.2-0.4 kg/ha (active ingredient) provides reliable control of egg and larva population.

The rice leaf miner *Hydrellia griseola* var. scapulasis Loew is a destructive pest of rice in the Far East. The black flies are 3.3-3.8 mm long and lay eggs on the leaf tip tissue. They attack rice in June. The maggots are yellow green 4-6 mm long when hatched and feed within the leaf working their way towards its base. The larvae pupate on the top of the damaged leaf which turns brown and lies prostrate on the water. Infestation leads to a reduction in yield. The rice leaf miner produces three generations of which the first two are most damaging to rice. Preventive measures include adequate weed control and proper water management.

The rice midge *Chirono mus* spp. is a destructive pest of rice in the Far East Northern Caucasus and the Ukraine. Only occasionally does the insect infest rice in Central Asia. Light attracts the midge and can be used to determine when the midge is attacking the rice fields. Such attacks usually occur in April. The eggs laid in water hatch yellowish translucent larvae within 2-3 days. The larvae first feed on organic matter and rice roots. During this time the injury to the rice is insignificant. The adult larvae 8 mm long infest the lower surface of leaves that are afloat and feed on the parenchyma. This causes the leaves to wither and reduces yield. The rice midge produces three generations and damages all rice seedlings regardless of the date of seeding. It is most damaging when the rice plants are excessively flooded and the leaves stay afloat for a long time on the water surface. Lowering the water level or draining the rice fields for 2-3 days provides effective control of the midge larvae. Treatment of the fields with a 20 per cent emulsifiable methafos at a rate of 0.2-0.3 kg/ha by aircraft sprayers is also effective on large larvae population.

The shore fly *Ephydra macellaria* Egg. infests rice in almost all rice growing areas. The fly is 4 mm long. Its thorax and abdomen are metallic green its legs reddish green. Its wings are large and translucent. It lays about 80 to 90 eggs in the water covering rice checks. The larvae are what is destructive to rice as they are adapted to live in water. Where they feed on young rice roots. Such feeding results in the withering and reduced rice plant stands. The larvae pupate where they feed i.e. on roots stems and leaves and emerge as flies within 8 to 12 days. The fly produces 3-4 generations. When larvae population counts are high withholding water for a day or two may provide adequate control. Treatment of field with 80 per cent emulsifiable chlorophos powder at a rate of 0.8-1.6 kg/ha is also effective in controlling large larvae populations.

The rice water weevil *Hydronomus sinuaticollis* Fst. is found in all rice growing areas of the Far East and Central Asia. The adult weevil is black 4-5 mm long and has two light spots on the elytra. The male water weevil is smaller than the female. In the post feeding stage the larvae overwinter in the plowed up soil at a depth of 5-8 cm. The larvae are milky white legless and about 7-8 mm long when fully grown. They pupate in the spring and emerge as weevils in May or June. The weevil feeds on germinating seeds and roots of young rice. Rice that is sown late is usually more susceptible to the weevil. Eggs are laid in the root zone. The hatched maggots live first in the plant and later migrate to prune the roots. Infested plants either die or grow more slowly forming small panicles with poorly set kernels. Rotations disking the stubble in the spring fall plowing and seeding at optimum dates help prevent and control the rice water weevil.

The rice leaf beetle *Lema suvorovi* Jacobs *var. oryzae* is a widespread and destructive pest in the Far East. The bugs 4-5 mm long have blue elytra and yellow head and prodorsum. They feed on rice leaves. The female bug lays chains of 6 to 12 eggs on the upper surface of the leaf in late May and early June. The eggs hatch and larvae emerge which feed on leaves and in mid June when they complete feeding they pupate and emerge as bugs 10-12 days later. The rice leaf beetle produces two generations the first of which is the most damaging to rice. Bugs of the second generation spend the winter in the soil or in dry grass straw and other material that affords them shelter. In the spring then they infest primarily the weed plants. Proper weed control and treatment with 80 per cent emulsifiable chlorofos at 0.8-1.6 kg/ha (in terms of active ingredient) reduces the number of bugs in subsequent season.

The cereal aphid Aphididae attacks rice in the Northern Caucasus the Ukraine and Central Asia. Aphids are most destructive to rice sown late in the spring on soils deficient in nitrogen. Some species are winged others wingless. The economically significant level of infestation (population threshold) is 1-2 aphids per square meter at leaf tube formation. The appearance of aphids in rice can be controlled by proper and timely weedings and treatment of fields with 20 per cent emulsifiable methaphos at 0.2-0.3 kg/ha (active substance).

Many other species of insects and various other pests infest rice fields by migrating to rice from the leaves and weed growths. Feeding on rice is supplementary for most of them so if rice cultivation practices are adequate the infestations seldom cause enough damage to reach economically significant levels.

19

Deepwater Rice

Deepwater rice is a variety of rice (*Oryza sativa*) grown in flooded conditions with water more than 50 cm (20 in) deep for at least a month. More than 100 million people in South and Southeast Asia rely on deepwater rice for their sustenance. Rice has adapted to deep water in two ways, known as traditional talls and floating rice. Traditional talls are varieties that are grown at water depths of between 50 cm (20 in) and 100 cm (39 in) and have developed to be taller and have longer leaves than standard rice. Floating rice grows in water deeper than 100 cm (39 in) through advanced elongation ability. This means when a field where rice is growing floods, accelerated growth in the internodal of the stem allows the plant to keep some of its foliage on top of the water. The Indica cultivar is the main type of deepwater rice, although varieties of Japonica have been found in Burma, Bangladesh and India.

Deepwater rice is a staple food that is grown on around 90,000 km^2 (35,000 sq mi) of land. The main areas where it is grown are in South and Southeast Asia where more than 100 million people rely its production for their livelihood. In South Asia the main area deepwater rice is grown in is the Ganges Brahmaputra basin in India and Bangladesh. In Southeast Asia the main areas of cultivation are in Burma in the Irrawaddy Delta, in Thailand in the Chao Phraya and Mekong in Vietnam and Cambodia. In these countries deepwater rice account for more than 25 per cent of the land used to grow rice.

Deepwater rice is cultivated less in West Africa than in Asia with approximately 4,700 km^2 (1,800 sq mi). Areas it is grown include the Niger river basin. Some areas in Ecuador grow deepwater rice.

Deepwater rice is grown in tropical monsoon climates normally around river deltas and their floodplains mainly in backswamps and natural levees. The nature of the flood is important for success of deepwater rice, with timing and the rate of rise of water affecting survival and crop density. Generally, the flood water comes from rainfall or rises in the water table. In places with low rainfall, water overspilling from rivers can flood rice producing areas.

Issues

When seeds are sown directly into the ground the seeds and young plants can be damaged by drought conditions before floods arrive. During this stage the plants can also suffer due to competition from weeds. Sudden flooding, where a large volume of water enters the field in a short time, can lead to a high level of seedling death.

Floating rice face additional problems due to the depth and time of the water it grows in. Water conditions such as turbulence and temperature can adversely affect the crop.

Natural disasters can also damage or destroy deepwater rice crops. Tropical cyclones are particularly a problem in Asia. For example, in 2008 Cyclone Nargis damaged 122,782 hectares of deepwater rice in Burma. If predicted sea level rises due to climate change happen, this would affect the pattern of flooding, causing deeper floods over a wider area and eroding the coast.

Deepwater rice is rice grown in flooded conditions with water more than 50 cm (20 in) deep for at least a month. Rice has adapted to deep water in two ways known as traditional talls and floating rice. Traditional talls are varieties that are grown at water depths of between 50 cm (20 in) and 100 cm

(39 in) and have developed to be taller and have longer leaves than standard rice. Floating rice grows in water deeper than 100 cm (39 in) through advanced elongation ability. When submerged this allows it to grow as fast as 25 cm (9.8 in) a day to reach a length of up to 7 m (23 ft) and survive in water as deep as 4 m (13 ft).

The Indica cultivar is the main type of deepwater rice, although varieties of Japonica have been found in Burma, Bangladesh and India. Deepwater rice emits the least methane, a greenhouse gas, of the wetland rice ecologies, producing approximately three times less than irrigated rice.

Floating rice is planted in dry ground and allowed to establish as young plants. The area becomes flooded which triggers the rice's elongation ability. This means when a field where rice is growing floods, accelerated growth in the internodes of the stem allows the plant to keep some of its foliage on top of the water. The stems are hollow and this allows gas to be exchanged between the plant and the atmosphere. Once the flooding ends the plant is left lying on the ground. The nodes at the top of the plant then start growing upwards towards due to gravitropic sensitivity.

The elongation is triggered when the plant is submerged through a mechanism involving ethylene gas. Ethylene is normally produced by plants and diffused into the air but when floating rice is submerged in water this process is disrupted as the gas moves more slowly into water. This leads to a build up of ethylene in the plant. This triggers the production of a hormone called gibberellin which causes the rapid growth in the plant. When the plant reaches the surface the ethylene gas can escape as normal and the rapid growth stops.

Upland Rice

Upland rice is rice grown on dry soil. Most rice is grown in flooded rice paddies.

Nearly 100 million people now depend on upland rice as their daily staple food. Almost two-thirds of the upland rice area is in Asia. Bangladesh, Cambodia, China, India, Indonesia, Myanmar, Thailand, and Vietnam are important producers.

Upland rice is grown in rainfed fields prepared and seeded when dry, much like wheat or maize. The ecosystem is extremely diverse, including fields that are level, gently rolling or steep, at altitudes up to 2,000 meters and with rainfall ranging from 1,000 to 4,500 millimeters annually.

Soils range from highly fertile to highly weathered, infertile and acidic, but only 15 per cent of total upland rice grows where soils are fertile and the growing season is long.

Many upland farmers plant local rices that do not respond well to improved management practices — but these are well adapted to their environments and produce grains that meet local needs.

Although the rice technology of the 1960s and 70s focused on irrigated rice, farmers in the uplands were not forgotten. Researchers produced cultivars adapted to poor soils, and with improved blast resistance and drought tolerance. Some have outyielded traditional rices by more than 100 per cent in evaluations. Scientists at national agricultural research systems have crossed these improved rices with local cultivars and farmers are now beginning to grow the progeny. But more improvements are needed to meet the new challenges.

New challenges are emerging in the world's upland rice farming areas, where already some of the world's poorest farmers try to wrest a living from fragile soils that are fast being degraded.

Population growth, the demands of urbanism and industry, and the increasing adoption of high value cash crop farming in the surrounding lowlands are leading to strong competition for upland terrain.

The uplands have traditionally suffered from drought and infertile soils, weeds and plant diseases. Soils there have been badly eroded and degraded as a result of the slash-and-burn agriculture that for many years followed logging.

Already the new upward pressures are resulting in a movement toward permanent agriculture and intensification of land use in upland areas. Those involved find themselves faced—in addition to the usual upland problems — with an urgent need to conserve the soil and the diversity of plant species, and to cope with increasingly frequent and severe weed and disease infestations.

Recently, scientists have been improving their knowledge of the genetics of resistance to the Blast fungus, one of the most damaging diseases of rice, and are using the techniques of biotechnology to develop cultivars with more durable disease resistance.

In the uplands, blast is particularly important because the environment favours its proliferation. Although many traditional upland cultivars show stable resistance to this disease under low-input cropping practices, they have other characteristics that make them difficult to use in intensified systems. So the risk from blast increases as cropping practices intensify and improved varieties are introduced.

IRRI scientists have been working with colleagues in the Upland Rice Research Consortium to better understand pathogen populations and to identify resistance genes found in some cultivars. Armed with this knowledge, they are working with IRRI's upland rice breeder to combine such genes with other desirable traits for incorporation into new upland varieties.

Consortium scientists are also trying to understand how upland rice farmers' cropping systems contribute to soil erosion, with the aim of proposing possible erosion control techniques. Studies in the Philippines have shown, for example, that hedgerows of trees, shrubs and grasses along hill contours can help reduce soil erosion up to 90 per cent. Rice or other crops are planted between these strips of permanent ground cover.

Leguminous plants in hedgerows make substantial amounts of atmospheric nitrogen available to both riceplants and annual crops and recycle other nutrients and organic matter.

Such legumes can simultaneously increase farmers' incomes and contribute to sustainability of the farming system.

Weeds are the most serious biological constraint to upland rice production. IRRI scientists are pursuing projects on managing weeds with less herbicide use. One approach is to search for rice plant species that exhibit a characteristic known as allelopathy. Allelopathic plants can affect the growth of nearby plants through the production of biological compounds they release into the environment. If an allelopathic rice — or other plant species — could be found that could inhibit the growth of weeds important in rice production, it might be possible through genetic engineering to develop rice cultivars that would provide their own weed control.

Most weed species also are victims of their own diseases. Purposeful application of the agents of such diseases to weed pests among rice crops could constitute another approach to weed control.

Researchers from IRRI, Maejo University and Chiang Mai University launched a study in 1993 of the interactions between weeds, crop environmental conditions, and farmers' practices in upper northern Thailand. The goals are to understand the diversity of farmers' practices and decisionmaking processes and to grade the factors that limit rice crop yields.

IRRI scientists are also studying how fertilizer and cultural practices influence weed communities. In one project on phosphorus management, they are investigating how weed communities change as soil fertility is improved over time in the Philippines, Indonesia, and Thailand.

Riceplant cultivars differ in their ability to compete with weeds in the field. Scientists in the Philippines tested the competitiveness of a dozen cultivars against weeds to help farmers choose the most highly competitive one. By planting this cultivar and enhancing its competitive ability through good management practices, farmers should be able to reduce the number of handweedings necessary while achieving maximum yields.

Research on farms in Thailand, Laos and the Philippines has confirmed what scientists had long suspected: that a lack of phosphorus in upland farms is limiting rice crop yields. Their suspicions arose from the fact that many highly weathered upland soils are inherently low in phosphorus and are acidic.

But the scientists found that the lack of phosphorus will limit production even if calcium is added to the soil to overcome the acidity, or if acid-tolerant cultivars are planted. Rotations of rice and legumes could lead to stable, higher value production, they concluded. But first it is necessary to ensure by adding phosphorus that soil quality does not degrade over time.

Eventually, the investment in soil inputs should pay off as added phosphorus exceeds crop needs and as other nutrients such as carbon and nitrogen are better cycled and used.

Breaking the Acid Barrier

The acidity present in the subsoil of many upland areas prevents plant roots from reaching the moisture and nutrients therein, thus reducing crop yield. Adding lime to the subsoil is not practical, but in 1994 IRRI and Indonesian scientists began experiments to see if components of lime applied to the soil surface could be leached down into the subsoil. This would be done by manipulating soil chemistry and using deep-rooted, acid-tolerant rice cultivars to help capture the leached components.

At present they are studying the processes that govern the rate of leaching of lime components and their accumulation in the subsoil. They plan then to construct mathematical models that will be used to develop practical technologies and to indicate under what conditions the technologies might be effective.

The experiments began at the Upland Rice Research Consortium site at Sitiung, Indonesia. French collaborators from l'Institut francais de recherche scientifique pour le developpement en cooperation are planning similar experiments in Thailand and Vietnam.

A rice plant that would not have to be planted annually could help reduce erosion by providing a permanent ground cover. Perenniality exists in several wild rice species from Southeast Asia, but their yields are low. These species, however, can be crossed with cultivated rice.

The challenge facing scientists is to produce a high-yielding perennial plant adapted to the poor soils of the uplands, and one that is highly responsive to low amounts of purchased inputs, and that resists diseases and insect pests.

It's a challenge IRRI scientists are currently working on. New biotechnology tools will be used to transfer the perennial characters into cultivated rice, and new knowledge of genetic diversity will be applied to develop pest resistance.

Upand rice has been replaced by other crops such as maize in onehand, in the other hand hand the landraces has been no more in farmers' field. Diversity of upland rice can be maintained at the sametime level of production can be increased using participatory techniques.

References

Bolens, L. (1997). "Agriculture" in Selin, Helaine (ed.), *Encyclopedia of the History of Science, Technology, and Medicine in Non-Western Cultures*. Kluwer Academic Publishers, Dordrecht/Boston/London, pp. 20-22.

Collingham, E. M. *The Taste of War: World War Two and the Battle for Food* (2011).

Crawford, G.W.; Shen, C. (1998). "The Origins of Rice Agriculture: Recent Progress in East Asia". *Antiquity* 72: 858-866.

Crosby, Alfred W.: *The Columbian Exchange: Biological and Cultural Consequences of 1492*. Praeger Publishers, 2003 (30th Anniversary Edition). ISBN 978-0-275-98073-3.

Douangboupha, B., K. Khamphoukeo, S. Inthavong, J. Schiller, and G. Jahn. 2006. Pests and Diseases of the Rice Production Systems of Laos. pp. 265-281. In J.M. Schiller, M.B. Chanphengxay, B. Linquist, and S. Appa Rao, Editors. Rice in Laos. Los Baños (Philippines): International Rice Research Institute. p. 457. ISBN 978-971-22-0211-7.

Heong, KL, YH Chen, Delaware Johnson, GC Jahn, M Hossain, RS Hamilton (14 October 2005). "Letter: Debate Over a GM Rice Trial in China". *Science* 310 (5746): 231-3.

Huang, J., Ruifa Hu, Scott Rozelle, Carl Pray (29 April 2005). "Insect-Resistant GM Rice in Farmers' Fields: Assessing

Productivity and Health Effects in China". *Science* 308 (5722): 688-690.

Jahn, GC and B. Khiev. 2004. Gall Midge in Cambodian lowland rice. pp. 71-76. In J. Benett, JS Bentur, IC Pasula, K. Krishnaiah, [eds]. New Approaches to Gall Midge Resistance in Rice. Los Baños (Philippines): International Rice Research Institute and Indian Council of Agricultural Research. p. 195.

Jahn, G.C., S. Pheng, B. Khiev, and C. Pol. 1997. Pest Management Practices of Lowland Rice Farmers in Cambodia. In K.L. Heong and M. M. Escalada [Editors] "Pest Management Practices of Rice Farmers in Asia." Manila (Philippines): International Rice Research Institute. 35-52. ISBN 971-22-0102-3.

Jahn, GC, NQ Kamal, S Rokeya, AK Azad, NI Dulu, JB Orsini, A Barrion, and L Almazan. 2004a. Completion Report on Livelihood Improvement Through Ecology (LITE), PETRRA IPM Subproject SP 27 02. Poverty Elimination Through Rice Research Assistance (PETRRA), IRRI, Dhaka.

Katz, Solomon. *The Encyclopedia of Food and Culture*, (Scribner, 2003).

Kogan, M.; Ortman, E.F. (1978). "Antixenosis a New Term Proposed to Defined to Describe Painter's 'non-preference' Modality of Resistance". *Bull. Entomol. Soc. Am.* 24: 175-6.

Leung LKP; Peter G. Cox; Gary C. Jahn; Robert Nugent (2002). 'Evaluating Rodent Management with Cambodian Rice Farmers". *Cambodian Journal of Agriculture* 5: 21-6.

Murphy, S, J Stonehouse, J Holt, J Venn, NQ Kamal, MF Rabbi, MH Haque, G Jahn, B Barrion. 2006. Ecology and Management of Rice Hispa (Dicladispa armigera) in Bangladesh. pp. 162-164. In Perspectives on Pests II: Achievements of research under UK Department for International Development, Crop Protection Programme 2000-05. Natural Resources International Limited. p. 206.

Mazoyer, Marcel; Roudart, Laurence (2006). *A History of World Agriculture: from the Neolithic Age to the current crisis*. Monthly Review Press, New York. ISBN 978-1-58367-121-4.

Saltini A. *Storia delle scienze agrarie*, 4 Vols., Bologna 1984-89, ISBN 978-88-206-2412-5.

Wells, Spencer (2003). *The Journey of Man: A Genetic Odyssey*. Princeton University Press. ISBN 978-0-691-11532-0.

Wickens, G.M. (1976). "What the West Borrowed from the Middle East", in Savory, R.M. (ed.) *Introduction to Islamic Civilization*. Cambridge University Press.

Zhao, Z. (1998). "The Middle Yangtze Region in China is the Place Where Rice was Domesticated: Phytolithic Evidence from the Diaotonghuan Cave, Northern Jiangxi". *Antiquity* 72: 885-897.

Index